THE INTERVENTIONIST

Joani Gammill, RN, BRI I

HAZELDEN®

Hazelden
Center City, Minnesota 55012
hazelden.org

Library of Congress Cataloging-in-Publication Data

Gammill, Joani, 1957-
  The interventionist / Joani Gammill.
    p. cm.
  ISBN 978-1-59285-894-1 (softcover)
  1. Gammill, Joani, 1957- 2. Drug addicts—California—Los Angeles—Biography. 3. Nurses—Substance use. 4. Opium abuse—Treatment. 5. Drug addicts—Rehabilitation. I. Title.
  RC564.5.N87G36 2011
  362.29092—dc22

                    2010051204

Editor's note

This publication is not intended as a substitute for the advice of health care professionals.

Alcoholics Anonymous, AA, and the Big Book are registered trademarks of Alcoholics Anonymous World Services, Inc.

The quote on pages v and 188 is excerpted from THE KITE RUNNER by Khaled Hosseini, copyright © 2003 by Khaled Hosseini. Used by permission of Riverhead Books, an imprint of Penguin Group (USA) Inc., Doubleday Canada, and Bloomsbury Publishing, Plc.

The lyrics in chapter 10 are from LOSING MY RELIGION. Words and Music by WILLIAM BERRY, PETER BUCK, MICHAEL MILLS, and MICHAEL STIPE. © 1991 NIGHT GARDEN MUSIC (BMI). All Rights Administered in all Worlds, now known and hereafter devised, by WARNER-TAMERLANE PUBLISHING CORP. (BMI). All Rights Reserved. Used by Permission of ALFRED MUSIC PUBLISHING CO., INC.

15 14 13 12 11   1 2 3 4 5 6

Cover design by Percolator
Interior design and typesetting by Madeline Berglund

To my parents, Aubrey Wilson Gammill and
Mary Ellen Kees Gammill, who lost their lives too young
as a result of their alcoholism and addictions.
And in memory of Father Joseph C. Martin,
who started my journey of recovery.

"How far do you go to save the life of an alcoholic?"
"You go as far as you can and then *one step more.*"

—Father Martin (quoting Austin Ripley)

In the stories that follow, some of the names and places have been changed to protect privacy. Some people portrayed in the book have chosen not to remain anonymous, and in those cases I have retained their real names. I give my heartfelt thanks to all the addicts, alcoholics, and families who have given me the privilege of telling their stories.

—JG

AND THAT, I BELIEVE, IS WHAT TRUE REDEMPTION

IS . . . WHEN GUILT LEADS TO GOOD.

—Khaled Hosseini, *The Kite Runner*

Contents

Foreword

It is an honor and a pleasure for me to write this foreword for Joani. She is one of the most dedicated and hardworking people I know, both in her personal life and in her professional life.

I first met Joani about fifteen years ago. She was struggling with an opiate addiction. She, like many in the nursing profession, suffers from chronic pain as a result of the lifting, bending, and other physical demands of the job, and, after many surgeries, she found herself in the midst of the battle of her life. Our initial introduction came as the result of one of her attempts at gaining sobriety. She was able to maintain that sobriety for quite some time, but, as so often happens with addicts, she returned to active use. Many of us in recovery find that returning to active use occurs more often when things are going well than when they are going badly. That was her situation. Over the years, her life was a roller-coaster ride: in and out of rehabs and various treatment programs, in and out of meetings, in and out of detox programs, with the same results—periods of sobriety and relapse along the way.

I am quite sure that in most of these attempts, she heard a statement that is very common in treatment, especially in the first couple of days. The counselor looks around the room and says, "Only one of you is going to make it." Now, statistically, we know that recovery numbers are not as good as anyone would like to see, but often we don't tell patients the rest of the story. And that is, "There is no reason why that person can't be you." I have personally been sober for over twenty-seven years and in the treatment field for over twenty-six years, and I have noticed that the people who make an attempt at sobriety fall into one (or more) of four categories:

1. The person who will not make it.

2. The "yo-yo" recoverer, or chronic relapser.

3. The "ninety-day wonder," who, somewhere during the first several months of recovery, starts to have doubts about whether he has a problem or not. He uses again, usually once or twice, scares himself enough to realize the seriousness of the situation, and returns immediately to his treatment plan.

4. The person who will make it.

Often, recovering addicts are not told that they have direct control over which of these people they become. I mention this because I have seen Joani go through every one of these possibilities. And, as a result of her determination, hard work, and dedication, true sobriety has been a major part of her life now for many years.

Joani initially trained as a nurse and provided years of comfort to many people along the way. Several years ago, she decided it was time to take that training and her own personal experiences on a different career path. She decided that it was time to "carry the message"—as commanded in the last Step of a number of Twelve Step programs— on a different level. The work she has done in the recovery community over the past several years speaks volumes about her commitment to her own recovery and the recovery of others. Her personal work in intervention has been a blessing to those in need. Based on my time and experience in the treatment field, I can tell you that the intervention portion of treatment is the most taxing and frustrating of all the services that can be provided. Joani provides a wonderful service to us all, and she does it with a sense of compassion and love.

The Alcoholics Anonymous Preamble calls on members to "share their experience, strength, and hope." Joani truly does that. Hers is a story of despair, courage, and triumph.

John J. McClanahan, PhD, CCDC, LCADC
McClanahan and Associates

Prologue

"We're used to the chaos," my husband, Brian, says to Dr. Phil McGraw (the popular psychologist who hosts *Dr. Phil*, a daytime television talk show) on the set of the prime-time special *Escaping Addiction*, which we have flown to Los Angeles to tape.

"You don't get it, man; you're going to bury your wife," Dr. Phil replies. "Where were you last night at four a.m.?" He continued to hammer at Brian. I am relieved that the focus is off me.

"Downtown L.A., looking for syringes for Joani," Brian answers sheepishly.

I pipe up and say, "I forgot my syringes," foolishly thinking this will make Brian's actions seem more respectable. Dr. Phil just looks at me like he cannot believe what he is hearing.

Focusing his attention back on me (I'm now thinking I should have kept my mouth shut), Dr. Phil says, "In fact, isn't it true, Joani, that you just shot up in my green room right before this interview?" Before I can answer, there it is in full living color, evidence of me injecting myself with buprenorphine prior to the show.

Trying to defend myself, I say, "You don't get it, Dr. Phil. If I hadn't shot up before coming out here, there would be no show or interview. I would be too sick to do it."

Which is a lie. Junkies active in their disease rarely tell the truth; protecting the addiction is our number one priority. I had plenty of sublingual Suboxone, the oral form of buprenorphine, on me. I just wanted the jolt of the needle before doing the interview.

When Brian and I flew to California to tape Dr. Phil's yearly special, I knew we would discuss my addiction, but my main focus was to get help for our four-year-old son, whose behavior had me increasingly concerned. I didn't expect the intervention that was to come.

I had never seen the *Dr. Phil* show in its entirety. Some glimpses here and there, sure, but I had no interest in reality talk TV. My life was hard enough without watching other people's train wrecks. I don't think I would have had the nerve to do a show if I had had a better idea of the tough opponent I was to face in Dr. Phil.

But here I am now, and frankly, I am too stoned to run. The crew has done my makeup, but even the industrial-strength stuff they use is no match for my constant tears. I rarely cry at home, but now, on the set with Dr. Phil, I cannot stop weeping. It's as if years of fear and anguish about my addiction have bubbled to the surface at lightning speed. Dr. Phil has a wonderful gift of getting right to the heart of the matter, and it is his gift that saves my life.

"I think you are here today because you want me to document your life and *death* for your children. This is your eulogy," Dr. Phil says.

As I break into a fresh puddle of tears, I feel like Ebenezer Scrooge looking at his own grave in *A Christmas Carol,* and, like Scrooge, I hope I'm not too late to save my life. The addiction, however, is not done fighting. "I will not go to boot camp rehab," I hotly tell Dr. Phil.

"Well, I'm not sending you to some spa in Florida to get well," he retorts. "I have some good folks here from La Hacienda treatment facility in Texas. I think this treatment facility is one of the best rehabs in the country, and that's where you need to go."

Now it's my turn to stare at Dr. Phil in disbelief.

He adds, "You know why you need to go to La Hacienda?" Before I can answer, he continues, "Because you don't want to."

I will steal that line from Dr. Phil over and over in my own intervention practice. His voice and wisdom resonate in my head when I least expect it and when I need it the most—when I am alone in the field trying to get addicts and alcoholics into treatment.

But the process of getting well and getting back to work is not easy, quick, or pain free. My path has twists and detours. My recovery is not perfect, and I'm a work in progress. I gain many things during my journey of recovery from severe prescription drug addiction. If you look closely, you also see what I have lost.

Addiction is a thief on many levels. Spanning generations, it will pop up and take those you love through tangled emotions and dysfunctional upbringings, and family will disappear. Professionals in the field of chemical dependency are aware of a sad but frequent phenomenon: when a person gets well, some loved ones can no longer relate to him or her. The ingrained family dynamics shift, perceptions and relationships alter, and sometimes the connections between people end.

In telling my story, I leave out my sister. She has her own story to tell, and it's not my place to tell it. In the end, I am left with an empty place that she used to inhabit, and to this day I have a hard time accepting her absence.

The story that follows chronicles my family's history of addiction. As I write my early story, I see through the lens of a child. But as my story matures, so does my view of my childhood and the people in it. Some of that maturity has come through being a parent who has not done things perfectly with her own two children, which has allowed me to see my parents in a much more forgiving light. I see more and more in shades of gray—no one is either all good or all bad. While writing this book I learned two important things: humans aren't perfect and to forgive others is to forgive ourselves.

Finally, this story is a wild ride through the interventions that I have been involved with. Each, like a little gift, embodies some memory from my own life, and I tell my story through those experiences. In the end, I am an adrenaline junkie, with a big heart for other addicts, alcoholics, and their families. I have found my passion in my life's work, or, more accurately, it has found me.

CHAPTER 1

A Beautiful Mess, and Near Death by Adderall

I am late this morning. My GPS has taken me to a downtown D.C. address. I need to cross the bridge into Arlington, Virginia. Feeling frazzled by the delay, I pull up in front of a lovely, early 1900s craftsman-style stucco home. The man who lives here has told his wife I'm coming. Technically, this is called an informational intervention.

Stacey is huddled on the end of the sofa. She is blond and sweaty, with menstrual blood smearing the bottom of her long skirt. She is unaware of this. Her feet are curled underneath her as she clutches a tissue, mascara under her red, swollen eyes. She is scared.

She does not get up to greet me. I look her way and instantly take in her misery. "Oh, honey, you feel like shit, don't you?" are my first words to her.

She smiles, laughs lightly, and the tears fall from her eyes. She is relieved. Someone finally knows. The truth does set you free.

I sit and gently take her hand. I gauge her comfort level with my physical proximity. She is accepting of my presence. I push back her bangs from her forehead as I whisper reassurance to her: "It will be okay."

I am filled with intense protectiveness toward my new charge. Without overwhelming her with too much information, I share my experience with addiction and recovery. My darkest past has become my largest asset, and I am eternally grateful for this opportunity.

Her home is filled with all the usual artifacts of family life. Pictures of her children grace the walls and the refrigerator. It is a warm home.

The call came, as usual, when I least expected it, disturbing my own mundane motherhood duties. The voice on the other end is always urgent and laced with deep sadness and concern. All the calls are similar in this regard, but the details differ, and I listen with my whole being. I listen as if it's the first time I am hearing the pain. I leave my shoes untied. I stop. I know this world. It is my passion, my responsibility, my duty as one who has lived through it.

The husband is articulate and educated, and has done his research. It's quick. We discuss options to proceed.

Then silence. His voice falters: "My wife is dying. . . . We have two small children. We can't lose her."

He pleads to me for her life, a stranger on the other end of the phone.

I take control. I gently and firmly lend him my confidence. I am a poker player at heart. I bluff when my own doubts consume me, which is with every intervention I do. No matter how many times I achieve success, my doubts hound me, yet I forge forward.

The devil is a powerful adversary. I respect the enemy. And I hate him, and I will win. My prevailing doubts are his weapons, and I will not back down. I am in the battle for someone's life. And I love it.

As I prepare for tomorrow's intervention, it's late summer. The air continues to be heavy with humidity and last-chance thunderstorms. The rain slows, and I hear the melody off my side porch. I follow the song and look out the window. A faint light appears as the clouds break up.

This could be the last night this woman, this mom and wife, has to live with this hell. And I am filled with purpose.

She and I walk together as one on this night. God is near. And it is this way every time for me before an intervention. A stranger consumes me.

Three years earlier:

I am also a mom of two small children, my little boy still in diapers. I am a wife and a registered nurse. I work weekends at an alcohol and drug rehab facility where I am the supervisor.

It is cold and just six days before Christmas. Historic Annapolis, Maryland, abounds with colonial holiday festivities. It is beautiful in a way that only old America can be at Christmas. Our homes, in their old age, ooze memories of Christmases past, whispering of carols sung and candles lit.

I wake up early. Fear of death is my constant companion. Today he will come to me, though I do not know this.... All I know is, the joints in my hands are so sore I can't make a fist without crying out. I need a shot.

I walk quietly downstairs. I'm the first one up. I'm trailed by my four-and-a-half-pound Chihuahua, Lucy. She is my ever-present friend, the only breathing thing that is witness to my 24/7 suspended state of consciousness.

She will lick the blood off my arm, exhibiting both her primal instincts and what I think is a gentle and fierce love of me. Frequently, tears fall from my chin onto her back, as the evidence of my injection disappears onto her tongue. I am grateful for her presence. I am not alone. She follows me.

In my bathroom, high on a shelf, nestled in an antique bowl my aunt gave me, is my salvation and my gun. And above the shelf is a picture—a finger-paint print of my son's three-month-old feet and his sister's three-year-old hands.

I see the picture as I reach for the syringe.

Addiction trumps everything. Even love of my children.

This hard fact is difficult to comprehend, but it is very true. It is not personal. Addiction trumps everything. On this morning, I love my children as much as any other mom waking to a new morning with her babies. And I cannot stop the addiction.

I have drawn up the liquid opiate the night before and gently placed it in the bowl with a tourniquet that I stole from the nursing unit at work.

I love the tourniquet. I miss it still. It is the perfect stretchy rubber, easy to wrap around my arm. In the early years of my needle addiction, I would attempt to tie off with ordinary household implements— blow-dryer cords and winter scarves.

I am wearing a floor-length, pure white cotton nightgown. I push up the long sleeve of my left arm to past my elbow. The nightgown's wrist has elastic in it, keeping the sleeve in place above my antecubital, the soft spot in the crook of the elbow.

I am right-handed, so the left arm vein is preferable. Taking the tourniquet, I apply it tightly around my arm, using my mouth to tug it ever tighter.

I examine the vein. It's plump this morning, but I tap it with my middle finger, teasing it to fill even fuller with blood. You never want to miss the vein. If the liquid drug seeps into the tissue, the high is missed. The sickness will slowly abate, but there will be no euphoric payoff. This is a universal truth known to all junkies: do not miss the vein.

Satisfied with my vein, I reach for the syringe. This will be the best part of my day. Another universal truth among the walking dead: the first hit is the best.

I draw up the liquid opiate but will inject only half with the first shot. The whole load makes me too sleepy. As Lucy gazes at me with love that I cannot comprehend, I prick my skin with the needle. I anxiously wait to see the blood return to the syringe. This tells me I have achieved my goal of hitting the vein.

Seeing the blood, I slowly depress the plunger, injecting half of the liquid. Releasing the tourniquet, I take the needle out. While bending my elbow to stop the blood flow, I recap the needle. Gently, I replace the remaining drug and needle back into the antique bowl, to be used later in the day.

The ritual complete, I sit on the toilet, lid down. I watch Lucy, and my joints loosen up as my head is filled with a sense of well-being. The lie complete, I begin my day.

I will come close to dying in four hours.

The house fills with the usual noises. The coffeepot gurgles. The kids tumble down the stairs. I let the dog out. Mary watches *SpongeBob Squarepants* in the background.

My mind is drawn to the medicine cabinet above the coffeemaker. I have a new lover.

I always thought I would be faithful to the opiate narcotics Percocet, Vicodin, Lorcet, OxyContin, fentanyl, Tussionex HC, morphine, Demerol, Dilaudid, and buprenorphine. I'm sure I've left somebody out.

But like all long-term loves, I suppose the luster wears thin and a little pick-me-up is needed. Along comes Adderall, also known as "mixed amphetamine salts." I love the sound of that. Oh, the possibilities. Mixed amphetamine salts. I will spend hours at the nurses' station desk reading the *PDR*, the *Physicians' Desk Reference,* the bible of prescription-drug addicts, looking up lovingly all the names of the mixed amphetamine salts.

I had a problem.

The opiates made me so tired. With two small children and a dope habit, I was barely able to keep up or, more accurately, to stay awake. At times I would have to put the van in park at red lights for fear of falling asleep. Kids in the car seats, I was in danger of rolling out into the intersection.

I needed a solution for the fatigue. No one must die.

D. J. Shay, a counselor at La Hacienda treatment center, used to tell us inmates the story this way. Normal people have a solution for the problem. *They give the drug up!* What? A motley crew of faces in the lecture hall would look up at him.

No! we all seemed to shout, as we openly stared in response to his remarks. We simply didn't understand. It seemed somehow insane to us drug addicts. Give the drug up? Nope, just need to tweak the drug habit a bit. I needed to get some amphetamines. That was the solution. It seemed sane at the time.

My first dose of Adderall felt as if fireworks had gone off in my head. The euphoria enveloped my mind and body in a way I am at a loss to describe. It completed me. I would lie awake in bed, utterly still into the early morning hours. In my motionless state, I was at peace. My mind awash in a false serenity, I just lay there. I would spend the next few months doing everything possible to get my hands on a prescription for Adderall. It was far more difficult to obtain than opiate narcotics.

The first two Adderall pills were the first and last medication I diverted—a nice term for stealing—from the rehab facility at which I worked.

Armed with books on attention-deficit/hyperactivity disorder (ADHD), I convinced my psychiatrist that I was clinically in need of Adderall—and I needed higher and higher doses. He obliged me. This was no fault of his. My skill at conning physicians was my job, and I performed well.

I called it "the housewives' speedball." On the street, a speedball is heroin and cocaine. For me, it is buprenorphine and Adderall. *Valley of the Dolls:* one takes you up, and the other takes you down.

Reaching into the medicine cabinet on this morning, I retrieve two Adderall caplets. Washing them down with coffee, I contemplate my day.

I have Christmas shopping to complete, and Max's preschool holiday play to attend in the evening. He is to sing "Rudolph the Red-Nosed Reindeer," complete with a red nose. We have been rehearsing all week.

But I have a new problem, and no solution—yet.

I am unable to control my use of Adderall. To a certain extent, I was able to take a constant level of the liquid opiate narcotic buprenorphine. Adderall is different. My compulsion for amphetamines is even greater than my addiction to opiate narcotics. This has surprised me. I've been popping pill after pill, many times forgetting how many I've taken.

So on this hectic morning, my obsession begins. As the euphoria from the amphetamines takes over my brain, my head tells me I need more and more pills. It is this abnormal response to drugs that is the hallmark of the addict's brain. Our brains are not normal in this regard. We have no more control over our response to drugs and alcohol than the type 1 diabetic has over his or her pancreas and insulin reactions. It is this so-called "phenomenon of craving" that sets us apart from nonaddicts and nonalcoholics.

Three hours later:

It is Christmas cold. I am to pick Mary up at her Catholic school, Saint Mary's, at 2:40 p.m. Max will stay later at his school, St. Anne's Preschool for the Arts. I have a few minutes before picking up Mary. Popping another Adderall, I stop in Chico's to look for something to wear to Max's performance.

Skimming the sales racks of clothes, I need to pause and take a deep breath. Death is hovering, and I am still unaware. Is my heart beating too fast? A fleeting thought that is to be a harbinger of what's to come.

Leaving the car at the bottom of Main Street, I hurry to walk the incline to Mary's school. I can hear the constant ringing of the Salvation Army bell and stop to deposit a small amount of money.

I continue on up Green Street, passing our 150-year-old public elementary school. Maybe halfway up the hill, what is essentially the length of a city block, my first symptom of distress appears: excessive sweating.

Then, in lightning-fast succession:

Shortness of breath.

Heart beating wildly fast.

Chest pain that radiates down my left arm.

Crushing anxiety.

Nausea.

I need to puke badly. I bend over and gag onto the sidewalk. I look over at a planter by our friends Laura and Glen's house. The familiar is suddenly ominous.

In another lifetime, I sat on that planter.

But now I need medical attention, and I know it. I do not have the luxury of denial. Yet I also don't have the good sense to stop and let my heart drink in the needed oxygen. A deep sense of urgency is making me react irrationally.

I am overdosing on Adderall and am experiencing a cardiac incident as a result. Death is a real threat, and I am painfully aware of this, but I must reach my child. My two prevailing thoughts are this: One, I must get medical attention, or I'm going to die. And two, I must pick Mary up at school. She's waiting in the school parking lot at the top of the hill.

The more prudent thing to do would be to stay put and call 911 or knock on Laura's door. But my overriding concern is not to abandon Mary in the school parking lot, so on I climb, in spite of my physical symptoms and extreme fear.

I reach the parking lot, where hundreds of children have been released from school. A sea of young children in their school uniforms surrounds me. I feel dizzy as I take in the sight. They all look the same. I am disoriented. Oh, God, help me.

Mary, I mouth her name in a mute prayer, *please appear to me.*

I need help. I am drowning in nausea and arm pain. I fear I might pass out.

I speak directly to God, clearly in my mind now: *Dear God, take me, take me like my parents before me, but please not today, not in my child's school parking lot, five days before Christmas. Do not make this her last memory of me. Do not do this to this child. I deserve this death, God, but Mary does not deserve this. Please . . . please . . . please . . . .* It is my mantra, my prayer.

I am not afraid to die. I am afraid for my children. They are too young to lose me. They need me. They love me.

I do not negotiate or barter with God; I have nothing to offer up in return for my life. I have no hope that this will never happen again. I am a pragmatist at my core. I know my genetics and feel fucked.

My anxiety mounting, Mary appears. She sees me before I see her.

She is happy, like all children as Christmas approaches and school nears an end.

She is excited about something in her book bag that she made for the Christmas tree. I remember this moment more than any other. She is eager to dig her treasure out of the book bag to show me.

Over and over, I tell her I cannot look at it now. She does not understand. This is unlike me, so she persists in trying to show me her craft.

I feel extreme guilt as I recall this moment in time. I failed her in my inability to be engaged in this Christmas moment. It will never come again. Addiction is a thief.

Finally, with quiet urgency—talking is difficult for me at this point—I tell her I'm not feeling well and I need to get back to the car. She looks up.

"What's wrong?" she asks in her little first-grade voice.

"Mommy has a tummy ache," I barely whisper.

"Will you puke?" she wants to know.

"I don't know."

We walk in silence now, thankfully downhill. I feel the chest and arm pain lessen as we go down. My cardiac load has decreased, I think. This is good.

I fish out my cell phone. I call my husband, Brian, in his home office.

"Hey."

"Hey."

"I'm not well. I need to get to the cardiologist right away. I have Mary with me," I say in a matter-of-fact way. I don't want to alarm Mary.

Silence. He knows. The other shoe has finally dropped.

"Max will need to be picked up," he counters.

"Call Margaret," I add quickly, not elaborating.

In the short time it takes us to reach home, my aunt Margaret has arrived. Leaving quickly, Brian gives her instructions about picking up Max.

Brian has called the cardiologist's office and given them what little information he knows. They are expecting us.

Brian and I drive in silence. "No, I don't know what's wrong" is all I say. Sweat drips from my forehead, and the nausea is overwhelming. *Please hurry,* I think.

As Brian parks the car, I look over. "Drop me at the door, I don't think I can walk." My hand is gripping the dashboard.

Slowly, I walk up to the office. The door is so heavy. Approaching the desk, I weakly tell the staff I don't feel well at all. They immediately take action. I hear one staff member whisper how pale I look.

I'm escorted to an examining room; Dr. Kennedy is already there. Wrapping the blood-pressure cuff around my arm and placing the pulse oximeter on my finger, he starts firing questions at me. Accurate information is vital to diagnosis and ultimately to treat. I'm guarded with the truth. I am ashamed.

Dr. Kennedy listens to my chest for a long time.

"Okay," he says, and continues what feels like an interrogation. I hedge. He starts the process of having me take a stress test. Hooked up to an electrocardiograph, which will measure the effects of the test on my heart, I am instructed to walk slowly on a treadmill. Almost immediately, the doctor stops me. The EKG tracing is showing what my body already knows. "Sit down, please, and stay still," he instructs. "We're transporting you to the cardiac-care unit at the hospital."

Fuck, is my first thought. It was not just an anxiety attack.

The doctor informs me there are EKG changes associated with ischemia to my heart. Ischemia is a fancy word for lack of oxygen to the heart. We need to determine why this is happening, he tells Brian and me. *Shit,* I think.

For a moment, imagine that I was having a seizure related to an underlying medical condition. Would I withhold the truth of the underlying condition from my doctor? Of course not. That vital information is lifesaving.

But drug and alcohol addiction are different. Although they are recognized by the medical establishment as brain disorders, deep stigmas continue to surround them. Many people continue to believe we have "a choice" when it comes to our abnormal reaction to drugs and alcohol. We do not. In 1939 the book *Alcoholics Anonymous* (commonly known as the Big Book) stated what is still true today: "We have lost the power of choice in drink." No one would choose this hell. But misconceptions continue, and addicts and alcoholics feel ashamed.

So I stay quiet. I stare death in the face, and I am mute.

During transport to the hospital, my mind is racing. How will I conceal my addiction while hospitalized? It takes me only a short time to come up with a new and improved standard story.

First, I am addicted to opiate painkillers as a result of chronic back pain associated with spinal surgery. That will easily cover my addiction to buprenorphine. Second, I take Adderall for ADHD. As long as a blood-level toxicology is not done, I should be okay. If a blood level had been drawn on admission to the hospital, it would have been readily apparent that I was abusing drugs. The problem with middle-class drug addicts is this: we don't look the way people expect drug addicts to look. We blend in too well. Our education and economic level allow us to continue on for a long time with the disease.

Okay. Third, I have huge holes in my arms where I shoot my drugs. Track marks. *Fuck. . . . Think, think, think.*

Got it. I am allergic to latex. I donated blood, and my arms reacted. Bingo. Covered.

These four things together—opiate dependence, amphetamines for ADHD, track marks, and ultimately chest pain for unknown reasons—could have been a huge red flag that shouted possible addiction. But no one approaches me, and I continue to die, my addiction undetected and undiagnosed.

I am hooked up to an IV with morphine. I will undergo two cardiac catheterizations during my stay in an attempt to figure out my mystery "condition."

I sleep deeply. I'm in amphetamine withdrawal. I can't stay awake.

Huddled in a ball in the middle of the hospital bed, I'm slumped over and snoring.

And I miss Max's holiday preschool play. He is three years old. Mary is five.

Brian reports to me that Max stood on the stage but would not sing.

There are moments of time in our lives that we can look back on as turning points, or times when grace is near. My baby boy will deliver a gift to me on this night. My heart will break and ache in a way that science can never cure. In this pain, in this glimpse of time, I will begin to heal. But I do not know this now.

Visiting hours begin, and the noises and routines change in the rooms and corridors. The light has long faded on the December evening. I glance outside and see the twinkling of white Christmas lights strung around the hospital grounds. And I am deeply sad.

The kids and Brian bounce into the room. Dressed in their holiday best, they look so cute. Mary has on a red velvet dress with a small white bow on the empire waist. Max has on "big boy" pants with a collared shirt. Polished oxford shoes complete his little-man outfit.

"How was the play?" I ask, with false cheerfulness. Mary's standard, "Good," with her signature inflection, is the first response.

Max is quiet, standing at the foot of my hospital bed. "Hey, buddy, how was it?"

Then, oh so gently, Max touches his still-red-painted nose! What is he doing? Moving his head up and down, he starts to get the tempo! With endearing awkwardness, he gently and clearly sings "Rudolph the Red-Nosed Reindeer" . . . to his mom who's in bed from an overdose of amphetamines.

"Thank you, Max," I manage to say. My feelings are incomprehensible. Mary claps. Brian looks proud. We had our own private concert.

Max then crawls into my bed. For the next four days, he barely leaves my side. With him cuddled against me, I am secure for the moment. I am not dead yet. For months afterward, Max associates the hospital with security. He wants me to go back with him and stay there. "Watch cartoons in bed," he says, every time we drive by.

I am discharged from the hospital. The discharging cardiologist's parting words are "Your ischemia is a mystery." It's determined that I had coronary artery spasms that blocked blood flow to my heart. Spasms that were caused by an unusually high dose of amphetamines in my system. That is my unspoken truth.

I'm given a prescription for nitroglycerin tabs, to be placed under my tongue for future chest pain.

I'm home for two hours when I take my first capsule of Adderall.

Addiction trumps everything.

My story goes on like this for a few more painful months. I will be rescued by the most unlikely of saviors: Hollywood and the *Dr. Phil* show.

Still sitting on the couch with Stacey, I show her the glossy brochure for the rehab facility she's scheduled to be admitted to. Somehow I always think the shiny pages will entice my patients to spring out of their slumber and immediately agree to go with me. It never works like that. I don't think they give a rat's ass about the brochure at this point. I didn't. But still I try.

All the families say the same thing when I show them the brochure: "Wow, I wish *I* could go there for twenty-eight days!"

Somehow they think alcohol and drug rehab is Club Med. I assure them that if you need rehab it will not be fun at all, especially in the beginning. It's sort of like being in hell, actually, although the scenery is nice. And you don't even see the scenery for the first two weeks. Then, just as you start to get comfortable, you become scared shitless to go home.

As we are pretending to look at the brochure, Stacey's husband says,

"Why don't you two girls go upstairs and pack?" He seems to be in a hurry, which I appreciate. Once the patient agrees to go, I generally start rattling my keys. Best to get on the highway before any changing of the mind sets in.

As we walk up the stairs, I'm taken in by all the photographs of the children on the walls. I do not pause or point them out, though. I don't want Stacey dwelling on her children at this time.

Moms are the least-represented group in rehab. Mothers feel that no matter how sick, no matter how bad the chest pain gets as they climb those hills, *they must not abandon their children.*

So I say nothing about the beautiful photographs to Stacey.

From the bedroom closet, Stacey pulls out a tiny suitcase. I think to myself, *Oh my God, she thinks she is just going for the weekend.*

"Sweetie, do you have a bigger suitcase?" I ask.

She looks up at me. Blank stare. Then I am rewarded. She smiles, slightly at first, then, hands on knees, bent in half, she just laughs and laughs. I laugh with her. Not sure what we are laughing at, but we're having fun.

Finally, taking a deep breath, wiping her eyes, she makes more of a statement than a question: "I guess I'm going for a month."

"Yep, you are," I say, hoping I sound matter-of-fact.

She drags out the big suitcase.

"Take lots of underwear," I say. "Number one requested item," I add.

She stares at me. *Don't ask,* my returned look says.

"Okay," she says.

Gently, I add, "Honey, you have blood on your skirt."

"Shit."

"If you need to drink on the way to rehab, it's okay with me. Are you jittery?"

"No, I'm okay."

I ask her to please hold out her hands. She's jittery.

"Please," I say, "do you have some wine or vodka in the house?"

She doesn't answer. I know she has alcohol in the house. But this is common. People try to downplay the physical dependence.

We have a two-hour drive to the rehab facility. I don't want DTs on my watch. Alcohol detox is life-threatening. It's my job to get the patient safely to rehab. I take this very seriously. I am an RN.

Knowing she won't want to drink in front of me, I leave her alone upstairs.

Coming down the stairs, she looks less sweaty and more composed. *Good, she had a long snort,* I think to myself.

I am constantly assessing the situation. During this part of the process of getting someone successfully into a rehab facility I am the only health care professional on the scene. It's a big responsibility.

Her husband carries the suitcase as he walks us to my red Mazda van—"the piece of shit minivan," as I frequently and affectionately refer to it. Oh, if that van could talk!

Stacey is surprisingly devoid of emotion as she says her good-byes to her husband. One never really knows what goes on in other people's marriages.

She's the best straight man on the ride to the rehab facility, Father Martin's Ashley. She laughs and loves all my stories. She laughs especially hard as I recount my intervention with Dr. Phil. She's without a doubt the "most fun" transport I've ever done. Her sense of humor is unsurpassed.

I'm hopeful that with such a fun, loving spirit, she might beat this deal.

She doesn't beat it, at least not this first round.

Stacey is scheduled to be admitted to Father Martin's Ashley, a beautiful and highly respected alcohol and drug rehab center in Maryland. It is considered to be one of the best treatment facilities in the country.

It is both impressive in its beauty and formidable in stature to new patients. This is true of all the big rehab facilities. They can be intimidating at first glance.

I immediately personalize the buildings, pointing out the women's dormitory, cafeteria, chapel, lecture hall, and, in the distance, the beautiful Susquehanna River.

We enter the main hall—or the "Suddenly Clingy Room," as I call it—for admission.

Lots of hugs and will-I-ever-see-you-again words are the order of the day. I am honored and flattered that I have achieved a sense of trust and closeness in our brief time together. My job is done.

I hold Stacey close to me for a moment. Reluctant to let go, she cries softly in my hair. I end our time together as I started it, whispering reassurance to her.

The miracle is, she is helping me as I am helping her. I whisper reassurance to us both. The odds are not in our favor for surviving this disease.

I leave Stacey in the competent hands of the admissions staff. I am both exhausted and satiated after the completion of an intervention. On my way home, I always go through the drive-through at McDonald's. I love the fact that they put the cream in the coffee before giving it to me. Simple pleasures. With satellite radio blasting classic rock and roll, I return home. I feel complete, and I am sober. God is near.

My phone will ring again soon with another family needing my service as an interventionist. Once again I will stop and listen, as if I am hearing the pain for the first time.

CHAPTER 2

Threats, Memories, and Car Trauma

It's cold outside. There are many dry leaves on the uneven stone steps as I race from entrance to entrance trying to reach the door before Jeff locks us out.

Always wear sensible shoes. This is one of the important rules to live by as an interventionist. Early in my career I learned that running in heels is inadvisable. As with most careers, I think, it's the on-the-job training that proves to be the most valuable. And attention to what appear to be mundane details can sometimes make or break an intervention.

So in my sensible shoes I run from door to door. The sky above is gray. It's late winter. Even drunk, disheveled, and in his bathrobe, Jeff manages to reach each entrance before me, leaving me breathless and cold, locked outside along with his stressed-out family. His mom has stayed behind, and from the bottom of the driveway, where she is clutching her walker, she stares up at us, hope and worry in her eyes.

The call had come a week earlier. A frantic and personable sister telephoned from overseas. She is a professional with an extremely high-level job in a part of Europe most people will never visit.

I always try to answer my phone. I do this for two reasons. The first reason is that I assume it takes a huge amount of courage to finally pick up the phone and summon help for a loved one's chemical dependency. By the time an interventionist is called, this living hell has been brewing for a long, long time.

So finally the moment is here. The miseries, worry, and trauma can no longer continue. The interventionist is called. And she answers the phone! The caller's relief at hearing a voice at the other end of the phone is prize enough for me.

Well, not completely. I also do this for a living. Like many Americans, we are a two-income family with two kids. The person who answers the phone also gets the job. That's the second reason.

When Jeff's sister calls, I am driving up Route 2 on my way to the New Way Clinic in Crofton, Maryland. I'm scheduled to talk to a group of patients, many mandatory DUI clients. This is my second such talk, and I'm apprehensive. Sharon's call concerning her baby brother is a relief from my own self-absorbed insecurities.

Sharon describes a potentially desperate situation regarding her brother's condition. Neighbors and an ex-wife in the neighborhood report increasingly erratic behavior and isolation.

"He won't open the door completely when people stop by and won't answer his phone," Sharon reports. "He's behind in his rent and has not been seen consistently at work."

"When was the last time you spoke to him and the last time the neighbors reported seeing him?" I immediately want to know.

I sense her urgency as I feel my own escalate.

Single male alcoholics have one of the highest rates of suicide and accidental death.

"Three days."

Bad news.

Before we can talk about the logistics of an intervention, we must make sure this guy is okay. As luck, or fate, would have it, I'm driving insanely close to his house. Fate or luck—who cares, really? It's convenient, and I'm happy for it.

So from some faraway country way overseas, a desperate big sister stays on the phone and guides me to her brother's house.

He lives on a hill on a crowded and winding street back in the woods. Under other circumstances I would have called the neighborhood "quaint." Tonight it's dark and hard to see. I drive slowly past his house. I think I see the curtains move. Turning my van around for another pass, I look up and see a man peeking through the drapes.

I chuckle lightly to myself, partly out of relief that we have a sighting but also because of a comic moment: we've got ourselves a "window ninja." Paranoia is never pretty, but at times it's amusing. Either amphetamines or end-stage alcoholism can produce this paranoia, which inspires people to "guard" themselves from imaginary enemies.

Every little bit of information I'm obtaining I am cataloging for my next move on helping this guy. I'm on the job.

Sharon is still on the phone, and I ask, "Any cocaine or amphetamines in his history?"

"No," she says, "he has never been a drug guy."

I'm relieved; amphetamine psychosis can be very dangerous and unpredictable. I have found myself crawling on my belly under a locked airport bathroom stall, removing a needle from a woman's neck as she seized, her head rhythmically hitting the base of the toilet. In a beautiful seaside town, in a home so lovely it defied description, an accomplished man attempted to harm me with a power tool.

Cocaine is THE BEAST. Cocaine is an upper, a stimulant sold on the street.

But cocaine is not the enemy tonight. Alcohol is.

I stop the car and get out, with Sharon still on the phone. We have agreed to maintain verbal contact, if possible.

Jeff sees me from the window and seemingly in no time at all cracks the front door open. With only his head sticking out of the door, he stares at me.

"Hey, buddy, everything okay up there?" I ask. The phone is still to my ear, with his sister on the other end. I can hear her breathing as I reach out to her brother. I am the conduit between two siblings separated by oceans, miles, and alcoholism.

"Who are you?" Good, a rational question, I think to myself.

"I am a friend of your sister's. She's concerned that you haven't answered your phone."

"Don't feel like talking to anybody," he counters.

"Fair enough, buddy. We just wanted to make sure you're okay. I have her on the phone."

"Tell her I'm okay, okay?"

"You bet."

He closes the door. The curtain shudders as he watches me leave, back at his watch post.

I don't presume that I'm always right. And God, I hope I'm rarely wrong when it comes to getting a feel for the situation at hand. Active addiction is a dangerous game. I depend heavily on my gut reaction when confronted with addicts and alcoholics. This intuitive sense has served me well in my nursing career. No doubt the skill was honed growing up in my chaotic and challenging family.

Let me rephrase that. The family I grew up in was messed up, full of fear, and devoid of any real healthy love or guidance. I felt my mom loved me, but love alone without the benefit of good parenting left me psychologically compromised. My father, an alcoholic, showed absolutely no love at all. When he was present, the atmosphere at home was intolerable, the air heavy with tension and fear. My mother had personality changes when she drank her nightly beer. As the years progressed, she used tranquilizers as well. Her obsession with my father was complete, as she spent all her time trying to placate a man incapable of any visible joy. She offered no protection or guidance to me in my journey to adulthood. Because of my parents' problems, I was on my own from an early age. To survive emotionally and physically, I learned to read the mood of all the players. I would then calculate my next move based on the information I was collecting in my increasingly injured mind. The birth of exceptional intuition was the result; it was an unexpected gift.

I do not view myself as a victim. That ship sailed years ago with the help of my psychiatrist, Dr. James Kehler; the fellowship of ACA (Adult Children of Alcoholics); and simple maturity. I am merely stating the facts.

So, cold and curbside, I quickly size up the situation with the window ninja and give the sister my assessment and options. I base my information on the history that the sister has given me and on my observations. He is on an alcohol binge. He is a heavy, daily drinker who is having a private party. He is slightly paranoid but still able to talk rationally and stand up. Standing up is good.

The option that's always important to consider is calling 911. When in doubt, this is the safest thing to do. It allows paramedics to assess the patient and make the decision as to whether the person needs to be taken to the emergency room. In Maryland, the second option is getting an emergency petition through the local courthouse for a seventy-two-hour hold. Again, the patient is taken to the hospital, but this time the person is required to stay for three days for physical and psychological evaluations. Anyone, not just family, can request this of the court.

In the back of my mind, I am always balancing patient safety and my liability risk. An ugly fact of life for any health care provider is the need to remember the motto "Do no harm and don't get sued." Of course, you can do no harm and still get sued. This thought does not consume me, but I know in modern life it is a reality, and I weigh it accordingly.

"What do you think?" Sharon anxiously asks me.

"I think we have a few days to plan an intervention."

It's traumatic to be dragged off to the hospital. Generally you are put in the most uncomfortable emergency-room bed, way in back, guarded by some underpaid security guard, with crappy food and no TV. You are detoxed while there. Not fun.

If tough detoxes kept us sober, there would be no need for interventionists, rehab facilities, and recovery. I did a million detoxes. They don't stop people from using again. Somebody, I can't remember who, explained it to me this way: Detox is like mowing all the weeds down. Rehab, and especially recovery, is like pulling the weeds out by the roots.

By the time I show up to do interventions in the ER, you would think patients would be agreeable. Tired of the ER bed and having their freedom taken away, you would think that they would eagerly jump up and run off to the greener pastures of a respectable rehab.

Nope, they are pissed! With a foggy memory of cold handcuffs and a squad car dragging them to the ER and away from their beloved booze, dope, crack, and so forth, they usually loudly declare that *everything* is the family's fault. Counting down the seventy-two hours of prison, they call a cab and hurl obscenities at us. Because they have usually been stellar patients (ha!) in the ER, the staff eagerly calls the cab for them. I swear I've gone to the bathroom and come back and the patient has been discharged.

I do not like to do interventions in the ER.

So it begins. The sister and I plan the intervention, with her talking from airports as she makes her way from eastern Europe. It's my first private intervention. I worked for an intervention company out of Los Angeles in the beginning of my career. Now I'm on my first independent job, and it will rank as one of the hardest and most traumatic for me. It will inspire me to *always* have security on call. The memories it will invoke in me will take me by emotional surprise.

I do not like this man or enjoy being with him. This is new for me. There's a part of me that almost always falls in love with my fellow addict. Not this guy. Hate and fear will fill my car and my head during our time together.

Still, I must carry on professionally and get this man safely to rehab. I have a strong work ethic. Prayer will become my constant companion.

Sharon gives me the contact information of everyone to be involved in the intervention. I in turn introduce myself to them and send them a guideline to use in writing Jeff a letter that they'll read during the intervention. This is done through e-mail.

We decide on a location for the preintervention, a dress rehearsal, if you will. I like to do this the day before the intervention, not on the day of the job.

You never know what will come up at these meetings. Little unexpected stones will be upturned. One of the players will have a hidden agenda that threatens to infect the whole process. Everything from divorce warfare, to thinking a rehab will "cure" homosexuality, to my favorite, "I sleep on the couch with the big-ass knife stuffed into the cushions in case he comes at me again!"

You don't want to find this stuff out one hour before you are to do an intervention. It can be dangerous, and your client is not getting what he or she deserves from the process.

You would think you'd have all of the information beforehand; most of the time you do. But when the whole family gathers, it is amazing. Honesty about the situation is much easier to read in person. Families tend to rat each other out at these meetings if there is a strong issue looming.

Today's family is calm, articulate, and caring—outwardly, anyway. I am falsely lured into complacency.

Maybe if I had counted the cash the sister gave me as payment I might have had a better idea of how tough this guy was going to be. She gave me an $800 tip! This was the first and last tip I have ever received. I do not expect tips. Looking back, I think she knew her brother would be a complete pain to deal with, so she paid me accordingly—possibly so I would not bail on them (which I thought of doing the next day).

Having run from door to door, Jeff has locked us out. I knock softly.

"Jeff, your family is here out of love," I say. It's worth a shot.

"Get the fuck out of here," he counters.

Damn! I think. No need to try to negotiate, to agitate him further; he won't open the door, and I know it.

"Anybody have a key?"

"No, but his ex-wife has one," the sister informs us.

Knowing his former wife lives in the neighborhood, I ask Sharon to retrieve the key from her. She has declined to be involved in the intervention. She is done. Their teenage son is too fragile emotionally to attend. I will use these facts in the negative during the intervention. Someone's absence can be just as powerful as another's presence. I have a large, beautiful picture of his son with me.

Sharon quickly goes to get the key as we stand unified outside. I'm whispering encouragement to the group. Lying, basically. I don't feel encouraged.

When Sharon returns, I quickly turn the key and open the door. It's like pulling off a Band-Aid: it's going to hurt, so you might as well do it quickly.

Get in there and get this thing done. Never let the patient see you hesitate. Look confident. The interventionist and the patient are on the same team, but the addict doesn't know this yet.

There are two opposing parts of the brain in the active alcoholic. One side of the mind houses the rational person, the one who knows he or she needs help. The other side is swimming in irrational denial. It is this side that will almost always fight for survival. This is the interventionist's opponent.

As the opponent, you want to look like you're there to win.

Good—there's no resistance as I push the door open. I march in, with my soldiers, the family, behind me.

Jeff is standing in a small sitting area off of the kitchen with his back to us. He is peering out a sliding-glass door. He has miscalculated. Not expecting us at the front door, he is guarding the back door. Our lucky day.

Hearing us, Jeff swings around. Barefoot, he is standing in what was once a white terry bathrobe. He has not shaved in days and generally looks disheveled.

"Hey, Jeff, my name is Joani," I say, looking directly at him. "Your family has asked me here today to help you with the problems you're having with alcohol. Everyone is here out of love."

I gently walk toward him, registering his mood. I will take a patient's hand if he looks like he's not going to hit me. I'm not sure of this guy yet. Again, an interventionist's job is in the details.

I do not take Jeff's hand.

"Get out!" he bellows sloppily.

Can you blame him, really? Whether drunk or sober, people do not like strangers entering their locked home unannounced with a key their ex has given them. If you mentally put yourself in their shoes, you will more naturally communicate empathy. At least I hope so.

"I know, buddy. This isn't easy, but everyone here loves you and is worried about you. I'm a nurse and a recovering alcoholic. All you have to do is sit down and listen to some letters your family has prepared, and then you're free to do whatever you like. The choice of what you do today is ultimately yours."

The trick is to give them back the control.

In spite of Jeff's initial anger, he calms quickly as he starts to shuffle aimlessly around the room. Again I explain to him who I am and what we are here for. I suspect he is drunk.

With his brother helping me, I quickly assemble a seating group from a sofa and dining chairs. I pull over a desk chair from the far corner of the room. Somewhat wobbly and heavy with large arms, it will do for "the power chair." I always scan the room, looking for a chair that's different from the rest. This helps establish me, or at least I think it does, as the authority figure in the room, the one who runs the show. Alpha Joani. Sitting forward in my big chair, my props—reading glasses or a pen—firmly in my hand, I feel more in control. Do I project a confident image to those around me with this routine, or is this a figment in my mind from which I gather strength? It doesn't matter; it works.

Gently but firmly I ask Jeff to a have a seat on the sofa. I touch his arm as I move him along. Reading his body language, I am comfortable that he will not reject my touch or deck me.

He will touch me later in the day, during our trip to rehab. His ability to read body language is not as evolved as mine. His touch is unwanted and inappropriate, and ultimately very frightening. I think his motive is to scare me. It works.

I generally have the patient sit between the two people in the room he or she has the least amount of conflict with and is closest to. Today Jeff sits between his mom and his sister.

His mom has generic little-old-lady looks. Tight white curls crown her head. Her murky blue eyes transmit both pain and meekness. She is not the tough-cookie type. But I bet she is a crier. This I like. Tears of loved ones are my weapons.

Jeff's sister, Sharon, has arrived from Europe. She has fashionable, short blond hair. She is on the heavy side and exudes a sense of style and intelligence. I am hoping her intelligence, coupled with her natural care-taking tendencies, will be an asset at the intervention.

My ace, the landlords, are present. They want Jeff out if he refuses help. The house, their property, could be condemned by the health department. The bathroom had human feces in it, outside of the toilet.

Soon, though, nothing else much matters in terms of gauging a success-ful intervention. Getting Jeff to rehab will boil down to me yelling like a . . . a what? Like a foul-mouthed woman, pushed to the edge by his childish, rude, drunken, and hurtful behavior. All my professional teaching will fly out the window as I reach the end of my patience with this guy. This has never happened before, and it has never happened since. I lose my temper. And it works.

What I have suspected has become crystal clear: he is drunk. This makes the intervention difficult and unpredictable. I hate it.

The family and friends read their letters to Jeff, imploring him to go to rehab.

I will spare you the details. Jeff is nowhere in that room. It's amazing how families fail to see this. They read and talk as if the person can make sense of their words, feelings, and reasoning. He is just too drunk.

Jeff gets up and starts to stumble around. Strings of words come out of his mouth and go nowhere. He is getting drunker by the second but is not drinking. I suspect he guzzled a bottle before we started the intervention.

He staggers and hits the wall next to the refrigerator. Jeff opens the fridge door, and rancid smells smack me in the face. Between the feces in the bathroom and this, I'm in danger of gagging on my own puke. The inside of the refrigerator looks as though a hoarder lives in it; nothing has been discarded in who knows how long.

Leaning on the counter for balance, Jeff grabs something out of the icebox. Suddenly he jerks back against the wall, and, holding a syringe like a dagger, he slams it into his upper thigh. Groaning loudly as if a tremendous relief has come over him, he slides to the floor.

I contemplate calling 911.

Grabbing the syringe, I read the word "insulin" on it. He is diabetic. I didn't know this. I asked the family for a medical history, but this was omitted.

Why all the drama around a shot of insulin? I guess even in his drunken state, he knows that with all the sugar in the alcohol he will need his insulin. But the noise and drama around the injection is just weird. This guy is making me uncomfortable.

Now my RN side is kicking in. Gauging the units of insulin against his size and consumption of alcohol, I'm trying to determine what his blood glucose might be.

"Where is your glucose meter?" I ask him, as he slumps on the kitchen floor. He's sweaty, and again I'm contemplating calling 911. I inform the family of this.

Jeff is a loose cannon.

"You're not taking my blood," he mumbles.

"It's me or the paramedics," I counter. Holding his chin up and demanding that he open his eyes, I say, "Me or the ambulance." Again, drunks hate the ER.

He stands, and I help him to his desk. After an infuriating amount of drama and miscalculation, we manage to measure his blood sugar. It's low normal.

With his family gathered around, Jeff now agrees to go to treatment. I can barely write that down. It evokes in me a tremendous amount of agitation and frustration. He played mind games with all of us. He would agree to go, but then he would take an inordinate amount of time to pack. He would put conditions on going to rehab.

"I'll go in four hours." He went in five.

"I'll go after I clean the bathroom." He cleaned the bathroom. The landlords were thrilled.

"I'll go after I read my favorite porn." Really, he said that. I let him pack his "girlfriend," the porn magazine under his pillow, into his suitcase to read later (knowing the people at rehab would throw it out after they searched his belongings).

"I'll go after I do the dishes." That would have taken a lifetime; dishes and grime littered every inch of the kitchen space. His sister assured him she would do them later. And she did.

"I'll go after I take a shower." He forgot about this condition and never showered.

"I'll go after you all leave me alone for six hours. Nonnegotiable."

I try guilt. "I have two kids at home waiting for their mom; we need to go now."

"I'll go after . . . " And on it goes.

The whole time, Jeff's mom is trying to keep up with her walker. She looks sad and confused. Alcoholism is baffling to witness, even for me.

One more comment, and I lose it.

"I'll go after you help me put on my shoes."

His brother, bent in half, attempts to get his shoes on. Jeff, like a three-year-old, is making it difficult. I watch as his brother struggles.

I am seeing a spoiled, overindulged, grown man playing with his family. I suspect I'm witnessing a caricature of what has transpired within this family for years.

I grab the shoe from the brother.

"Get your fucking shoes on yourself and get your ass in my car now! I am done!"

We glare at each other.

The family is stone quiet.

I apologize to the group for my abrupt behavior and foul language. They assure me my behavior is fine and agree that it's needed.

Jeff's glare has changed to a smirk as he continues to look at me while holding his tennis shoe.

Quieter but firm, I say, "I am not fucking kidding. Get the shoes on now and get in the car or the landlords are prepared to evict you."

Reaching into my computer bag, I show him the document supporting this. Amazing—he suddenly has the ability to put his shoes on.

Back on the stone steps, I support his arm as we walk to the car.

"Nice car," he says, as I push his head down the way the police do when putting a suspect into a squad car.

His family looks like they've been to war as they weakly wave goodbye from the steps.

As we pull onto the highway, Jeff starts to howl like an injured dog. Bizarre. Slumped back with the seat reclining, he's howling as though he's severely injured. I'm not sure what's happening. The howling escalates as he arches his back and head up. Again I'm thinking about 911. I feel as if I'm in over my head.

Abruptly, he stops the horrid noise.

As my hands tightly grip the steering wheel, he grabs my upper groin, his hand grazing my crotch.

"You're a nervous driver," he says.

I suspect the howling was a maneuver to try to unnerve me.

"Get your fucking hands off of me," I say, as I glance at my cell phone.

It's clipped to my pants on my right hip. From this day forward, my cell will always be on my left hip, away from the patient, so he can't easily grab it.

I say a silent prayer. "Dear God, I need you, I need you, I need you" is my mantra. I take Jeff's hand from my crotch and jerk it back to his side.

But, oh no, he's not done with the game yet.

I'm on Interstate 95 North going seventy-five miles per hour.

He grabs the door handle and attempts to open the car door, but it's locked. "I should just go throw myself onto the highway and end it all."

Oh, for God's sake. The drama will not end with this guy. But I have precious little time to think about anything. I am in survival mode.

As he attempts to unlock the door, I click the child safety lock into place. My mom skills come in handy!

He laughs at me as he realizes he's unable to unlock his door.

"Clever little bitch, aren't you?"

"Listen, dick, anymore bullshit from you and I'm calling the police. Detox in jail, where when you puke on the floor they'll make you clean it up, or in a nice rehab, your choice," I say loudly and with more confidence and force than I feel. I'm scared shitless.

I feel that at any moment he could fling himself at me, force the car over, strangle me, and assault me.

He settles down, thank God.

"You're going the wrong way," he declares.

"Shut up," I respond.

"Really, it's down this way," he says, pointing to an alternate turnoff.

"Shut up, I know the way."

We make it to the rehab facility. Why didn't I call the police? I'm not sure. My strong work ethic, I think. I had a job to do: get this guy to rehab. Since that day, I have always had security on call and used it when I got the feeling either before or during a job that I might need backup.

I fear for my safety at a gut level. Something that rarely happens to us,

I think, in this life. And I'm taken back to another time, when a man in a car changed my life in ways I probably will never completely comprehend.

It was a time of confusion, fear, trauma, and ultimately the abrupt end of childhood. It took place, with one exception, exclusively in a car. It lasted approximately two years.

I was eleven years old when it started. I want to write that I was afraid, but I told myself when I started this book that I owed both the reader and myself the truth. To alter the facts, to rewrite history, will neither help me heal nor bring to light how it is that pedophiles perpetrate their crimes on children.

So let me say, I was not afraid. In my confused, naive child's mind, I interpreted the advances of a sexual predator to mean that I was loved, nurtured, and affirmed by a man. Confused, certainly, and in over my head, but even being sexually abused provided a distorted version of the attention I desperately needed and was missing at home, especially from my father.

It was a quid-pro-quo situation. He gave me love, and I gave him oral sex and my childhood. I needed the love that badly.

My family had just moved to Arizona from California. While our house was being built, we moved into an apartment complex. We were living down the street from a family of four: Bruce, Naomi, and their two children, a boy and a girl. Naomi used to make the best meatballs every Sunday. Every weekend they had a huge Italian meal.

Naomi pierced my ears. Kissing my cheek and placing an ice cube on my ear lobe, she told me I was beautiful. Their family was everything mine was not. They were noisy, outwardly affectionate, and generally happy seeming.

Bruce was charming, affectionate, and talkative. His daughter, who was just a bit younger than me, was frequently in his lap, absorbing his attention and interest. I do not recall my father ever having me in his lap or touching me in any way. When I say my dad was devoid of any emotional closeness, I mean this in the extreme. My main emotion toward him was great fear. He was completely alien and unavailable to me in any way. He was an alcoholic.

I am sure Bruce recognized the emotional landscape of our home. Our dysfunctional, emotionally barren, and fear-ridden home was a pedophile's orchard. The child was ripe for picking.

We had heavy drapes in the living room at the apartment. Did he know I was home alone? Of course he did. Why would I still persist in thinking that his every move with me was not completely calculated? Innocence lost dies hard, maybe even now. He knew I was home alone.

I heard a tiny tapping noise at the window. I can't remember if I responded at first or not. Eventually I peeked around the drapes. I saw Bruce standing by a heavy cement column that supported the walkway above.

He stared at me; I don't remember if he smiled. I remember his eyes, the intensity of his gaze. A grown man's lust for a little girl, I presume now.

He moved from behind the column, coming into full view. His penis was exposed outside of his pants.

I was shocked and utterly confused. I was a child.

I had seen a penis only one other time in my life, when I saw my father in the reflection of the mirror as he stepped from the shower. I had no brothers.

I moved back from the window, and the heavy drape quickly dropped back into place, momentarily protecting me. And that was the end of my initial indoctrination.

Things become fuzzy. I remember that after the window incident, Bruce continued to be friendly as if nothing had happened. He continued to foster a strong friendship between us. The grooming process was under way.

The first time it happened, I can't remember why I was in his car.

Over the years, the car rides revolved around his picking me up to babysit for his children. We had moved from the apartment complex, and I was the family babysitter. As I write, I realize this was odd. His daughter was one year younger, and his son was about my age or slightly older. I was young to babysit.

He always had a box of tissues on the dashboard of the car and never seemed to expect me to swallow after he ejaculated. He never instructed me to, as far as I can recall. His penis seemed huge to me, and foreign. I had no idea what was happening in sexual terms. We never kissed. He never fondled me. I sucked, and that was all. It did not seem to take much time. He would tenderly wipe my mouth with a clean tissue when we finished.

This all took place in a car until one night. My memory is very foggy, but I remember that we went into an office. The lighting was dim. I recall that he was on top of me as I lay on a sofa. Funny, the things I do remember—the beige leather sofa, shiny with no arms, modern style.

His penis was just on the outside of me, between my legs. I'm not sure if I had panties on or not. My mind tells me he ejaculated before entering me. And that's all I have ever been able to recall.

It ended soon afterward. I told a school friend what was happening, and she told my mom. I don't know why I told my friend, but maybe, feeling that the intensity of the situation had shifted, I could no longer keep the secret.

When my mother approached me about it, I was sick with shame and refused to discuss it. She in turn told Naomi, who came rushing over to our house.

I was hastily preparing to leave the house. As I quickly ran from my home, Naomi caught up to me. Throwing her arms around me, she brought me to the curb, and the two of us sat, side by side. She held me and cried, repeatedly telling me to just think of it as a "bad nightmare."

It would come to my knowledge, through my mother and her investigation, that Bruce had a strong history of pedophilia, as well as a gambling addiction at the horse track. Apparently, the family had owned a car dealership on the East Coast. Through civil legal action taken against him for similar pedophile behavior, they had lost the family business.

If my father had a reaction to the molestation or was even told about it, I don't know. I do remember my mother saying it was "better that your father was out of town and knew nothing of this. He would kill the guy." I assume she never told him.

Naomi must have known what was taking place between her husband and me, all those times he and I were alone in the car after babysitting, and she did nothing, allowing it to continue. This violation, above all else, is what hurt me the most as I matured and began to understand the situation.

I remember telling my mother that Bruce threatened me, saying if I told anyone he "would cut me up, including my ears." That was a lie—a lie told by a kid who felt guilty.

Twenty years later, my mother was dying, and I was helping her die. It would be a special time for both of us. Lung cancer was killing her. Her addiction to cigarettes had caught up to her.

We were watching the story of actress Patty Duke on TV. Molestation is a part of Patty's story. My mother, for the first time, asked me a question that must have been on her mind for a long time. When you know your time is limited, you start finishing up unfinished business.

"Why did you never tell anyone what was happening between you and Bruce? I don't understand why you went along with it."

My heart crumbled. Her inference was clear. It was my fault for being a willing participant.

I broke down. Through my tears I could barely speak. I attempted to explain to her how the relationship works between an opportunist pedophile and a little girl needing love. No Hollywood ending here, in my mom's last days.

She could not or would not understand. I believe that for her to take any responsibility for the dysfunctional home environment that fostered the relationship between Bruce and me was beyond her emotional capabilities. Even within our flawed family, I always knew my mom loved me. And I loved her. I was unwilling to hammer out our family's dark past as we attempted to say our final good-byes. I could not hurt her in that way. Sometimes, forgiving others is a gift we give to ourselves, too.

Bruce always smelled of Brute cologne. For a while after the abuse, I secretly kept a bottle of it in the bottom drawer of my dresser. Uncapping the bottle, I would breathe deeply. I was a young girl remembering a man who had preyed on me, leaving me with a lifelong wound. Breathing in the cologne, I felt a conflicted nostalgia: still so indoctrinated that I was oddly comforted . . . and very confused. No criminal or civil action was ever sought against Bruce.

Jeff is not done with me yet.

My cell phone rings.

"Joani, Jeff is refusing to sign himself in," the intake staff at the rehab facility tells me. "He's threatening to leave."

"Put him on the phone," I say, sternly. The only thing he responds to is my extreme emotion, a style I have never needed to use again.

"Listen, dick, you are free to leave, *but* you have nowhere to go. The landlords are changing the locks, and you have no money. So good fucking luck!"

"Will you go to the movies with me when I get out of rehab?"

What? "No."

Jeff did well in rehab. He did his time in a halfway house and followed up with a local psychologist and recovery meetings. He did call me months later, but he did not ask me to the movies.

He thanked me for my help.

CHAPTER 3

Putting the Pieces
Back Together

Drew has long red hair in dreadlocks. I know this, but I never see his hair, which he keeps balled up in a knit, seventies-style hat.

He walks up from the basement bedroom on the morning of his intervention with his bedspread wrapped around him. He has perpetual sleepiness in his eyes. His nails are bitten to the quick, and he has a snarly teenage attitude. He is in his early twenties. I suspect that years of pot smoking have dwarfed his emotional maturation.

His father makes the initial call to me. He is distraught, concerned, but also close to the end of what he is willing to tolerate in his son's behavior. His kid has racked up some legal problems in their conservative state. He has been caught selling marijuana to an underage boy, his best friend. Dad is hoping an intervention and drug treatment will mitigate the sentence his son will receive in court.

But the state in question has mandatory sentences for the charges Drew has been convicted of. No amount of pleading with the promise of rehab to come or to be completed will change that, Drew's lawyer informs the father and me in a conference call.

Dad is fed up with his son's addictions and the subsequent behavior and consequences, but he also deeply fears what prison will do to his son. His voice cracking, he breaks down as he discusses the possibility with me.

"Prison will serve no purpose with him. It will break him," he tells me repeatedly.

The decision is made to try to get the court case postponed long enough for Drew to complete three months of rehab.

But Drew shows no signs of slowing down. Instead, he is contemplating getting a tattoo. His dad feels he is glamorizing and identifying with the prison "life" even before his sentencing.

My goal is to get this kid off the streets fast, before he does any more legal damage. He needs a good extended-care rehab center that can get him in the best psychological health possible, a center that will help prepare him for a year in a penitentiary.

As upfront as his dad is with me about Drew, his mother is much more reticent about sharing with me her son's history and her feelings about him—in words, at least.

She is petite. Sitting on the sofa at both the preintervention and the intervention, when things get intense, she draws her legs up. Hugging them to herself, her chin down on her knees, she almost disappears. Periodically and silently, tears fall from her eyes. Mom agrees that hard limits need to be set for her son. She says this, agreeing with me and her husband, but her body language tells me she is grieving and ambivalent about it. My job will be to keep both parents on the same page. An intervention can fall apart if a kid smells a divide.

Drew's grandparents drive eighteen hours to be at the intervention. A cousin flies in from the Midwest. Neighbors who have known him since boyhood are present, including an African American lady who tells him the way it is with an honesty and vigor that impress me.

Drew makes the long ascent from the basement to meet the group. I can't tell you how many sons I have had to drag out of their parents' basements. They never seem to reside on the same floor; they are always living in The Basement.

As usual, I feel my heart rate go up as I hear the patient coming up the stairs. I start wondering what life is like for people who don't do interventions.

I stand back just a bit until Drew gets through the door before I make my presence known. His uncle is outside, standing guard at a basement window in case Drew decides to bolt. Coming through the door, he sees the unexpected family reunion. He looks confused. I step into view.

"Hi, Drew, my name is Joani. Your family has asked me here today to help you. I'm an RN and an interventionist."

"What?" is all he says as he scans the room with his eyes. He has that beautiful and wonderful combination redheads possess: his eyes and hair are exactly the same color.

"I'm an interventionist and a recovering drug addict, Drew. Your family feels you're having continuing problems with drugs."

"No way am I doing this," he says. The popular TV show *Intervention* on A&E has increased people's knowledge of the process of intervention. The kids especially catch on quickly to what is taking place. Some even think it's cool to have an intervention done to them. I love it. I'll use whatever tools of persuasion I can get.

So Drew quickly sees what's happening, but he doesn't think it's cool. His face reveals his disdain as his family gathers to give him hugs before we begin. Limply, he puts his arms around each person. His dad doesn't attempt a hug.

"No fucking way am I going through an intervention," he says, directing his comment to his dad.

"Why don't you get dressed?" I suggest.

"Good idea," he says to me with contempt.

As he turns to go back to his bedroom in the basement, I direct his cousin to follow him.

"Really, go down there?" His cousin looks scared.

"Yep, keep an eye on him, be casual."

The uncle who has been keeping guard at the window outside has joined the group. A few minutes go by, and there's no sign of either boy. This happens almost every time. When the patient gets one person off by himself, a litany of bullshit, defenses, excuses, and deflection comes out. Never do an intervention alone. You will not win.

I make the long journey downstairs.

Interrupting Drew's discourse on how perfect his life is, I say, "Hey, guys, come on up. We have some folks who love you, Drew, and who just want a little bit of your time."

"Yeah, right."

I gently touch his arm. "It's not so bad, buddy. And it's kind of cool to have an intervention."

"Okay, let's get it over with."

Music to my ears. He is willing to listen. He doesn't know it, but he has started to negotiate. I have him sit on the couch between his grand-mother and his mom. I love grandmothers. They seem to have an easy, natural relationship with their grandkids. The patient generally behaves when they are around.

Not Drew. He is argumentative, snarly, and nasty. He spirals down into extreme emotional anxiety exhibited by repetitive physical actions like pulling on his eyebrows over and over, then quickly switching to twirling his dreads, and finishing by biting and picking at his toenails. This extreme agitation scares me more than hostility. The group continues to read their letters of love and concern as I keep a close eye on Drew.

"Will you accept the help we have found, Drew?" each person asks in turn after reading his or her letter. His responses:

"Hell no."

"Fuck no."

Laughter.

Picking his feet and toenails as he ignores us.

Dramatically tearing up the rehab-center brochure and throwing the pieces at me.

Tearing up his airline boarding pass and throwing that at me, too.

"Rather go to jail."

"Bite me."

Telling his mom, "Shut up," as she is curled in her little ball.

"You drove how far to say this shit to me?" he asks his grandmother, who cries.

It is like watching Linda Blair in *The Exorcist*. His head is spinning around, and he's spewing ugliness all over the place.

I always tell the family and friends at the preintervention to stay calm and don't, for God's sake, don't take the bait. A good fight can deflect the group from the primary purpose of motivating the person to accept treatment.

But I also like to think I'm a flexible person. So when the African American neighbor lets loose, I find myself being the silent cheerleader.

"You disrespectful, spoiled little shit. Your grandparents drove all night to be here to try and help you, and this is how you act? I have half a mind to smack you upside the head. Look at your mother. She loves you and has given you the world. Car after car you have wrecked, and they give you another one. College tuition, beautiful home, their unending support. And now you respond to the offer of even more help with this filth?"

Drew is looking down at his bare feet, which are propped up on the coffee table.

"Look at me!" she demands.

Drew looks up, his chin quivering. Suddenly he looks like a little boy, not a young man facing prison time.

Quieter now, she continues. "Have some respect, Drew; listen and act like a man."

With tears in his eyes, he again starts the disgusting habit of picking his feet and toenails. He does not seem to realize that he's surrounded by a group of people and that this is inappropriate behavior. Getting past the grossness of this habit, I'm concerned about his emotional state. He appears overly agitated and anxious. I watch him closely.

"Mom, I need to talk to you, alone outside," he says.

No way. His mom alone will cave to his demands. He knows it. I know it. I agree to a family conference with Dad included.

"Oh, I see they need *your* permission to talk to me, huh?" Drew says with extreme disdain.

"Yes, I'm directing this meeting. It's my job," I say, in a neutral tone. This kid will need firm boundaries from me if I'm going to get him to the treatment center in Texas.

Up to this point, his father has been quiet, taking my instructions well. He and Drew have been at such odds of late that I know they could be very volatile together. But I need him now to help Mom hold her ground, and I know he's up to the task.

Drew reluctantly agrees to talk with both parents outside. Leaving the group, Drew and his folks go out back.

It's an oppressively hot and humid East Coast summer day. I watch from the sliding-glass door as the three of them sit on a low brick wall and talk. Drew is smoking frantically as he pleads his case and lays out his plan. I am not looking forward to going out there. I hate the heat.

Giving them no more than five minutes alone, I slide the door open. A huge wave of August heat smacks me in the face.

"Can I come out?" I ask confidently, and maybe a bit too cheerfully. I do not feel cheerful. I am exhausted, and I still have to get this kid and myself on a plane to Texas.

"No," Drew barks at me.

"Five more minutes," I say, and retreat back into the air conditioning. I'm giving him some control so he feels he has some power in the situation. When I return outside, I don't ask permission to enter the conversation.

"Please, please, Mom." He is crying, and imploring, and trying every maneuver that has most likely worked in the past to get his way.

I can't let this go on long or Drew's mom, in her emotionally fragile and exhausted state, might give in to him, just as a mother in a grocery-store line gives in to the toddler who wants candy. Her fatigue overcomes her judgment, and she gives the child the chocolate. It's my job to make sure Drew's mom does not give him the candy.

Drew can see I am about to regain control of the meeting. He quickly pulls out his trump card and hits his mom in what he must know is her most vulnerable spot.

"Mom, if we get the court date postponed, I can stay around the house with *you* and do stuff before I go to jail."

Dad comes to Mom's emotional rescue.

"Translated, Drew, that means you'll hang out with your friends, get stoned, sleep all day, treat us rudely, get a tattoo, go to a three-day concert next weekend, possibly get arrested *again,* and live in our basement while we continue to supply you with a roof over your head and food in your belly.

"You have two alternatives. There are two bags in the house. One small one you can use to pack and move out with *now,* or a large one that has been packed for you to take to the treatment facility in Texas."

Mom looks as if someone has stabbed her in the heart.

"No way, Dad. Fuck! I won't do this!" Drew yells at his father.

I step between them.

"Okay, guys, let's stay calm and go back in, sit with the group, tell them the choices on the table, and listen to what Drew has to say."

Again I'm giving Drew control, allowing him to talk to the group about his feelings. Sitting with them, he cries in earnest, restating his twisted logic. I need to dial this session back and get to the finish line. Drew is just too worked up.

"We need to make a decision," I say. "The plane is leaving in two hours."

"I am not going to fucking Texas, and I am not moving out," Drew says, his arms folded across his chest as he stares at his dad.

Dad stands up. From the hall closet he retrieves the small suitcase, then flings it in Drew's direction. Taking his cell phone out, he aims it in

Drew's direction and heatedly tells his son, "Pack and get out, or I'll call the police and have you evicted. I mean it, Drew, I am done. Get treatment or you're on your own. You have five minutes before I call the cops."

Mom is again curled in a ball.

Everyone is stone quiet. I look at Drew, and bless his heart: like putting together a jigsaw puzzle, he is piecing his torn-up boarding pass back together. I know at that moment that he will go with me. You can do it, Drew, you can put the pieces back together. Not easy, quick, or painless, but in recovery it is possible.

Standing up, I say, "Come on, buddy, let's get your stuff together."

When he goes downstairs, I stay behind momentarily to talk with his parents about making arrangements for Shawn, his cousin, to fly with us to Texas. In that brief amount of time, Drew finds his stash. When I enter the basement, he has a clear plastic bag in his hand.

"Can I take a hit of X for the plane ride?" As I open my mouth to say I prefer that he not take it, he answers his own question. "Oops, too late, I already did." He looks like the Cheshire Cat with a mischievous grin on his face.

I'm worried. I have had no experience with the drug Ecstasy. As I search the archives of my mind for anything I can remember about it, Drew is pulling what looks like an instrument case out from under his bed. Opening it, he shows me his bong. It is the largest, most ornate pipe I have ever seen. He is obviously proud of it, as he gently removes it from its protective covering.

Producing another plastic bag, he loads the bong with pot, lights up, and inhales deeply. Eyes half closed, he holds his breath, maximizing the effect of the cannabis. Earlier, during the intervention, I had given Drew permission to smoke pot before we left for Texas, but the Ecstasy pill takes me by surprise.

Almost every drug addict and alcoholic I take to rehab uses prior to the trip. It's okay with me, and in some cases it's preferred if physical withdrawal is a possibility en route to treatment. Some withdrawals are life-threatening. Feeling shitty going to rehab never accomplishes anything.

"Shit, where am I going to hide my stash while I'm gone?" Drew says, scanning the basement as he packs.

Seeing a guitar in the corner, I say, "Put it in the guitar. Your folks won't look in there." I am rewarded with a big smile.

"Wow, good one! You *are* a drug addict!" he says, as he stuffs his pot into the belly of the guitar.

The marijuana and Ecstasy calm Drew considerably at first. But at the airport, as we're walking to the boarding gate, he becomes agitated, calling his mom repeatedly, begging and negotiating for his release from my care. His dad is texting me frantically as I watch Drew talking to his mom. Cousin Shawn is trailing behind with his roll-on suitcase.

Dear God, when will the fucking plane take off with us on it? is the question running through my head. I can almost see the *People* magazine in front of me and hear the airplane engine humming in my ear, with Drew next to me sound asleep.

The boarding has started on Southwest Airlines. We're lining up like obedient passengers. As we take our places in line, Drew announces to me that he needs something to drink.

My heart rate rises sharply. "Drew, the plane is boarding. Get a drink on the plane."

"No, I'll be right back." As he quickly takes off, I instruct his cousin to go and stay with him at all times. One of my worst fears has always been losing track of a patient at the airport. I practically stalk the person, even as he or she uses the restroom. With males, I have even asked strangers to go in and check on them.

I'm left standing with all of our bags as the plane continues to board. As I wait anxiously, I contemplate a new career. I also realize I do not have the cousin's or Drew's cell phone numbers to text them. I feel adrift with no means of communication as the plane continues to board.

I text Drew's dad for his son's number. As I'm texting Drew, Dad is repeatedly texting me, wanting to know what's up. Dad is telling me of Drew's anxious calls and texts to his mom. We are in texting hell.

As the last passengers board the plane, Shawn and Drew appear, with Drew holding a bottle of Orange Crush. Sometimes a soda is just a soda. Still, I want to smack him.

When we board the plane, there are still two seats together.

"Hey, buddy, want to sit here?" I ask.

"Fuck no," he replies, as he shoves past me.

Lovely boy.

The flight is uneventful. It's early evening as we make our way down the escalator in the Austin airport. I see two people from the treatment center waiting at the bottom of the escalator holding a sign with my name.

Thank you, Jesus. I am beat and need to hand this kid over. It's like a relay race: pass the baton to someone with more energy and a fresh perspective. Dealing with these kids *is* the war on drugs, up close and personal. It is tough. Really tough.

The men from the rehab center—an employee and a patient who have been at the facility awhile—introduce themselves to Drew. He is having no part of it. He tries to look cool and nonchalant as we wait for our luggage.

At the hotel, Shawn and I climb out of the Texas-size SUV. As the boys grab my bag from the back, I open the back door to say my good-byes to Drew.

"Hey, buddy. It has been my privilege to get you down here. Thank you." I reach my hand out to him. He does not reciprocate.

"Yeah, yeah, yeah, skip the sincerity and get the fuck out of my face."

"He doesn't mean that," his cousin says.

"Yes, I do," he yells from the back seat.

I need coffee, badly. As I walk through the hotel lobby, I asked at the front desk if they have any. I am directed to the bar.

I approach the bartender, who is very accommodating.

"Do you need cream?" she asks.

"I do."

"Right back, just made a fresh pot!" She is so perky. Probably just being nice to me because I look like roadkill.

As I stand waiting, I see a well-dressed woman sitting alone at the bar. Her legs crossed, she is drinking red wine from a large tumbler wine glass as she flips through her BlackBerry. The wine looks good, really good. I can almost smell the deep burgundy wine as I longingly gaze at the glass. Red wine was a favorite of mine and my dad's. In high school, I would fill an ugly plastic drinking glass with wine from his cheap gallon bottle, which he kept on the kitchen counter. Lighting a joint, I would sip from the glass in between tokes of marijuana. "Mellow" was the word we used in the seventies to describe the feeling that would come over me.

The devil wants to dance. He hits when you are down, exhausted, and stressed. But not today.

The bartender returns with my coffee.

I am grateful as I make it to my hotel room. Kicking off my shoes, I sit back in the chair, feet on the ottoman. I find a rerun of *Seinfeld* on TV. Drinking my coffee and laughing, I am relieved my work day is over. As I relax, I start to reflect on the effect marijuana had on my youth.

As with Drew, marijuana was the first and primary drug in my life for many years. A boyfriend introduced it to me.

The molestation I had gone through with an adult neighbor in Arizona ended when I was in seventh grade. During that year, I had a boyfriend who was eighteen and in his first year at Arizona State University in Tempe. My parents never seemed fazed by our age difference or that he was a college student, dating their daughter who was in middle school. I can't remember how or when we met.

John was at our house frequently. He was from a wealthy, well-known family. He always brought food and gifts to the house for me and my mom. I remember lots of candy bars. He would bring a case of Milky Ways for the freezer.

John and I had sexual contact, but not in a way you might expect. I had just started to develop physically and certainly could not have been emotionally mature. We would not make out, kiss, or pet. I would sit on John's lap, he would finger me to orgasm, and that was it.

This book is not intended to be about sexual molestation, yet it is alarmingly clear to me that the issue of molestation and the disease of addiction were born dangerously close to each other. Sexual issues became a reason for using, and sexual compulsions haunted me on and off, even during my recovery from narcotics.

John introduced me to marijuana in his dorm room at the university. It initially made me anxious. The dorm room was in a high-rise cinder-block building. The room was dark, with unmade beds. I recall another young man, a roommate maybe, lounging in the dim room. He made a snide remark about me. The exact words elude me, but the feeling was that I was "a sweet find." I remember a vague feeling of being frightened for my personal safety. And I wanted to go home.

John sat in a chair at his desk. Pulling me onto his lap, he pulled a joint out of his pocket, lit it, and handed it to me. I hesitated. I remember these words: "Don't be a cold fish, try it." He used to accuse me of not being sexually responsive to him by calling me a cold fish. I took a small puff, letting the smoke drift out of my lips.

"No, like this," John said, showing me how to inhale the smoke, the smoke that would alter my consciousness, my life, and my brain development for years to come. Marijuana is a gateway drug. Studies and science support the detrimental effects it has on the still-maturing brain of a young person. It is a strong, statistical predictor of future addiction.

John eventually drifted out of my life, sometime in my eighth-grade year. I am not sure exactly when or why, or whether the parting was friendly. Much of this relationship is foggy in my mind. I know I was intensely important to him. But that is all I'm left with.

By ninth grade, marijuana was a weekly, sometimes daily habit. I smoked with friends, both male and female, and at home alone. I was expelled from high school early in the ninth grade. I almost never attended school. Instead I wandered from the house of one friend to another when their parents were at work, and I smoked weed. Aimless, I was sent to reform school by my high school administration.

I was arrested during my time in reform school. I was with a group of people hiking up Camelback Mountain. We would make our way through the Wrigley estate to a huge water tank. Stoned, we would all strip and swim in the water tank. On this hot night in the desert, we were arrested by narcotics officers who were impersonating hikers. After we offered them a toke, they took out their badges. We were handcuffed and taken to the station.

I was a natural caretaker, giving me the illusion of maturity. This is a characteristic that is common among children of alcoholics. We grow up fast as a result of taking care of our sick parents. My friend Lynn was nearly hysterical. As we sat on the bench with many intoxicated Native Americans, I tried to calm her down and stop her incessant crying. The strip search didn't help.

My parents were unreachable, and I was released to Lynn's parents. My mom finally answered the phone, and in her nightgown and robe she came to retrieve me. Not much was said. She was angry, but the focus seemed to be that she was angry she had been woken up. I was charged as a juvenile with trespassing and marijuana possession. My father was the head administrator for a large and prominent law firm in Phoenix. The next day, when he approached me about the night before, he simply said, "Don't get caught again."

The charges against me disappeared, no doubt because of his contacts. I was the only kid who did not have to appear in juvenile court. I felt lucky.

My father had three DUI convictions in the year leading up to his dying drunk at the wheel of his car. As far as I know, he never suffered any legal consequences for the DUIs. His ability to make charges go away and his alcoholism cost him his life at the age of forty-seven. And at the age of forty-seven, I would end up nearly dead with a needle in my arm. Like father, like daughter.

I was readmitted to Saguaro High School in Scottsdale in the tenth grade. I continued to smoke marijuana, but I never missed school again, and I went on to college. Reform school actually worked for me on some level. I came away from that year knowing I wanted to attend a regular school and graduate. More than a few of the kids who attended reform school with me that year died young.

My marijuana habit continued into the 1970s. I would smoke pot at home watching *The Waltons*. My mom would watch TV with me, not smoking my pot but drinking her Budweiser beer. As my father drifted further from us, my mom's drinking increased. She had frequent mood swings and cried often. Her world with my father was crumbling, and she was sad and sleeping much of the time. My heart ached for her.

I recall those times together fondly, me smoking pot and her drinking beer. I miss them still, miss her still. I would be intensely high, engrossed, and giggling at the TV show, and my mom would tease me, saying I acted like a child after smoking pot.

Eventually my cannabis habit became expensive. I was working at a local diner as a waitress and trying to save up for a car, but my tips were literally going up in smoke. I needed a plan, a business plan.

I do not recall how it came about—it seems odd to me now—but I ended up buying large amounts of pot from my mother's supervisor at an insurance company where she worked. Pushing our cranky cat off a round, black-and-white speckled fifties-style Formica table, I would spread out the marijuana a pound at a time. I would clean it up, removing the sticks and stems. Nobody wants to buy sticks and stems. Using a scale and clear plastic bags, I would measure out one-ounce bags.

My mom would watch the process. Her approval was implicit. She seemed proud of her entrepreneurial daughter.

Sitting on the laundry-room floor, with my back to the washer and the olive-green phone cord wrapped around my knees, I would call my buyers, friends, to come over and bring cash. I smoked and shared more of the profits than I ever saved.

My high school days and nights were defined by marijuana. The night the state troopers came to give us the news that you expect other families to get but never your own was no different from many others. Stoned and having the munchies, my friend Betsy and I were in search of a Whitman's Sampler chocolate box. And my dad was driving around looking for another bar. He lost his life to addiction just as my addiction was gaining force.

A few months have gone by since Drew and I parted in Austin. My cell phone rings. His voice sounds different. Where did my snarly boy go?

"Hello, this is Joani."

"Joani, it's Drew. Do you remember me?"

"Sweetie, how are you?" I am delighted beyond description.

"I am great, really great. I cut my hair. You wouldn't recognize me."

"I bet you look very handsome," I say, reminding him that I never saw the infamous red dreads that were tucked into his cap.

"You didn't miss much, all ratty and shit. Glad they're gone."

Then, with a deep breath, he takes the plunge.

"I wanted to thank you for helping me and also to say I'm sorry for treating you rudely. It was wrong of me to treat you like that."

"I appreciate that, Drew, and I'm happy to accept your apology." With tears in my eyes and joy in my heart, I add, "Really, buddy, this call means everything to me."

Drew returns home after three months in treatment to serve his one-year sentence in a state prison. The plan is for him to return to the treatment facility after his release.

He does not get a tattoo before serving his time.

And I tell his parents about the pot in the guitar.

CHAPTER 4

A Dentist, a Dad, and a Convertible

In the predawn light, we quietly get out of our cars. The air is thick with a cool spring fog in this Northeast coastal town.

Twelve men are with me this morning. Most are retired professionals; one is a well-known politician. We line up the automobiles on a long, winding driveway. We have planned our approach the night before at the preintervention.

The patient, Dave, and his two children are in the house. His kids—a daughter, eighteen, and a son, twenty—are part of the intervention and have unlocked the door for us this morning.

I approach the car in front of me. The man inside is slightly disabled with a bad hip. I help him make his way up the driveway, holding an umbrella over our heads. A slight drizzle has begun.

I shush the group. The open lawn is carrying the sound of so many male voices, voices that are familiar to Dave. These men have been friends since high school. They tell me they have been through so much with each other: marriages, divorces, deaths of parents, career changes, affairs, births of children, vasectomies, girlfriends, Christmases, golf games, and many, many poker games. And now they are gathered for an intervention.

These men are a true inspiration, not only because of the longevity of their friendships but because of their commitment to helping one of their own, in trouble with alcohol at age sixty-two. They also have an amusing and endearing trait of talking about each other to me when no one else is around. By the time we part, I know everyone's idiosyncrasies, and what and who drives each of them nuts. They are a lovely group of men. I envy their seasoned friendships.

This is my first intervention organized and carried out primarily by friends. The patient is divorced, and his former wife is not involved in his life. His son and a daughter participate, but they are dwarfed at times by the influence of these powerful men.

We meet the night before at the local Marriott hotel. With such a large group, I reserve a meeting room. I set up the tables in a long row so they can sit on either side. I sit at the end, facing the group.

I am rarely intimidated anymore when meeting groups of people before an intervention. I was early in my career, but like all jobs, the more you do it, the more comfortable you get. With this group, however, I feel nervous. I think the fact that it's composed primarily of professional men has me a little on edge.

My anxieties soon lift as I look down the long table. In the middle of all these men, sitting so still and quiet, is Dave's daughter, Julie. She stands out not only as the only woman but also because she is not joining in the conversation with questions or comments. She has a slim, athletic build, dark hair, and big brown eyes. She is the only one who has not yet written her letter to her dad, to be read at the intervention.

I am drawn to her instantly. There is something in her nature I identify with. Her presence in the room calms my nerves. She is just eighteen, one year older than I was when my dad died drunk at the wheel of his car. My concern for her overtakes my insecurities about addressing the men. I am at my best when someone needs me.

As we discuss the details of the next morning's intervention, Julie remains quiet, stoic almost, until I open the floodgates.

"I hope a few of you are the emotional, sentimental type. Dave will remember the feeling in the room more than your actual words," I say, focusing my attention on Julie. "So I hope a few of you cry!" I say, with an inflection of humor. Softer now, I add, "This is all about love."

Julie's eyes are bright with tears, which then slip down her cheeks. It is my desired effect. It isn't easy, but I need to get to her feelings so they can be dealt with and also to allow twelve of her dad's best friends to support the most injured person in the room.

It is wonderful to watch. All these accomplished men become clucking hens as they direct their attention toward Julie. They surround and support her with their words. Those close enough reach out to touch her.

She cannot control her tears.

Her brother, Joe, comes up to her from behind. In a gentle gesture, he hugs her shoulders as he puts his chin on top of her head. Men love to fix things.

"It will be okay, Julie," one of the men says. "We'll get the job done tomorrow."

She nods as she blows her nose. Another interventionist rule: always have tissues.

"He loves you," another one of the men says.

"Don't worry, sweetie, everything will be okay."

She says little. "Okay, I'll be okay," she manages to get out. "Just go on."

I continue the meeting with a core feeling that there is much sorrow in Julie's relationship with her dad. There usually is when a lifetime of alcoholism has come between two people.

I finish the meeting with my pep talk for the day to follow and the details needed to make it happen. As the men pack up to leave, I ask Julie if she can stay behind and talk with me. She agrees.

With just the two of us there now, I put a couple of chairs together, with no table between us.

"You okay?" I ask, as I look directly into her eyes. "I know I'm glad you're here. I wouldn't want to be the only girl!" I usually find that a little levity can go a long way.

She smiles. "Yes, it does feel like the boys club!"

"Really, though, I know this is tough," I say, bringing us back to the point.

"It is," she says to her hands in her lap. "You know what bugs me? These guys got the best of him, and I barely knew him." Not crying now, she seems angry. "The most he has done for me is pay my college tuition. And now I'm supposed to come up with all this love and shit."

I am quiet, letting her finish.

"He was always around but never there." That statement sums up what every person who has ever lived with an alcoholic feels to some degree.

"Julie," I say, "love written in the negative can be effective in an intervention. This intervention is as much for you as for your dad. Tell him how you feel in your letter. I would bet your dad has loved you all along, but the alcohol got in the way."

As I speak to her, I speak to myself.

"My dad died drunk at the wheel of his car when I was about your age. No one ever approached him about his drinking and his behavior. We never had a chance to establish a relationship. It's my greatest privilege to be here with you tonight. In helping you and your dad, it makes it seem that my own dad's death was not in vain."

Every time I say these words to a family, I get goose bumps and a lump in my throat. And I feel honored beyond measure to be doing the job that I do. I have found a passion in the ashes of my family's past. Nothing could be greater.

I tell Julie how invaluable the Twelve Step program of Adult Children of Alcoholics was to me in my journey of healing from the trauma of growing up with alcoholic-addict parents. I give her a pamphlet about the program. I don't tell her how many years I attended before getting some psychological relief. I do emphasize the importance of participating in the family program at the rehab clinic while her dad is a patient. I hope she hears me.

Going back to the table, we take out pen and paper. She writes her dad a letter, stating her disappointments, hurts, and hopes for the future.

The next morning, between the predawn light and the dense fog, an eerie feeling descends on me as we make our way to Dave's back door. I am not superstitious, but the setting has the feel of a Hitchcock film. I hope it's not an indication of something bad to come. I keep my thoughts to myself.

The kids have done a good job. The sliding-glass door, under a balcony, is unlocked. We quietly make our way to the living room, one floor above. I see Julie and go to her, giving her a quick hug of support. She is to sit next to me during the intervention. She looks nervous.

Dave is expected at his dental practice this morning. He doesn't know it, but his partner has cleared his calendar and put Dave's more complex and pressing cases on his own schedule. This is an important point. The number one objection men assert as grounds for not being able to go to treatment is work. Men's jobs, more than women's, define them as a person. They equate work and their ability to provide material comforts and necessities with the expression of love. It took me a while to truly understand and appreciate this quality in men. Now I always try to make sure I have a man's work covered, which greatly increases the odds that the intervention will succeed.

Dave walks down the stairs, freshly shaved, with what appears to be coffee in a to-go thermos. He sees us as he comes down the staircase. Stopping at the bottom, he stares at us.

"Hi, Dave, my name is Joani. Your friends and children have asked me here today out of concern for you and the role alcohol is having in your life. I am an RN and interventionist, also a recovering alcoholic. Please come and sit down."

As I direct him to the living room, he takes a sharp right and heads for the kitchen without saying a word. His buddies all follow him.

"I can't believe this," he mutters under his breath. Slamming his coffee down on the kitchen counter, he turns and faces the group. "Really, I can't believe this."

"Believe it, Dave. We're all here because we're worried sick," one of his friends says.

"Please, Dave, just come and have a seat," I say. "Your friends and kids have some letters to read to you, and then you are free to do what you like."

I am giving the control to the patient, and this fact is true: after listening to the letters, the patient is free to do as he or she wishes. There are no handcuffs at my interventions.

Rolling his eyes, Dave picks up his coffee mug and walks to the living room.

"Come on, guys. Give your buddy a hug," I say.

Some of the men hug Dave; others slap him on the back. His son holds him tight. They seem to have a close relationship. I will find out later that they frequently drink together.

Julie hangs back from the group. She's wearing a pale yellow, button-front sweater. I think of spring when I look at her.

Dave informs us, "I only have so much time for this. I have patients to see."

"Dave," I tell him, "we've taken care of that for you this morning. Your calendar has been cleared for this important meeting."

"Shit," he says, shaking his head.

After each letter is read, Dave is emphatic that he will not go to treatment. He is polite and listens, but as each person ends and asks if he will accept the help that has been found, he simply and strongly replies, "No."

But there is one person, one letter with its reasoning, that gets through to him.

Sadly, it is not Julie and her letter. She reads last, and it's distressing to watch. The lack of connection between her and her dad and his inability to respond emotionally to her infuriate me, even as my professional side stays neutral.

It is Dave's retired former business partner who connects with him.

"Dave, the community is starting to sense you're having difficulties with alcohol addiction. The incident in the office a few weeks ago, the day you nodded out during a procedure, is on the gossip circuit. This is a small town."

Then he made the observation that sealed the deal.

"You're close to the end of your career. I know the books and what your practice is worth. If you continue with this behavior, your practice will suffer, and you will not be able to sell it and have the retirement you want. In short, the value of your practice is decreasing as your alcoholism increases."

"How will my practice be covered if I go?" Dave rightly wants to know.

"Your partner will take on the pressing cases, and I'll do your routine hygiene checks," his colleague tells him.

"Okay, I'll go."

I lead the group with clapping and cheers. My favorite part of the intervention!

"First, though, I need to go to the office and sign some checks."

I hate when people need to make pit stops before going to treatment. But I sense Dave is earnest in his desire to take care of business. His friends feel the same. And he agrees to have one of them accompany him to the office.

As promised, Dave returns, and after he quickly packs, we leave for the treatment facility. The trip is uneventful. He speaks mainly about how moved he is that all his buddies would assemble for an intervention.

In the end, Julie gets to tell her dad her feelings. Love in the negative: "I never felt love from you. Your friends and alcohol were always more important to you than me." In contrast to her emotions of the night before, now in her dad's presence, she is devoid of tears.

Dave does not try to refute Julie's words, and like his daughter, he does not express much emotion toward her. The void between them is wide. I think the best I can say about the exchange is that a conversation has been started between them. But clearly there is much work to be done to repair their relationship.

It is sad to watch and is eerily reminiscent of my father's and my relationship from so many years ago. I think back to my early-morning foreboding as I approached this home and wonder if my old wounds linger, intuitively knowing they will be felt anew.

The relationship between my father and me was strained and difficult, and had far-reaching negative effects on the entire family. His attitude and demeanor toward us all can be summed up in the story my mom would tell about the day I was brought home from the hospital following my birth. My mom, after a few beers and feeling resentful of my father, would tell it to me periodically. I believe the story is true because it's characteristic of his pervasive, never-ending dark and brooding mood—a mood he didn't seek help for until weeks before his death. And I never knew my mom to be a liar. She could be contrary when drunk, but not a liar.

I was born in early May, generally a beautiful time of the year in Maryland. Coming out of the hospital, my dad took me to the car in a carrier of sorts. As he fished out his keys, he placed me on the top of the car. He got into our Ford and started it up.

"Gill, the baby is on the roof!" my mom shouted.

Without a word, he got out, retrieved me, and placed me in the backseat.

"Your dad was so annoyed in the car the day we brought you home, you know, the *mood*," my mom would tell me. And I knew exactly what she was talking about. He was that way for a large portion of his life. "He was angry that we had had another baby. What a shit he was."

He said nothing on the drive home. He appeared annoyed, his mouth in a grimace as if sucking something sour. The presence of me and my mom seemed to cause him an inordinate amount of irritation. Despite his total silence, his mannerisms screamed the total imposition we were to him.

My dad seemed unable to take pleasure in most things, and everything revolved around his black mood. If you attempted to engage him in a conversation, he would answer with a one-word sentence and say nothing to encourage further discourse. My mom walked on eggshells as she attempted to alter her behavior to his liking.

I was afraid of him for most of my life, and fear was the one enduring emotion I felt for him. I do not remember being physically or sexually abused by him, but my terror of him was complete. My inner voice continues to tell me I was physically assaulted at some point. As my mother was dying, I tried to get the facts from her, but our conversation led to little, other than an almost-too-dramatic denial of any wrongdoing on my father's or her part. Still, although I can't quite access a memory, I feel anxiety, nausea, and a hard-to-describe sense of utter disgust and anger when I try to remember specifics of the past. My mom's frequent threat, "Be quiet, or you'll get the shit beat out of you with your father's belt," is an indelible memory. Could threats alone elicit such strong feelings? I don't know.

My dad did not play an active role in my life. He never attended any of my school functions, and I don't remember any questions about or assistance with schoolwork. I rarely had friends over, and never had a sleepover or a birthday party, because these normal activities would disturb him too much. Again, our existence revolved around keeping him from becoming annoyed.

I never saw my parents engage in a conversation, hold hands, or kiss, although my mother told me my dad had an unusually high sex drive. Not only did he have sex with her frequently, but with numerous other women outside of the marriage. This caused her much pain. Her moods and drinking would become erratic as she became increasingly obsessed with his outside activities. Our household suffered crab lice more than once when I was young. Even after my parents divorced, he would swing by on the weekends. They would go upstairs and shut the door. After coming back down, he would promptly leave, saying nothing, as usual.

The door was also shut at mealtimes, as he ate in his room alone. I would bring him his plate of food and refill his wine glass from time to time. He would join us for dinner on holidays, and I hated it. It was strained and plain odd for us to have him at the table, and even at those times there was little or no conversation. He would eat and then leave us alone, retreating to the solitude of his room, wine glass in hand. To this day I have a hard time sitting down at a dinner table, a simple act that seems foreign to me. Like a duck lacking early patterning, I find myself missing some social skills. I do try, but it's not perfect. I'm painfully aware that I possess many of my father's traits and his genetic makeup.

My father was an alcoholic, like his father before him, and like me today. His childhood was far from easy. For many years, my grandfather made his money running alcohol during Prohibition. During some of the rare times he spoke, my dad would recall those days, telling me that they would frequently run from the law with a trunk full of booze. He attended any school that happened to be close by. They were so poor that he rarely had shoes to walk to school in.

My father had an intense hatred of his mother, though he would never say why. I suspect there might have been some physical abuse in my father's early years. My cousins, who briefly lived with my grandmother, said they suffered some brutality while in her care.

My dad left his family at seventeen and joined the army. On the GI Bill, he obtained a college degree at the University of Maryland in economics and political science. He was the first person in his family to go to college, and he went on to have a respectable business career.

There were times when I was alone with my dad that were less strained. Away from my mother, he was more talkative and less sour. Our family lived in the Bay Area of San Francisco before relocating to Arizona, and my dad and I would spend time exploring the city or golfing in Oakland.

He was an avid golfer most of his life, his clubs always at the ready in the trunk of his car. He loved the Chinese New Year and Golden Gate Park. He was like a tour guide, pointing the sites out to me as we took the trolley car around town. Even on these outings, though, he had an aloof quality. He never let you in, and he certainly never expressed his emotion in words or physical touch in the seventeen years I knew him. Except for one unusual day the week before he died.

Sunsets over the desert in the fall are brilliant in color: red and orange mixed with the fading blue sky. It is my favorite time of the year, with the summer heat finally giving in to cool autumn breezes.

That fall, in 1974, marked one year since my parents' divorce. I would see my father most Mondays when he would visit the diner where I worked as a waitress. He would always sit at the counter, order the meatloaf dinner—and leave me a quarter for a tip! He was notoriously frugal and predictable. That's why his invitation took me by surprise.

"Hey, do you want to go to the Unitarian Church with me this Sunday?" he asked, hesitantly.

"What?" I was clearly confused. Church? How bizarre. Church? Really? Why? "Aren't you coming to Mom's for Thanksgiving?" I asked.

"Yes, next week, but I thought you might want to check this church out with me," he said.

I did not know my dad *ever* to go to church. And I had no desire to go to church with or without him. His attempts to have a relationship with me were a bit of an annoyance at this point in our history. I simply did not know the man. And I was seventeen. I had places to be, or so I thought, being consumed, as most teenagers are, with their own lives.

"Okay," I agreed. "I'll go." I didn't want to disappoint him.

He picked me up Sunday morning in his Mustang convertible. It was a soft baby blue, and because it was warm, the top was down.

"Got your rubber band?" he asked, as I jumped in.

"Yep," I said, as I took it off from around my wrist.

As I pulled my long, blond hair into a ponytail, we took off, classical music playing on the radio. We rode in our usual silence.

The Unitarian Church is in Paradise Valley, just north of Scottsdale. I was surprised to see a round building with a domelike roof. It didn't look like a church.

I remember we all sat in a large circle. I don't remember if there was a sermon or the words to the song we sang. I wish I could remember. My last day with my dad, and I long to remember every detail, but I cannot.

As we sang, we all stood in a large circle and held hands. I don't recall ever holding my father's hand before. When I was a child and he needed to get me across the street or keep me close on an outing, he held the back of my neck with his hand as he led me around. I hated it. It seemed he held you with the least amount of physical touch he could get away with. Having my hand in his for the first time felt both foreign and strangely comforting.

At the conclusion of the song, my dad turned to face me. Bending, he kissed my cheek and uttered words I had never heard him say before and would never hear again: "I love you, Joani."

I don't remember saying anything in return. I felt uncomfortable. I didn't know what to say. My mom had never told me she loved me. I don't think I knew how to respond. So I just stood there. Now I was the one who was mute.

"Bye, Dad, see you on Thanksgiving," I said later, as I got out of the Mustang.

"Okay, see you then."

He died five days later in the Arizona desert. He was drunk at the wheel of his car, overshot a curve on Carefree Highway, and went into a skid. Making the fatal error of turning out of the skid instead of into it caused his convertible to flip into the air. He was thrown from the car and hit his head on a rock in the sand. He was dead on arrival at the emergency room from a cerebral hemorrhage.

A woman passenger, his date, was pinned under the car and died forty-eight hours later in intensive care. The one survivor was a stranger to my dad and his date. He was on an out-of-town business trip and had gone along for the ride simply to find another bar and party with his new friends. My dad's golf clubs, in the trunk, came through the crash unscathed.

My son and daughter whisper to me from across their pillows.

"Mom, tell me about the day I was born."

"Well, it was a hot day in July," I tell Mary. "Well, it was a cold day in February," I tell Max. "It was the middle of the night. You had just finished breast-feeding. Daddy was asleep on the cot and snoring loudly!" That part always gets me lots of giggles.

"I suddenly heard this whooshing noise from the window."

"What was it, Mommy?" they ask, with big eyes, even though they have heard the story dozens of times before.

"It was a lone white dove."

"What did she want?"

"She wanted to know if I was happy with God's gift. She was a messenger from heaven."

"What was the present, Mommy?"

"You are my present! You were in heaven, and God sent you down to me.

"I told the dove to go back to heaven and tell God thank you. That he has sent me the most precious gift in the whole wide world!

"Again I heard the whooshing noise from her wings as she quickly and softly flew back to heaven to tell God I was pleased with the gift of you."

As I speak to my children, I speak to myself.

Four days after Dave's admission to rehab, I get a phone call from one of his friends.

"He's leaving. Can you fucking believe it? Four damn days and he's bailing," he laments.

"I'm sorry, but it happens," I say.

"I'm done helping him."

"You have planted powerful seeds," I tell him. "His drinking will never be the same. The conversation has been started."

Since that phone call, I have never had another update about Dave.

CHAPTER 5

The Birth of Pills

Three beautiful and thoughtful friends have organized an intervention on an old college friend of theirs. The four girls had been roommates in the dorm at a prestigious college on the East Coast. Now a few decades out of college, they all have diverse careers and families.

I am envious of their continued connection and commitment to one another. I spend precious few hours in this life feeling sorry for myself. Playing the victim is a waste of energy and an old game of mine that has lost its appeal. As Alicia, a counselor at La Hacienda treatment center, once told us patients, "Victims do not get sober." But I must confess, I do at times feel envious when I see a group of people coming together to help a friend or family member in crisis with addiction. That is not a part of my story.

Diane's addiction is to pills. I know pills well. Pills were my one true friend that took me through the years and seasons of my life. They took all my pain, anxiety, and self-doubts away. They created a false sense of euphoria in my mind, so I was able to enjoy life more. Until they turned on me. In the end, the pills delivered far more pain than they ever alleviated, a cruel joke so acutely felt that I wanted to die. When I get a call for an intervention on a pill addict, a part of me still gets anxious. I am hypervigilant over my own recovery at these times. The memories of those years still have the power to haunt me, whispering their empty promises, calling me home.

Diane is like me in other ways as well. She is a mom of two young children and is married to a quiet man, Tim. He is an anxious dad and husband, small and physically nondescript. Tim is included in the planning of the intervention, but the organization is primarily carried out by the three friends.

It starts when I get a call from Sherri. She and Diane had attended the wedding of another friend in Pittsburgh, and Diane had fallen asleep at her table.

"When she woke up, she couldn't remember a thing," Sherri tells me. "She had no recollection of having been at the wedding. It was so weird and scary to witness."

Diane's father, a physician, is included in the intervention. After communicating by e-mail and phone, I usually meet with an entire group for the first time at a preintervention. But Diane's dad asks for a private meeting with me. I have a gut feeling something big is coming, a secret of sorts, and I am right.

Diane's mother is still alive but declines to be involved. She feels there would be too much stress on her if she were at the intervention. She also declines to write a letter to be read to Diane on her behalf. I try to stay nonjudgmental, but it's not always possible. I silently wonder, *If this child of hers had cancer or any other potentially fatal disease, would she decline to be involved in the process of helping her get well?* Misconceptions about addiction persist even in this modern age. But I have no opportunity to talk to this woman—her lack of involvement is absolute, and the reason for her silence is never revealed.

As Diane's three friends and husband make plans for the intervention, the dad and I meet at a local Starbucks. I am first to arrive. Finding a table in the back with a bit of privacy, I sit and wait. The father is easy to spot as he enters. All parents going through this have the same look when we meet. A combination of deep worry and anxiety radiates from their faces. Rarely do they appear comfortable.

My job as the interventionist is to impart confidence in the process of intervention and to convey a profound sense of hope that people do recover from the disease of addiction. This comes naturally to me after doing this job for years and from my own personal recovery. This morning, though, I feel unsettled. I have a nagging dread about why this father needs to see me privately. I smell a complication concerning the intervention coming on as the dad walks over to the table.

"Hi, you must be Dr. Johnson," I say, as I extend my hand.

"Yes, call me George," he replies.

"Please sit down," I say, as I direct him to a chair.

We exchange the usual pleasantries, discuss the weather and parking, then settle in for the heart of the matter.

"Is there something specific you needed to discuss with me?" I ask.

"Yes," he says, slowly, without elaborating.

"This must be difficult for you," I offer.

Taking a deep breath, he jumps into the deep pool of regret.

"Over the years I have prescribed controlled substances to my daughter."

I say nothing, waiting for him to continue.

"She was a high-strung kid. She would get anxious about taking tests, so I would give her a Valium from time to time to take the edge off. Was that wrong of me?" I think I hear his voice crack.

"How often did you give her medication, and were tranquilizers the extent of what you gave her?" I ask, without answering his question. Flashbacks of the tranquilizer Ativan, given to me as a teenager, are swimming in my mind.

"She played lacrosse; she was a great athlete in high school. Sometimes if she had an injury and pain, I would give her a narcotic for the discomfort."

His pale, watery blue eyes transmit sincere concern. Diane is his only daughter, only child.

I still need to know to what extent he prescribed medications for his daughter. Was it once in a while years ago, or was it much deeper? The information I gather I will pass on to the patient's therapist at the rehab center. This will give the therapist a leg up on helping the patient.

"How often do you give her these meds, and what age was she when you started?" I specifically ask. "And are you still prescribing?"

He hesitates. "She was fifteen years old or so. I gave her medications about two to three times a month."

I wonder if he is underestimating; probably so. Giving teens mood-altering drugs is a dangerous game played with a not-fully-developed brain. Early drug use can negatively affect the growth process of the frontal lobes and be a precursor to addiction. I could be the poster child. Tranquilizers at age fifteen; needle in my arm at forty-five.

"Are you prescribing medications for her now?" I ask again, hoping against reason that he says no.

"Yes," he says. "But since the wedding incident, I have cut back on the amount."

Diane is close to forty! This takes enabling to new heights. Many doctors and nurses, including me, seem to believe a pill can fix just about anything. But it's hard to fathom that this dad, a doctor, has been prescribing controlled medications for his daughter all these years. It is going to take a team of family therapists to figure out and fix this family. I'm rethinking why the mother has excused herself from this intervention.

"Does your daughter have a chronic pain condition or an existing medical diagnosis that I need to be aware of?" I ask.

"Well, she has complained of back pain on and off in her adult years, but in spite of workups, nothing has ever been diagnosed."

I have heard enough. Again, this dad/doctor needs the help of a family therapist at a rehab center. I cannot figure this out or solve it.

Again he asks me, "Is all of this my fault?"

Most physicians receive very little training in addiction; the average amount of time devoted to it in medical school is six hours. So patiently

I answer, "Well, current medical knowledge believes that certain individuals with a propensity for addiction can be negatively impacted by taking mood-altering medications. The adolescent brain is especially vulnerable to exposure to certain drugs."

My answer feels incomplete and sterile in light of his admission of prescribing narcotics to his own daughter for twenty-five years with *no* medical diagnosis.

He stares at me in silence. His eyes seem to be imploring me for something I can't provide: forgiveness. What I can offer him is something I'm good at providing, and that is a chance to move forward and salvage the situation at hand.

"Thank you for your honesty; I admire that," I tell him. "I'm sure divulging this information to me is not easy."

With his head down and his hands covering his face, he momentarily breaks down, then quickly regains his composure. I wonder if there is more to their history. My radar is humming. But I leave my thoughts and questions to myself. I am the interventionist. My job is to get the patient to treatment. Let the therapists at the rehab center figure it out. They are the angels of the industry, generally an amazing group of professionals.

Pulling my napkin out from under my coffee cup, I hand it to him to wipe away his tears. "Are you willing to tell Diane at the intervention that you will no longer prescribe drugs for her? And are you willing to follow through with this?"

"Absolutely," he says, without hesitation.

If I didn't believe people could change, I wouldn't be in this business.

"Good," I say, as I reach over to touch his arm. "Let's get that in writing with your letter to Diane."

The intervention takes place on a mild summer day at the home of one of the friends, an old Sears house tucked back on a heavily tree-lined street. Bright colors and large pieces of modern artwork adorn the walls. The three friends, the dad, and I wait in the family room, around the corner from the kitchen. A pitcher of homemade lemonade is on the table before us. The usual nervous chatter takes place as we wait.

Diane thinks she is coming for Sunday brunch. I feel ambivalent about the deception that's sometimes needed to get someone to an intervention. When someone expects food, I usually try to make sure there is something to eat. A half-truth makes me feel better anyway.

"Here she comes," one of her friends announces quietly.

Looking out the window, I see a petite, slightly overweight, pretty blond. Her hair is in a stylish, chin-length bob with no bangs.

As her friend greets her at the door, Diane gives her a big smile while handing her a bunch of baby pink roses. I almost feel guilty, knowing her smile will soon disappear. But it's for the greater good, I assure myself.

Waiting until she's well inside the door and her husband is behind her, guarding the door as we had planned, I introduce myself.

"Hi, Diane," I say, taking her hand. She smiles a big smile. She thinks I'm a guest she has not yet met.

Placing my left hand over our already engaged hands, in a gesture that I hope imparts my sincere concern for her, I say, "My name is Joani, I am an RN and interventionist." As her smile fades, I continue, "Your friends and family have asked me here today to help you. I am a recovering prescription drug addict."

Her hand slips from mine as she wordlessly stares at her friends.

"Come on, guys," I say. "Give your friend a hug." They surround her, taking turns holding her tight, and she hugs them back. A good sign.

Her dad stands back from the group, waiting in the family room. I direct Diane to come in and take a seat. Seeing her dad, she approaches him and kisses him lightly on the cheek, as he touches her shoulders. I watch the two of them closely. Her brief interaction reveals no animosity toward him.

Taking a seat on the sofa between two of her friends, Diane gently asks for some lemonade. Her demeanor is almost timid, a very unusual affect in my experience for someone who has just found out an intervention is taking place. "I've been waiting all week for some of this lemonade," she says, and everyone giggles in relief. Apparently this is her friend's specialty, and I'm secretly happy that at least part of the brunch is available to her.

The first friend reads her letter. It's full of college memories, that magic time in many of our lives. I can almost see the campus and their dorm as she relives their happy, crazy college days.

"Will you please accept the help we have found for you?" the first friend asks, as she finishes her letter.

Covering her face with her hands in the identical gesture her father had made the day before, Diane cries, nodding her head in a wordless yes. I am thrilled; it is highly unusual that someone agrees to treatment right out of the gate.

"Yea," I say quietly, not wanting to overwhelm this reserved woman. "Everybody tell Diane thank you."

Her friends flanking her on the couch hug her, while her husband and dad beam from their chairs. The very air in the room seems to breathe a sigh of relief. We continue to read the letters even though she has agreed to accept the help. Next to read is her husband. His letter is full of wedding and baby memories of the two of them and their children.

The person who has the most emotional weight with the patient generally reads last at an intervention. It's like saving the trump card for the end. If the person has not consented to accept the help, the hope is that this last person will have a powerful influence.

In most cases it is a parent speaking to a child, or a child speaking to a parent, that has the greatest potential to break through the river of denial that runs deep in the addicted mind. No matter the age, it is this connection above all others that influences people the most in interventions.

So Diane's dad is to read last. I can hear the ice cubes shift in my lemonade as Dr. Johnson prepares to read. I have warned the friends about what to expect, that he had supplied Diane with many drugs through the years. The friends then hoped to hear words of contrition and responsibility from him, but I also told them that this is just the beginning of a long road of recovery for both of them. In other words, they should not get their hopes up too high.

All eyes are on Dr. Johnson as he pulls out of his breast pocket a handwritten letter, a deviation from the computer-generated copy I had seen. A handwritten letter gives the correspondence a more personal feel. I'm glad on the one hand that he has done this, but I still have an uneasy feeling about their relationship and am troubled by his going rogue with a new version of the letter.

His letter is folded into a million little squares. He methodically opens it. "Diane," he begins, and then pauses as he tries to get hold of himself, choking back tears. "I have loved you since the moment you were born," he continues, reciting the kinds of family and childhood memories that I have asked people to put in their letters. He continues to struggle to read his letter, his emotions and tears getting in the way of his ability to speak.

His son-in-law offers to read the letter for him.

"No," I say, gently, "just give him a second." In my early days as an interventionist I would bail out people who were having a tough time getting through their letters, but I rarely do it any longer. It's highly effective, I have found, for the patient to witness the emotion and pain surrounding their addictions. It is also therapeutic for the person reading the letter to get feelings out in a protected and supportive environment. On a personal level, I have gotten more comfortable with emotion as I have matured as a person and as an interventionist.

So we wait as he collects himself. Diane is silent, looking at the coffee table.

"Honey, look at me," he asks. Putting down his letter, he speaks from his heart.

Without moving her head, Diane lifts her eyes up to meet her dad's. Her eyes are blue like his, but darker, with tears lacing her lashes. As often happens, my heart aches as I watch the two of them.

"Baby, I am sorry. I always wanted the best for you. No more narcotics, *we* can't do it anymore."

What does he mean by "we"? Is he implying Diane was somehow responsible for the years that he prescribed for her, or is there more to the story? Again I am rethinking why the mother is not here for the intervention. God, I hate it when people ad lib. This is why letters are written, reviewed, and read from at the intervention.

It's time to wrap this thing up, I silently tell myself. Diane has agreed to go to treatment, so the crazy family stuff can wait for later. Also, in many ways, interventions are like sales. Once the person has said yes, you do not drag out the pitch; you could lose the customer in the process.

Diane ultimately has no response for her father. She is without a doubt the quietest, most compliant, best-behaved patient I have ever dealt with. This in itself is disconcerting. No opposition at all. I can't help but wonder what I'm witnessing.

The drive to the treatment facility is uneventful on one level. Diane is silent even as I try to engage her in conversation, her only request being that I stop at a convenience store so she can buy a sweet soda. Opiate addicts love their sugar.

On another level, my midbrain, the devil's home, is playing games with me. The midbrain is the where the compulsion for addiction arises. In my case, the compulsion for drugs will subside for long periods, and then, like a jack-in-the-box, it will pop up. It is cued, so to speak, by some stimulus. As Diane gets out of the car at the store, I feel compelled to look in her purse, just a little peek at those pills. Knowing that she has pills, my one true love, has cued my brain to crave. Actually knowing what process is taking place helps me get through the craving. Like a wave, the desire will peak and flatten out. I have learned to wait it out with a combination of cognitive reasoning and prayer. For now, it's working for me. My vigilance, born out of deep despair and suffering, is ever present, but as history has shown me, it is fallible.

She climbs back into my van with her soda, and we continue our drive to the rehab clinic. Diane's silence is unrelenting. I feel self-conscious trying to engage her in conversation, so I ask, "Would you like me to be quiet, Diane?"

"Yes, please, I would appreciate that," she says, without looking at me.

I honor her request and leave her to her thoughts. I will be unable to bridge the gap between us, but that's okay. It is what it is, and I leave her safe at the rehab clinic. My job is done.

My first exposure to mood-altering pills was innocent enough. I was fifteen years old. My family was in a state of chaos for the two years leading up to my father's death. The flimsy and peculiar marriage between my parents was unraveling. My dad rarely came home before two in the morning and was always impaired. My mom was increasingly depressed. She cried frequently and slept an inordinate amount of time, taking tranquilizers for anxiety. She drank beer nightly, which made her angry and spiteful toward my father. As a teenager trying to find my way following the years of molestation, I was alone. My parents were just too caught up in their emotional marital battle and their substance problems to pay much attention to me. Until I got physically ill.

I was a sophomore at Saguaro High School in Scottsdale. I had been mainstreamed back into a regular school after spending my freshman year in a county reform school because of excessive truancy. I started having headaches. At first, the pain was nagging and dull, but it quickly escalated to a searing and debilitating temporal throbbing on the right side. I started popping aspirin like M&M's. Bruises began popping up on my body from excessive aspirin intake. Aspirin affects the clotting factors in the blood; the more you take the more you bruise. Hot showers especially seemed to cause increased pain. After showering, with my hair in a towel, I would lie on my bed and wait for the pain to subside.

I complained to my mother about my head pain, and she no doubt witnessed my unending consumption of aspirin. She was typically very resistant to taking me to the doctor.

Finally, with my headaches persisting, she took me to a gynecologist for the first time. I was already on birth-control pills; I cannot remember who prescribed them, when, or why. I just don't know.

I showed up for my first Pap smear complaining of severe and frequent, if not constant, headaches. The nurse's name was Paula. She had short dark hair and a pretty face, and was dressed in a white nurse's uniform. She was chatty and cheerful as she put the blood-pressure cuff around my arm. Pumping up the cuff, she watched the numbers on the wall. Her cheerful expression changed to one of deep concern. She pumped up the cuff again, this time squeezing it tighter on my thin arm.

"Let's try the other arm," she said.

She pumped up the cuff on my other arm, and redid it several times with ever-increasing pressure on the arm. Satisfied with her performance, she stopped.

"Your blood pressure is unusually high," she told me. "It is 180 over 100. We never see this high a reading in such a young person. It certainly explains the headaches you're having."

Even though I was ignorant of normal blood-pressure levels at this point in my life, I could easily recognize the alarm on her face and in her voice. That and the word "never" were disturbing, even though I was relieved she had so easily found out why I was crippled with headaches.

At this point the doctor came in, and as he approached me, I felt a high level of anxiety and dread as he got near my body. He was standing too close to me; I could not breathe. I thought he sensed my anxiety. He asked me to hold my arms straight out, and he saw my hands tremble. He took my hands and commented on my nails.

"Your fingernails are bitten to the quick," he said, with a tone of clinical observation.

As he proceeded to do the Pap smear and vaginal exam, I felt acutely anxious. But I tolerated it. Paula, the nurse, was at my side, and she continued to look concerned.

This day marked the beginning of a phenomenon in my life that would take decades to subside. Whenever men were in close proximity to me, I would experience extreme anxiety, sometimes to the level of panic. As time progressed, this same reaction would happen with women as well. Later in my life it was given a name: general anxiety disorder with social panic. But on this day, I was a teenager with angst and severe hypertension.

The doctor advised me to quit my pack-a-day Marlboro habit, get off the birth-control pills, start to exercise, eat healthy, and try to relax. At age fifteen, I was being given lifestyle advice that most out-of-shape, overweight fifty-year-olds get. My marijuana habit wasn't on the list of things to give up because no one asked me about drugs, and I was not offering the information. But I was asked about my sex life.

Before I left for the day, the nurse instructed me to sit in the doctor's personal office and try to relax. "Sit in here, sweetie, and take some deep breaths," Paula said. "We want to see if your blood pressure will come down some. Back in a bit." When she closed the door behind her, I was left alone in an impressive-looking office, with medical degrees and member-association certificates adorning the walls. I was not alone for long.

The door opened and the doctor appeared. He touched my shoulder lightly as he walked behind his expansive, dark-wood desk. He had a medium build and dark hair, like his nurse. He wore an official-looking white lab coat and had a stethoscope casually draped over his shoulders. His name was sewn into the lab coat above the left breast pocket. Sitting down at the desk, he took off his glasses, folded his hands together, and looked at me intensely. He then proceeded to ask me questions about my sexual experiences. It was just the two of us, no other staff or parent present.

"Do you have orgasms?" he asked.

Please, for God's sake, I thought. I was horrified and trapped. I could not get up and walk out. He represented authority to me, so I sat and answered his question. Was he a pervert, or did he have my best interests at heart? Maybe he was doing a research project on sexuality and the teen. Or was he a dirty old man and an opportunist taking advantage of a young patient with his power and authority? To this day, I sometimes panic in a doctor's office. The sweet assistant at my primary-care physician's office today knows to never close the door when leaving me in the exam room alone. I will suffocate.

Paula rescued me from further questioning by tapping lightly on the door.

"Let's see how your blood pressure is," she said, cheerfully.

It had crept even higher, and my head was ready to explode. If I was prescribed a blood-pressure medicine I don't remember it. I was sent home with a referral to see a cardiologist and with a prescription for the tranquilizer Ativan, the Valium of the seventies. The love and obsession was about to begin.

Having had the prescription filled at the pharmacy downstairs from the doctor's office, my mom and I made our way to our car. I didn't tell her about the sexual interrogation. I was confused about what had taken place. I still am. That was my first Pap smear, and I thought that might be part of the process and exam. I remember standing at a street corner waiting for the light to change. With the Arizona midday sun blaring down, my head was throbbing. I needed to sit down. Heat from any source seemed to exacerbate the pain. I could feel my heart beating on the right side of my head, and I feared I might puke.

I got into the car and dug around my purse for my aspirin. My mom reached across the seat and handed me the tranquilizers.

"Here," she said, "take one of these. They might help."

"Okay," I said, weakly, hoping the medication would alleviate the unrelenting pain in my head. And it did. The sun got softer as my mind and body let go. I put my head back on the car seat and soaked up the peace. And that's how my love affair with pills began.

I had a complete workup with a cardiologist. After numerous procedures, including blood and urine tests, an EKG, an ultrasound of my kidneys, and a chest X-ray, it was determined that I had essential hypertension and tachycardia (fast heart beat) at the ripe old age of fifteen. Even with the Ativan, my blood pressure remained elevated when I was at the cardiology office, so they added phenobarbital to the mix.

I hated the diagnosis, but for the most part, my headaches were gone. I did quit smoking cigarettes, stopped taking birth-control pills, and started riding my bike everywhere. My bike and exercise became a big part of my life for years to come. So, as with most difficult challenges in life, some good things came from this situation. Admittedly, I have wondered from time to time if more good could have come from it if someone had taken a moment to ask me what was happening in my life and at home. Did anyone ever consider psychological counseling for me? If it was recommended, I never heard about it.

I continued to smoke pot during my last two years of high school, but I was not as consumed with it as I had been. I continued to see the same cardiologist for the next seven years and was prescribed tranquilizers the entire time.

Today my blood pressure is excellent, and I no longer take tranquilizers. But there is much more to the story of how I got to where I am now. My pill addiction, which started out innocently enough, has had many, many twists and turns, escalating to dangerous proportions and taking me to a living hell.

A few months after dropping off Diane at the rehab center, I get phone calls from one of her friends and from her husband. Diane has relapsed.

"Stick to the boundaries, Tim," I tell her husband. "Don't let her drive the kids around," I say, feeling relief that I never killed my children while I was behind the wheel of my minivan.

Diane is no longer getting pills from her dad. Her husband tells me he was adamant about no longer prescribing for her. I am extremely proud of that father; old patterns of behavior die the hardest. And change is taking place in the family system. Sobriety is a process, rarely smooth or quick.

Diane is doctor shopping for her meds now, according to Tim. No doubt she is good at it.

I did look at the pills in Diane's purse when she went into the store to get a soda. I couldn't help myself: I had to uncap the bottle and look at them. The ground was shaking. I took the top off the bottle and poured the beautiful and deadly pills into the palm of my hand, counting them out of an old habit. I registered their shape and color as I studied them. Slowly, one at a time, I slipped them back into the bottle, listening to the familiar noise as they clinked back in. Tenderly, I replaced the cap. Not today, old friend. But we will meet again. Even as I know you will strangle me, I want you still.

That is addiction.

CHAPTER 6

The Beast Cocaine, and a New Love

Nancy's father calls me as I am driving to the gym. His accent is so heavy and difficult to understand that I'm forced to pull over and listen. He has gotten my name from a rehab center.

The dad is a pragmatic man who works for a large government agency. He is deeply concerned about his daughter, her addiction, and her subsequent lifestyle, as well as about the cost of my services. We talk about an intervention for an inordinate amount of time as we haggle over the details and cost. This is his right, of course, even if it does get tiresome on my end.

Later, when we meet for the first time, I find out that he is an interesting, handsome, self-made man who moved to the United States from southern Europe. His wife is equally attractive, also has a heavy accent, and is from northern Europe. She is as fair as he is dark. Together they have worked hard to create the American dream in their lives. And their wonderful combination of genes has produced a stunning, exotic-looking daughter. Those same genes, coupled with social and psychological influences, have also created the most fragile cocaine addict I have ever dealt with.

After he has gathered all the information from me over the phone on how to do an intervention, Dad tries to do the job himself. Nancy readily agrees to go to treatment when her father approaches her, but she tells him she wants to experience a professional intervention! *Wow, this will be easy,* I think. I have never done an intervention *after* the patient has agreed to go to treatment. Perhaps that is not technically an intervention, but it is still an opportunity for family members to support Nancy and to make clear their feelings about her and her drug use.

Nancy has a college degree in early education and was a nursery school teacher until her cocaine habit demanded more cash. She first started exotic dancing—that is, stripping—at an upscale gentlemen's club part-time on the weekends. She quickly learned that the income is far greater in the erotica industry than in teaching, and the cash is immediately accessible from down in her G-string. No taxes, no waiting for a check to clear—a drug addict's dream.

Nancy was eventually fired from the club. Having her panties stuffed full of cash, she couldn't resist the temptation to leave her shift and score cocaine. She was not reliable, and the club let her go. By the time I meet her on the day of the intervention, she is working in the section of the city known as "the block," filled with low-end strip clubs, prostitution, drug dealing, and gambling. No commitment is necessary here; girls just drop in to the sleazy clubs and work as needed. The block is in the grimiest part of the city, in an extremely dangerous neighborhood.

I pick up Nancy at her house in a cozy, working-class, inner-city neighborhood. This is a first for me—picking the patient up for the intervention. As I go through a metal front-door gate, I hear barking. I look up and see a little snow-white dog in the window. I can't help but see a correlation between cocaine and her pure white dog.

Nancy takes her time getting to the door. I hear lots of scrambling-about noises. She finally answers, wearing the shortest shorts possible. She has a cute, perky bottom, and sweet, long, light-brown legs. Her breasts are perfect—and manmade. (She tells me later that a client paid for them.) Her nail polish is bright red and stylishly chipped, that look that only young women can get away with.

Best of all is her face. She has impossibly big, brown, almond-shaped eyes that look naturally lined. Her beautiful, full lips form a smile that is warm and sad at the same time. Her only flaw is her nose. She points out this "defect" almost immediately upon meeting me. I would never have noticed. But there is a concave area on the top of the bridge. Her nose is caving in from chronic cocaine use. She has an unusual amount of mucus buildup because of this condition, and she coughs and spits frequently. Her voice has a raspy quality that she also attributes to her cocaine habit.

I like her immediately. Behind her severe addiction there is obviously a warm heart.

"Hi, Nancy, I am Joani," I say. "Can you believe it, this is your lucky day!" I stand there with a happy look on my face, as if she has just won the lottery, and that is how I feel. This could be the last day she ever has to live in this hell. "Can I hug you?"

"Sure," she says, in her sexy, raspy voice that matches her short shorts. She does not look as happy as me. She looks scattered, like she needs direction.

"You all packed?" I ask. She knows that after the intervention that's not really an intervention, I will be driving her to rehab.

"No, almost, not completely. I'll be right back." And she scampers up a flight of steep, narrow stairs, the kind that one-hundred-year-old row houses have. "Watch TV," she yells over her shoulder.

Her family sent me to pick her up for a reason. The girl cannot get away from the coke long enough to pack and get anywhere on time. I take advantage of the time alone to look around.

Piles of magazines are scattered on the living-room floor. A few panties and bras are thrown about. The TV is set to *The Price Is Right*. Sticking out of one of the pages of a magazine on the floor is an uncapped needle. Good thing I have my shoes on. I am very careful as I look around, not wanting an unexpected needle stick. If this young woman is not HIV-positive, I'll bet she has hepatitis C; virtually all needle addicts in the city do.

As I enter the narrow kitchen, I see an open bottle of whiskey and a single, bright-red plastic cup. Her refrigerator is a vast wasteland, containing almost no food. The freezer holds an open bag of ice cubes, which are spilling out. The girl likes her whiskey on ice.

Nancy's life can be sadly described by looking around her house. She sits in front of the TV doing coke. As the euphoria from the cocaine overtakes her brain, she looks at the magazines and TV shows, fantasizing about what she sees, as if it is somehow her life. Intense euphoria allows her to dissociate from reality.

Her world of illusion is complete until one of two things happens: she goes too far, or she runs out of cocaine.

If she injects too much, her euphoria is replaced by paranoia and psychosis. With the dreadful premonition that this is about to happen, she will start to drink whiskey to bring herself down. Sometimes it works; other times she has to ride it out in hell. She likely has been hospitalized several times with seizures and psychoses brought on by cocaine overdoses.

If she runs out of coke, she then picks up the bras and panties from the floor and prepares to go to work. She goes to the block for her temporary employment. She no doubt has regulars who come to her. She still looks good.

"Nancy, I'm coming up," I warn. We will be here all day and night if I wait for her.

"Please don't, I'll be right down," she counters.

"Sweetie, I'm a drug addict. There's little I haven't seen."

"Really?" she says, while peeking her head around the corner. She must be on her knees; her head is at the bottom of the door jamb.

"Yep, and I even have the track marks to prove it," I say, as I roll up my sleeves. My darkest past has become my largest asset, just as the Big Book promised me it would.

"Amazing, you don't look like a needle junkie," she says, as she looks at my track marks.

"We come in all shapes and sizes," I say, smiling. I am proud to be a sober junkie.

She is on her knees, at the altar of her drugs. On a small, low table, with a round mirror, she has her cocaine laid out. Some powder is loose, and a spoon and needle are nearby. There are also small, cloth-wrapped containers holding the drug.

"Do you shoot, snort, or smoke?" I ask, already having seen the needles and her concave nose.

"Snort or shoot. Hate smoking crack, it bothers my sinuses terribly."

"How do you decide which you will do?"

"I am more and more afraid to shoot. I've had some bad reactions with seizures and acting crazy," she says, "and I have a hard time finding a vein that still works. The one vein that still works keeps getting infected." With that she pulls up her sleeve and shows me a discolored, swollen, rock-hard mess of a vein. "I am on antibiotics for it now. Not too long ago after I shot up, I ended up running down the street naked and screaming nonsensical bullshit to strangers. Not cool. I ended up in the ER."

"But you still shoot from time to time?"

"Yep. Sometimes I just can't get where I need to be, you know, not jacked enough with snorting, so I end up with the needle. If I can get my vein to work, I try to shoot as little as possible."

It is like looking at a time bomb. With this sort of history and habit, Nancy is likely to die of her cocaine addiction. I feel like I'm in the presence of someone who is terminally ill. In my experience, addiction to a powerful stimulant like cocaine or methamphetamine is the granddaddy of all addictions. The euphoria produced in the brain is so extremely seductive that a rat in an experiment with such a drug can't help but go back and push the bar for more reward. I was that rat, and it almost killed me.

I watch as Nancy snorts the rest of her stash. No addict I know leaves any coke behind before the long march into rehab. Almost immediately, even before the effects of the last hit have worn off, she is lamenting the fact that she has no more.

"Shit, can we make a stop on the way to my sister's?" she asks, looking distracted and frantic.

"No, we're already late, everyone is waiting."

She is a prisoner; invisible handcuffs have her chained to this drug. Cocaine is a beast.

The intervention is at the home of her married sister, Carol, who is as beautiful as Nancy, but in a more traditional, less exotic way. She has long, dark, shiny hair with no bangs. Both women embody the word "sexy." Carol is also educated and articulate, and she loves her sister with her whole being.

The intervention goes as planned. It is emotional, sweet, and affirming. Instead of asking the usual, "Will you accept the help we have found and go to treatment today?" everyone ends by saying, "Thank you for agreeing to go to rehab." At its conclusion, I drive Nancy to the local treatment facility.

But this is not the end of our time together or the story. It's a cliché for sure, but the worst is yet to come.

Nancy does her thirty days in rehab. She is reported to be a compliant and receptive patient. Within a few weeks of her discharge, however, I get a worried phone call from her sister.

"Nancy is in a hotel by the train station in the city," Carol tells me. "It's not good; she has stopped answering our calls. I'm sure she has relapsed."

There it is, that awful word—"relapse." No other word is so laden with the connotation of failure. Many diseases are chronic, but we do not imply moral failing when those diseases need further treatment. Bad behavior, in all its numerous forms, is, unfortunately, the way the diseases of addiction and alcoholism manifest themselves. I have often said it is this manifestation that people hate about addicts, not the disease itself.

I call Nancy's father and make plans for her to enter a more comprehensive rehab center, for a longer stay, in a state far away. I will need to transport Nancy by airplane.

"Okay, give me the address of the hotel," I say. "I'll see what I can do." My gut tells me to be careful approaching her. A hotel connected to a train station screams transient drug and prostitution activity.

The hotel has a beautiful lobby, not the scuzzy atmosphere I expect of a hotel down by the train tracks. The hotel staff, citing the usual privacy policies, will not give me Nancy's room number. I have to get creative with the security guard and a police officer in the lobby to find her location.

"Yeah, we have our eye on that girl," the police officer tells me. "The room is trashed. Bill was paid one week in advance by some guy."

A john, pimp, or drug dealer is my assumption. "Can you give me her room number, so I can check on her?" I ask, nicely.

"Really can't, privacy policies," the security guard informs me.

"Listen, guys. Her family has sent me over her to check on her." I take out my business card. "I'm an RN and interventionist. This girl is a fragile cocaine addict with a history of seizures. I have no doubt illegal activity is going down in there. I just need to find her and get her to a treatment center."

They stand and stare at me, weighing the options. Possible seizures and death, illegal activity, trashed room—or let this lady get her out of here. These guys know each other well. A nod from the cop to the guard, and I am told the room number.

"Thanks, guys, I appreciate it, really. Hey, any chance you could come up with me?" I'm really not that brave, although the Big Book says on page 102, "Your job now is to be at the place where you may be of maximum helpfulness to others, so never hesitate to go anywhere if you can be helpful. You should not hesitate to visit the most sordid spot on earth on such an errand. Keep on the firing line of life with these motives and God will keep you unharmed." I am thinking that maybe God sent these guys!

"Sure. We peeked in there yesterday, out cold on the bed."

"Was she breathing?"

"She wasn't dead," the cop says.

On the ride up in the elevator, the security guard tells me he is in recovery for heroin addiction. His cop buddy is beaming.

"So proud," he says.

I love these guys.

I knock loudly on the door at regular intervals. I can hear that the TV is on, but there is no response.

"Nancy, it's Joani. You in there, sweetie?"

Still nothing.

Before the security guard opens the door, I need to get something clear with the cop. "Hey, if you see any drugs lying around, please do not arrest this girl. I need to get her to long-term treatment, not to jail."

"We're on the same page," the cop says. "As long as there's no violent crime going down, we're okay."

"Thank you."

The security guard opens the door with a universal pass key hanging from his belt.

Nancy is lovely, even in a deep, post-cocaine-binge slumber. Lying on her stomach with one leg slightly off the bed, she looks like a sleeping child—a child who played dress-up, with too-heavy makeup smearing her face and pillow.

"Thanks, guys, I'm okay. Thanks for your assistance."

I look around the room. In her purse is a wad of cash. She must have danced last night. Opening the small door under the bedside table, I find a small amount of cocaine. It's her wake-up stash. A drug addict's rule: never go to bed without a wake-up stash.

Sitting on the side of the bed, I gently rub Nancy's back. Surprisingly, she wakes easily. Recognizing me, she gives me a big smile. A hopeful sign, I think to myself.

She pops up. "Hey." She looks sheepish now, as she pulls her long, brown hair from her face.

"Hey," I reply. "You okay?"

"No, no, I'm not," she says, while shaking her head. "You talked to my family, huh? God, I don't want to see my dad. He must be disgusted with me."

"He's worried. He wants you to fly with me tomorrow to another, more comprehensive, longer-term treatment facility."

Amazingly, she again readily agrees to go to treatment. I get on the phone and make the arrangements with her dad to get her out the next morning. She refuses to talk with her father on the phone.

As usual, in the hours before transporting an addict, things get crazy. I make plans to pick her up at the Days Inn the next day so we can drive to the airport together, and while I am in the hotel room helping Nancy to leave, there is a knock at the door.

"Fuck, that's my drug dealer," Nancy says quietly. "Be cool; if you run out now he'll get suspicious of me. Just sit down."

Now I am afraid. This girl is living a hard-core lifestyle of drug addiction and erotic dancing in a city known for crime and violence. Meeting her drug dealer is not on my bucket list. I make sure my cell phone is within reach. I sit on the couch by the window.

As Nancy opens the door, I see a large African American male, probably in his twenties, with shoulder-length dreadlocks, small gold earrings, and a black leather jacket. He is good-looking, but also scary-looking, considering the circumstances.

Nancy is unusually perky with him. As she stands on her tiptoes to kiss his cheek, he encircles her waist with his hands. As he does so, I hear the crinkle of his leather jacket.

"Where were you, girl?" he asks, at the same time noticing me over her shoulder.

"This is my friend Joani," she says, adding, "She's a drug addict." Seemingly afraid he will not believe her, she continues, "She has track marks."

Crap, I think. I want to be anywhere other than in this hotel room. As he approaches me, I assess the door to the room, trying to determine whether I can escape if I need to.

"Hello," I say. Skipping the usual handshake, I stretch my arms out, elbows down, for his inspection. Inspect them he did. Both arms, carefully, before speaking to me.

"You in recovery?" are his first words to me.

"Yes, my track marks are healed, but they never seem to go away."

"She's cool," Nancy adds.

"Nice to meet you," he says, as he grabs the desk chair. Flipping it around, he places it in the far corner of the room, allowing him to see everything. I'm nervous.

Nancy goes into a long-winded explanation of where she was the night before and what she had been up to. I'm still not clear what they're talking about. She seems anxious to make sure he believes her story. He continually hammers at her about her activities, accusing her of lying. This exchange goes on and on and back around again.

Their bantering has a friendly edge to it, but because I don't know what's happening between them, I continue to feel uneasy. I stay alert, constantly assessing the situation. I'm afraid his friendly banter could turn nasty. From my seat on the couch, I'm not sure I can make it to the door before he can catch me. I'm wishing my buddies, the security guard and cop, were still with me.

"Well, you got it?" Nancy finally asks.

"Yep. Got the money?" he counters.

"I told you I was fucking dancing last night," she insists, while fishing the cash out of her purse.

Getting up, he slings maybe a dozen small plastic balloon bags of cocaine on the bedside table. So he *is* the drug dealer.

"Here babe, for being a good customer," he says, throwing down on the bed an extra bag, filled with cream-colored powder. The other bags hold pure white powder. This odd bag is heroin. Nancy's heroin habit is periodic, not steady like her cocaine dependence. He is like the department-store saleswoman who gives you a free perfume sample in the hope you will come back and buy it in the future. Sales are sales, I suppose, no matter the industry. But perfume never killed anybody.

"Need anything?" he asks, looking at me

"No, those days are over," I say. God, I hope forever.

"You a counselor?" he asks.

"Yes, sort of, an interventionist and a nurse."

He nods his head, saying nothing.

"Okay, Nance, be a good girl," he tells her with a quick hug, and he's gone.

With all this cocaine, it will be a miracle if Nancy is around, let alone in any shape to fly, in the morning. I give her a stern lecture about being on time the next day, and she promises she will be here in the morning.

But she isn't. Just as I am about to give up hope on making it to the airport in time to catch our flight, she comes running in. Although her hair is disheveled, her eyeliner and mascara are smeared, and her thong is sticking out the back of her tight low-slung jeans, she still looks sexy, like a girl in a music video. She is frazzled but still committed to going with me. We rush around throwing everything into her luggage. I call back the taxi that I had put on hold, and off we go.

In the taxi, I tell her, "If you have drugs or paraphernalia on you, Nancy, you need to lose it. We need to make it through airport security."

"I can't make it to the West Coast without some coke. I won't go without it," she says, defiantly.

I take her purse and dump it out onto the seat of the car. Needles and old coke balloons—tiny plastic containers that hold the drug—spill out with the rest of the contents.

"Where is it?" I want to know.

From her bra, she pulls out what is left of her stash.

"Do you think that's wise, to take that through security?"

Without a word she scrounges around the disheveled mess of her purse contents. Finding a tampon, she takes the cotton out and replaces it with cocaine and a needle. Without apparent modesty, and with the cab driver sneaking peeks in the rearview mirror, she pulls her jeans and thong down, and inserts the tampon into herself. She rolls down the window and throws spare needles and used cocaine balloons onto the highway.

I express my concern to her, but she is firm in her decision to carry the drugs onto the airplane.

As we approach security, Nancy looks every bit the coked-up, unkempt hooker. The top of her G-string is still visible, pointing to a tiny tattoo on her lower back. She is continually rearranging her boobs by pulling up her tube top, and her high-heeled sandals clip-clop along as we hurriedly make our way.

She plops her carry-on luggage and purse onto the conveyer belt to be screened by security, then starts chatting up the guard. I'm quietly trying to tell her to cool it, but she's having no part of it. I feel as if she has a beacon flashing from her head that says, "Look at me, I have cocaine stuffed up my crotch."

I am amazed that we make it through security. She immediately heads for the ladies' room.

"Nancy, please be cool with the drugs in the bathroom," I urge. At this point our relationship starts to become strained.

"I'm fine. You're the one that'll get us busted with all your fretting," she hisses. She might be right, so I try to calm down.

We find our gate, and Nancy announces that she's going to the bathroom. I trail her, keeping watch from outside the lavatory. Too much time has passed; I feel an intense urge to check on her.

"Nancy, it's me. Where are you?"

"Down here."

I follow her voice to the end stall. With my face pressed against the door, I peek through the crack. I can see she has the needle in her mouth as she scans her arm for a vein.

"Shit," I quietly hiss. "Nancy, pleeeeease put the needle away. It will take you all day to find a vein. Fuck, just snort it and be done with it!"

"Leave me the fuck alone," she quietly barks back.

It will be a long day.

Nancy saunters out of the ladies' room, coked up and ready to shop. Heading to the nearest kiosk, she starts spending what little money she has with her. She buys a cheap pair of gaudy sunglasses that she's convinced looks fabulous on her. Almost anything this girl puts on manages to look good on her, but right now she appears so ugly to me. She is not present in her body. Her whole being has been hijacked by cocaine. I do not know the girl in front of me, and I feel a deepening sense of dread about our trip together. I contemplate canceling our tickets.

With her big, black sunglasses on, we board the plane. The second we sit down, while other people are boarding and placing their carry-on luggage in the compartments above, she insists on going into the airplane bathroom. Like a salmon desperately swimming upstream, she pushes her way to the lavatory, looks of annoyance clear on the other passengers' faces.

Shit, I think. I sit and wait. With the plane engines on, the flight attendants start to bang on the bathroom door, insisting that Nancy take her seat. Finally she comes out and sits down. I want to smack her. She is up and down the whole flight. Then, God help me, we have a layover in Denver. Really, I will need God's help soon.

Nancy heads back into the bathroom in the Denver airport. I continue to plead with her to slow down, which makes her even more incorrigible. As I stand outside her bathroom stall, she verbally abuses me. Leaving her alone for less than five minutes, I go to buy a bottle of water.

I return to the bathroom and approach the stall, but she doesn't respond when I call her name. I can hear a rhythmic pounding noise coming from inside.

"Nancy. Nancy. Shit," I say, breathless as my heart races, terror filling my head as I realize my greatest fear was becoming reality. Rushing into the stall next to hers, I stand on the toilet and peer over. She is having a seizure and is unconscious, with drool sliding out of her mouth. The noise I heard was her head pounding the base of the toilet as she seized.

Jumping off the toilet, I crawl on my stomach on the filthy bathroom floor to reach Nancy on the other side. As I try to hold her head still while she is seizing, I see the cocaine needle sticking out from the left side of her neck, blood oozing around it. Dear God, no. My fear is that she missed the vein and injected the cocaine into an artery. Injecting into an artery instead of a vein makes the effect of the cocaine on the brain stronger because blood flow from arteries is far more forceful. The dangers from having the drug and anything else in the solution go directly to the brain include strokes, seizures, weakening of the blood vessel wall, and nerve damage.

With a wad of toilet paper, I pull the needle out of Nancy's neck, and then apply deep pressure. Even in this charged situation, the nurse in me is aware of the danger the needle poses to me. I immediately throw it into the toilet as I keep sustained pressure on her neck, hoping she didn't puncture an artery.

Reaching for her wrist, I'm reassured to feel a weak pulse. Her breathing is shallow as her seizure subsides, and her color remains a pale pink. It's not the worst seizure I've seen, but I'm still shaken up. Nancy is disoriented as she regains consciousness; she quickly realizes what has happened. This must have occurred many times before. I give her the option of calling in paramedics, but she adamantly refuses. Reluctantly, I agree to board the plane to California, knowing that getting Nancy to long-term treatment is her best hope of finding the real help she needs. This is a tough decision for me, and it includes both my clinical knowledge and prayer. I feel tremendous stress.

Nancy insists that all the cocaine is gone and her one needle is now in the toilet. How can you tell when an active addict is lying? When her lips move. I naively think this potentially catastrophic experience will temper her actions for a bit. I should know better. My own history with amphetamines, including my overdose and subsequent usage coming out of the hospital, is not a whole lot different. How quickly we forget.

On the plane again, Nancy starts to cry, telling me she'll die from her addiction. No argument here. Then as quickly as her tears dry, she is up again and going to the bathroom. Storming to the back of the plane, I slam my fist on the lavatory door. Cracking the door open, she claims to be sick to her stomach, showing me the puke in the sink. Okay, maybe.

Nancy stays in the bathroom for the rest of the short flight. The attendant keeps watch, coming to my seat to tell me, "Your friend is still sick to her stomach." She never returns to her seat, even for the landing. All the passengers have deplaned, and the cleaning crews have come onboard, when Nancy finally comes out of the lavatory.

We walk to the baggage-claim area in silence. I am exhausted, and she is angry with me. Or maybe, more accurately, it's her brain on cocaine that's mad at me. The addiction will always fight to survive. I struggle to remember the girl and her smile that I fell for not too long ago.

While we are waiting for our bags, she again needs to use the bathroom. Dear God, I am so tired of this bathroom scene. Once again, against her wishes, I follow her.

"Get the fuck off my ass," she yells.

"No, I'll stay with you until I hand you off to the rehab. It's my job!"

"Fuck you."

"Fuck you back," I say, as she glares at me.

She enters a stall, and I go into the one next to hers.

"You can go, I am fucking peeing," she says.

"You aren't the only one who needs to take a piss," I reply, lying. Climbing onto the toilet, I peek over, and there she is, sticking another needle into her neck. "Get that fucking needle out of your neck, now!" I scream at her.

"Fuck you, I said *leave* me alone."

"Get it out *now*, Nancy, or I will leave this bathroom and get the police. I would rather see you in jail than dead on the bathroom floor!" She repeatedly jabs at her neck, trying to find a vein. Then I utter the threat I should have used miles ago, one that finally has an impact on her: "Get the needle out of your fucking neck or I am calling your father."

Bingo. Out comes the needle. I can't help but wonder how it is that her dad has this much influence on her at this moment. I suspect it is a deep, abiding fear of his disapproval. Whatever it is, it works. She stops jabbing at her neck.

I hand her off to two people from the rehab center. After hearing about our trip west, they meticulously search Nancy and her belongings for any contraband. This would normally be done at the center, but considering her recent history, they feel it's best to do it immediately.

We do not hug as we part company. As she smokes a cigarette curbside, she glares her wordless good-bye to me. I say nothing, silence being the best I can offer her. She has made our brief time together a living hell for me. I am worn to the bone and, frankly, ready to be rid of her.

We will meet again shortly.

It was my birthday. "Happy twenty-first birthday, Joani" was creatively and lovingly spelled out on a mirror in cocaine lines for me. It was a present from my boyfriend, Jack. I was in Scottsdale, Arizona, home from Yavapai College in Prescott and waiting to take my registered nursing boards.

Cocaine had replaced the marijuana habit of my high school years. I had needed a new drug because marijuana no longer worked for me. It turned on me. As much as I tried to retrieve the old feelings of relaxation and distraction that pot had provided, I could not. What was left was pervasive and unrelenting paranoia every time I smoked. The fun was gone, never to return. So as marijuana left the stage, cocaine and alcohol joined the ever-present tranquilizer Ativan.

Jack's and my relationship revolved around cocaine. We met through a mutual friend and quickly started to date. Distance separated us much of the time. I lived in a college dormitory in the mountains of Arizona, and he lived in Scottsdale, more than one hundred miles away. But when I went home most weekends, we would hook up.

It was the late seventies. *Saturday Night Live* parties, disco, water beds, and powder cocaine were in their heyday. And Jack always had cocaine. Coke did not grab me right away. It was a slow burn that built over time. I became a heavy binge user. After college, the binges escalated with free-basing, known today as smoking crack cocaine.

Jack was a generous boyfriend; my sense of comfort around him, as with other men, was almost always achieved through chemical alteration from cocaine and tranquilizers, such as Ativan or Quaaludes. I would be perched on a garbage can in the dorm hallway, pay phone to my ear, and Jack would ask, "Did you get the coke in the mail?"

"Yep, got it. When are you sending more?"

"When are you coming home?"

"When are you sending more?"

And on it went. I was his girlfriend, and he spoiled me and supplied me with cocaine. We had a term for this type of relationship, which is probably still used today: coke whore.

But I had a problem: I was worried about my blood pressure. I was in nursing school now and knew the dangers of hypertension and using stimulants. I bicycled and played tennis frequently, and I no longer smoked cigarettes, but I knew I was playing with fire when it came to my cardiovascular system and my cocaine use.

The night of my twenty-first birthday was like many nights before it. I had a bizarre ritual. Sitting crossed-legged on comfortable white wall-to-wall carpet in Jack's living room, I contemplated the lines of my birthday message laid out before me on the mirror. Before snorting my first lines with a rolled-up dollar bill, I placed a blood-pressure cuff—a specially modified cuff that makes it easy to take your own blood-pressure reading—around my left arm and pumped it up with my right hand. Jack watched with what seemed to be intense curiosity as I inflated the cuff to get a baseline reading before snorting the first line of cocaine. With a stethoscope in my ears, I slowly deflated the balloon to get an accurate reading. Good, 118 over 78.

With the cuff still on, I snorted a line. Then I pumped up the cuff again and anxiously awaited the reading as the cuff slowly deflated. Immediately, and maybe predictably, considering my unstable cardio-vascular system, the reading jumped to 140 over 90.

"Not too bad," I told Jack. "Let me snort four more lines."

After snorting each line, I would repeat the blood-pressure check. Every time I inflated the blood-pressure cuff, my hands would visibly shake as the cocaine was absorbed into my bloodstream, affecting my nervous system.

"Shit, 160 over 98," I told Jack.

In an attempt to justify doing more coke despite my elevated readings, I offered to take Jack's blood pressure. I needed data to validate my excuse that everyone's blood pressure is affected by cocaine. I repeated the process on Jack. His blood pressure did rise because of the cocaine use, but only in small increments. Besides having a coke habit, he was a nonsmoker and avid tennis player. He would go from an initial low pressure to an acceptable 120 over 80. This disturbed me. But my false euphoria affected my judgment and drove my need for more cocaine, despite the evidence before my eyes that cocaine affected my blood pressure far more severely than it did Jack's.

I had a rule. If my systolic reading, the first number, went above 180 and my diastolic went above 100 and I got a headache, I would slow down. That is, I would wait for them to go back down and then snort more coke. If I overshot the mark, I would take an extra Ativan. I did not like to do this because the tranquilizer would dampen my high from the cocaine. And on it went, in an exhausting attempt to have the drug cocaine without stroking out. This is what I did for fun.

The night of my twenty-first birthday was a blowout, with more cocaine than I had ever seen or consumed, and I did not sleep at all. As the sun rose, I dragged myself back to my mother's house. I always preferred to sleep alone; the ability to be intimate beyond having sex was completely out of my emotional range and comfort level.

So with the early morning desert heat already on the rise, I made my way home. I was twenty-one and profoundly depressed that day. Sitting on my mother's couch, I was in a stupor of tears and utter blackness. It was my first experience of complete despair after the cocaine ran dry. So I downed a handful of Ativan and slept it off. I would bounce back in a few days, only to repeat the cycle the following weekend.

Jack and I eventually broke up over money. I loaned him seven hundred dollars he owed his coke dealer, and he never paid me back. I was outraged, and that was the end of Jack and Joani, but not of my relationship with cocaine.

My cocaine use escalated shortly afterward, when I moved into my first apartment. Armed with my registered-nursing license and my first hospital job, I settled in with a roommate named Maria. Maria and I had met poolside at our moms' condominium. I loved Maria. She was a wonderful friend on many levels, but birds of a feather find one another. Our drug use together reached dangerous proportions. We were two professional young women, working by day, drugging by night—many times all night.

The apartment we shared was lovely; the balcony overlooked a park. During spring training, baseball teams played just below our windows.

Maria's sense of decorating style and cooking abilities made our first apartment a home. She was a brunet beauty, with a figure I envied. She was from Brooklyn, New York, and had an odd inflection to her speech, unlike the usual mild and benign accent of the Southwest. Her mannerisms were always exaggerated, and I found her pleasant in every way.

Despite our increasing and erratic drug use, we both tried to act responsibly about our jobs and our careers. We rarely called in sick; we were punctual and accountable. But it wasn't long before I "diverted" my first narcotic from the hospital where I worked as a staff RN on a GYN medical-surgical floor.

Cocaine and Quaaludes were our amateur version of a speedball. The real speedball on the street is cocaine and heroin. The first takes you up, the second brings you down. Boyfriends came and went for me; Maria had one regular, Chris. He taught us how to freebase cocaine by cooking and smoking it. He was also our consistent supplier of Quaaludes.

At some point I stopped checking my blood pressure. When smoking coke, the assault on your cardiovascular system is sudden and intense, the euphoria is beyond description, and it leaves you almost immediately wanting and needing more, oblivious to all other priorities. Needing to know my blood pressure became insignificant to me. Despite the dangers to my health and even my life, I continued to smoke coke. This is the definition of addiction.

The sun would come up, the coke—and the boy of the moment—would be gone, and I would feel desperate. Throwing back a handful of Ativan, I would close my bedroom curtains tight and wait for slumber, one of the few places I found peace.

Another place I found peace was at work. Despite all the chaos in my personal life, I was a responsible nurse, never going to work under the direct influence. I worked the evening shift, three to eleven, in a beautiful, all-private-room hospital in the Southwest desert. Evening breezes would drift in from the patients' balconies, lifting the curtains and bringing with them the sweet smell of orange blossoms. At the nurses' station, an expansive, half-moon window showed off the brilliant sunsets.

I loved the patients and the nursing profession. Hospital nursing can be a grind, but for the most part it fit me well. I was friendly, caring, efficient, and knowledgeable. I was also the typical addicted nurse: an overachiever, bright, efficient, and generally a good worker. My parents, despite their own struggles, had instilled in me a strong work ethic. My dad, a man of few words, did give me a glimmer of his wisdom. Whenever I complained about my menial high school jobs, he would say,

"Never forget the day they hired you and that they are paying you to do a job." Then he would add, "Go to college and *always* be able to take care of yourself." Maybe he sensed that he would not be in my life for long. I was a hard, reliable worker.

I don't remember what I was thinking the first time I stole a narcotic from work. I don't think it was premeditated. At the time it seemed like pure necessity, in my mind anyway. I was going on a date after work with George, the hospital pharmacist. I never felt comfortable with men and always took an Ativan or Quaalude before a date, sometimes overshooting the mark and becoming far more sedated than I intended. I have a foggy memory of one time when a man whom I had met at a bar brought me home—carried me home—probably scared to death by my near-comatose state toward the end of our first date.

So as my shift neared its end, I fished around in my purse for an Ativan—but no pill. I felt that familiar sense of panic start to rise up as I anticipated being in a man's company. I so badly wanted to make a connection, to experience that sense of ease, love, and companionship that seemed to come so easily to others. But I could not; as badly as I wanted to achieve closeness, the majority of the time I was paralyzed with crippling anxiety. Even a school dance with a boy standing close to me could send me into a panic.

To my relief—and I remember this clearly—I realized I was surrounded by pills! Looking through a file, I scanned the medications my patients were prescribed. None was taking tranquilizers, but they were all on the opiate Percocet for postoperative pain. To make sure enough time would elapse if the patient asked the incoming nurse for a pill, I charted that the patient took a Percocet at a certain time and slipped it into the side pocket of my white uniform pants.

Walking down the hall on my way out, I stopped at the drinking fountain. I took the pill from my pocket and expertly tossed it to the back of my throat. Bending over the drinking fountain, I pushed my bangs from my face and let the cold water splash in my mouth. With one quick gulp, a love affair began that would span decades. Eventually I would find my ability to obtain opiates impeded by a job change, but my love of them never died. Surviving that long period of time away from each other, we would be reunited, and the love would grow even deeper and increasingly more dangerous.

But that evening I was an insecure young nurse on her way out the door on a late-night date. I remember stopping by the nurses' station across the hall. I needed to start an IV quickly for one of the nurse's patients. I always had an uncanny ability to start IVs. When there was a difficult job, I would get called by other areas of the hospital to help out. And I always obliged. I was proud of my skill as a nurse at just twenty-three.

I had no idea how the narcotic would affect me, or how much time I had before it kicked in, but I figured I had a few minutes. Throwing my purse down in the nurses' station, I approached a colleague.

"Hey. What do you have?"

"Oh, man, she is a tough stick. We have all tried. Elderly woman had her gallbladder out yesterday. Room 217."

"Everything in there?" I asked.

"Yeah. IV cart outside the door."

"Thanks."

The first sign that the narcotic had reached my brain came as I approached the room. I did not know this was a symptom at first, but I came to recognize it as one over time: my nose would start to annoyingly itch. In my attempt to hide this from my husband, Brian, years later, I would take Benadryl with my narcotics to quell the itching. The itching was a dead giveaway for him that I was using.

So scratching my nose periodically, I wheeled the IV cart into the room to assess the patient. A nice, white-haired old woman greeted me on arrival. "Sweetie," she said, "I hope you're good at this. I feel like a pin cushion."

Smiling, I reassured her. "Yep, I'm good at this. That's why they called me. Don't worry, it'll work out," I said, as I confidently took her paper-thin arm. Her skin was so loose it slid around as I scanned it for vein access. I saw multiple bruises where veins had burst as soon as a needle was inserted. She was frail and somewhat dehydrated, making my job more difficult. But I always loved an IV challenge.

Bending her elbow up, I looked at the underside of her forearm and—bingo!—I saw a virgin vein, which was protected by a bit more fat. I placed a tourniquet *lightly* around her arm; this is the trick to keeping a vein from blowing as you insert a needle.

Then it happened. A sense of subtle but powerful calm descended on my mind. It was lovely, and so welcome. It almost defies description. Often when I lecture on narcotic addiction I tell the audience, "I guarantee that if Percocet made you feel how it makes me feel, you would be doing Percocet, too."

Stopping momentarily to absorb the feelings I was experiencing, I chatted with the elderly woman. I was suddenly euphoric, everything was subtly more alive, and I felt completely engaged in my surroundings.

I returned to the task at hand. As I stood behind her to reach the back of her bent forearm, I took her frail arm and expertly held back the loose skin, firmly but with a light touch. With my right hand I slowly and gently slid a small bevel catheter and needle into her vein. I was rewarded with dark, rich blood flowing back down the catheter from the vein. Still being very gentle, I slowly pulled the needle out while advancing the catheter, and it was done. Using less-abrasive paper tape so as to not tear her skin, I anchored the catheter and tubing to her arm.

"You did it!" she said happily.

"Yep, I did," I said proudly, as I patted her thin white hair and gently tucked it behind her ear.

I learned three lessons that night. One, I could use narcotics and still work productively. Two, it was easy to steal the drug. And three, I loved the feeling it gave me far more than cocaine or tranquilizers.

Cocaine and Ativan were still in my life, but my use of them started to wane against the tide of my new obsession. My addicted life would morph once again. Much like a parent who makes room in her heart for a new baby, I made room for a new drug.

George and I hobbled along for a while. I would not say we were a couple. I was never sober when we went out or had sex. I never achieved a sense of comfort with him, and he eventually left me. Perhaps he sensed my substance-abuse problem, or maybe it was my inability to connect. Either way, he was gone.

Two weeks after I leave Nancy curbside, we meet again at the rehab center in California where she has been living. I am there on a personal trip to pick up my own sobriety chip, the tokens we give each other in recovery to mark our time sober.

I approach her as she relaxes on a large wooden deck with other patients, soaking up the southern sun. I am unsure how she will respond to me, our last interaction having been so contentious. But upon seeing me, she squeals with delight, hugging me tight and long. I hate cigarettes, but as a peace offering, I bring her a few packs.

"I love you, Joani," she says, immediately and amiably. Her voice has lost its raspy edge.

The girl I had glimpsed is back. She is beautiful once more, with clear eyes and an open heart. As we sit through a Twelve Step meeting together, we sweetly hold hands. I will tear up periodically with gratitude that this lovely girl is no longer actively held hostage by the beast cocaine. She is alive and safe.

But it does not last long. After I return home, I receive a report that she has been dismissed from the rehab center prematurely. Apparently she engaged in disruptive behavior that was unsettling and dangerous to the community at large. Knowing this center as I do, her actions must have been severe and extremely unruly to get her kicked out.

Once home, Nancy relapses again. She ends up in intensive care at the hospital with an overdose of cocaine. Her physical state is so life-threatening that she is placed on a ventilator as the nurses and doctors attempt to save her life. They do save her, but upon waking, no amount of persuasion from her family can motivate her to accept help again. She goes back to the seedy hotel where she had just overdosed, and that is the last I hear of Nancy.

CHAPTER 7

Alcohol, and a Psychiatric Diagnosis

My Chihuahua, Lucy, and I frequently hang out at Pronto, our local coffee shop in Annapolis. It has Wi-Fi and the best coffee and baristas ever. I affectionately call it my office, and Lucy is a star there with many fans. With her licking my arms clean of blood after my own drug use behind us, she patiently sits in the chair next to me as I work—my loyal companion in good times and bad.

I find that I work best with lots of noise and distractions around me. I'm not sure why. And this is where I am when many of the calls from distressed families come in. Today, a husband and father named Joe has called to say that he can no longer tolerate the pain of living with his alcoholic wife, June, and that she is opposed to going to treatment. "She's extremely resistant about going to get help," he tells me. "It will be tough."

I hear this all the time, and my reply is always the same. "If she was not resistant, you wouldn't be calling me. This is what I do every week; this is what an interventionist does, motivates people to enter treatment in spite of their unwillingness. Don't worry. I can help you." My aim is to instill a sense of hope and confidence in the process of intervention.

Although my responses to family members are predictable, the circumstances surrounding each particular intervention continue to surprise me, sometimes catching me off guard, as they do in this case.

Joe reports that June is chaotic and out of control from alcohol. She has a history of pill addiction as well, but at the moment, alcohol is the problem. They have two young children, and Joe is overwrought as he juggles managing the prominent company he owns and attempting to keep the home front from imploding. It's a familiar story.

As I get to know Joe better, it becomes evident that he is invested in the very thing he is complaining about; although he bitterly objects to June's drinking, his role as caretaker becomes his identity, and it gives him a great deal of control over his wife. The intense control-taking can also be a way to try to manage the stress of the situation—creating order from the chaos swirling around the family.

So once Joe and I initiate a working relationship, I have to set the boundaries, because he attempts to do my job. To his credit, he takes direction extremely well, which is sometimes hard for a powerful businessman.

"Joe, that's my job, don't worry about it," I frequently reply to his comments.

"Okay" is the simple answer I get from him on my BlackBerry.

I like him from the beginning, but I am clear with him that he needs treatment as well as his wife for codependency. I remember well my treatment at La Hacienda and being outraged that I was in rehab, away from my children, and that my husband, Brian, was not.

"You are just as fucking sick as me and I am the one in rehab again. You get to stay home with the kids, and then you have the gall to put me on the prayer list at church *and then* you get all the sympathy with casseroles and kisses! The poor husband, my ass!" I would scream, as I flung another phone at the wall in my room at rehab. Maybe I was not appropriately expressing my anger and frustration that Brian needed help as well as I did, but he got the point. He became active in individual therapy and Al-Anon, a sister program to AA. Al-Anon is a recovery group for those who live with and love alcoholics and addicts. I often say that Alcoholics Anonymous saved my life and Al-Anon saved my marriage. Brian and I continue to work on issues in our marriage. It's not always easy or perfect, but most of the important things in life aren't.

So I try to relate to Joe our marital experiences, struggles, healing, and growth at the preintervention meeting. I don't think he hears much of it, though. He is too caught up in the hell of the moment. The respectable rehab center we are sending June to will approach this issue with him and will have specific programs for him and their children. All good rehab facilities do. As a general rule, spouses cannot get sober alone; the family has to be involved in treatment to achieve any measure of success.

The preintervention meeting is on a dreary, bitterly cold mid-winter evening in Manhattan. It seems to be just on the verge of snowing. The hotel is high-end and has valet parking, a small luxury I happen to love.

The meeting is uneventful on one level. Why is it, though, when I am bestowed with a glimmer of lasting wisdom, it is from the most unlikely sources and at the most unlikely time? So it is on this night.

Joe and June live in an extremely affluent neighborhood outside New York City. They represent a social-economic class that I have never been a part of. I am comfortably middle class. The income I generate for our family is not a luxury; we are a typical two-income family with kids, one of whom has special needs because of autism. These facts alone have probably been a factor in saving my life. Necessity is the mother of the internal motivation needed to get well from addiction. There is nothing like impending financial ruin from reckless, wasteful spending and a child who needs you even more than your other child to motivate you to get off your ass and do what is suggested to get well and stay well. I do not envy the wealthy when it comes to this. Except for making it possible to afford great rehab centers, having money does not stack the deck in their favor when it comes to getting well from addiction and alcoholism. Father Martin of Father Martin's Ashley rehab center used to say that the two things that deter people from getting well from addiction are wealth and youth: both the rich and the young feel invincible. So even if I grumble at times, it has served me well to have a two-income family, with a precious little boy, Max, with autism, and of course Mary, my daughter and the light of my life.

As I plan for the intervention with women from June's neighborhood, I imagine what these wealthy, stay-at-home moms will be like: pampered, snotty, fake, and pretentious.

I am completely wrong. The three friends participating in the intervention from this exclusive suburb could not be more loving and real in their concern for June and her family. I am put to shame and happily shift yet another prejudice in my mind. This little bit of growth is an unexpected gift from this intervention, and I am better for it.

The morning of the intervention, the skies continue to be gray, the snow just will not come, and the cold persists. I park my minivan, as we have planned, behind Joe and June's expansive garage, preventing her from possibly seeing me from their house. My Mazda minivan is a workhorse, with a few battle scars evident on its body. I tell people it keeps me humble, because it still displays the dent I acquired driving it while high on the amphetamine Adderall. But just as it symbolizes my addiction, it also has signs of my recovery and career. A cameraman from GRB Entertainment, the company that tapes the TV show *Intervention* for A&E, inadvertently broke the side door handles by gingerly pulling on them as we sped away in pursuit of an alcoholic on the move. And I have never fixed them.

Still, as I park behind a Ferrari and three other expensive vehicles on this chilly morning, my little minivan feels, well, shabby. She has a strong, proud ego, though, so holding our heads high, we wait patiently for the others to arrive. And they all do arrive—in more expensive cars. Oh well. Joe, having dropped the children off at school, is the last to join us.

"She's up; looks like shit, but she's up," he tells the group, as he nervously checks his watch. His nails are bitten to the quick.

"Okay, guys, let's go in," I say. "Remember, she'll sit between her brother and Theresa." Theresa is one of June's friends.

"And Joe, once again, and I say this respectfully, do not speak until I ask you to. Got it?"

"Yeah, I'll try," he tells us.

The group giggles nervously, knowing it's almost impossible for Joe to be quiet and not try to run the intervention.

"Really, Joe, the intervention could fall apart if you get heated or try to fix things," I say. "Let me do my job. You've paid me to do this job, so let me do it. You wouldn't expect me to do your job, would you?"

This he understands. "You've got a point. Your show, Joani."

"Thank you."

We all enter through the garage door into a spacious kitchen. The kitchen overlooks a pond with a cascading fountain and, farther back, a Barbie-doll-type guesthouse with an indoor-outdoor pool that flows under a deck and pergola.

As we make our way in, a pretty but disheveled blond looks over her shoulder from her place on the sofa. She is wearing an impossibly fussy pink bathrobe. A welcome fire is blazing in the stone fireplace in front of her, with a large TV mounted on the wall above. Kelly and Regis are bantering back and forth about some inane point as we proceed into the family room.

She is speechless, silently staring at the group as we march forward.

"Hi, June," I say. Walking in front of her, I crouch down on my knees and take her hand in mine. Her hand feels cool to my warm touch. "My name is Joani; I am an alcoholic and drug addict."

"Oh, God, you guys," she says, as she pulls away. Disengaging our hands, I continue: "Your family and friends have invited me here today to help you with the issues you're having with alcohol. I am an RN and interventionist."

"You know you need help, baby," Joe says quickly. I immediately throw him a stern look that translates to *"Be quiet!"* If his way of communicating to his wife had worked before to get her to enter treatment, I would not be here. He gets the point and backs off.

"Everybody give June a big hug," I say. Quietly, and with some tears, everyone hugs their hellos.

"June, all you have to do is sit and listen to some letters that have been written and absorb the love in the room. Stay right there; your brother and Theresa will sit next to you."

"Can I get dressed first?" she asks.

"Sure, go throw something on," I tell her. "Please don't take too much time."

As she leaves to go upstairs, I instruct Theresa to go with her. Many people ask to be allowed to get dressed first. Even though this is a reasonable request, you don't want too much time to go by because as it does, they are able to come up with excuses why they can't enter treatment. And you want someone to go with them so they can't take a drink or slip some substance into their body when unattended. It's much harder to get people to agree to get treatment if they are under the influence.

"Don't you think you should go up there?" Joe wants to know. He just can't help himself.

"Give them a few seconds, and then I'll follow up," I say.

As everyone mills around unsettled, I slowly go up the huge staircase. The foyer in this house is as big as my entire downstairs. I'm wondering what the utility bills are. The upstairs is a maze of one beautiful room after another. Even as I hear voices, I'm having a hard time finding June and her friend.

I call out, "Hey, guys, where are you?"

"Oh, down here," Theresa calls back.

Going through a bedroom door with a paper sign that is curled up on the corners and reads "Knock before entering," I wind my way through a large dressing room to find the two women.

"You *are* beautiful," I say to June, as she applies subtle lip gloss. "Your husband was right." My statement is true, but I always find flattery to be helpful at interventions.

Ignoring my comment, she meets my eyes in the mirror. "You know, I *used* to have a problem with pills, but I detoxed a month ago."

Here we go: the addicted mind is crafty and never-ending with denial. As an interventionist, you never fight it. You will not win. This begs repeating. *Never* fight denial. You will not win!

"I know. Your family told me you were in detox a month ago. Let's just go downstairs and listen to their letters. Your job is to absorb the love. Come on, sweetie," I say, as I gently direct her back downstairs.

We all take a seat; the only sound is the crackling of wood in the fire-place as the group waits for my direction. I glance out the window; it's still overcast with no snow. The weather is on my mind because the rehab center I'm scheduled to take June to is up a mountain with narrow, winding roads. As I worry about the ice and snow, I have no idea that the biggest risk will come from the patient herself. I would never have thought a size 2 blond could cause me so much trouble—and bruises. It will be another long day on the job. But I don't know this yet.

They all take turns reading their letters. Joe is obediently silent throughout, occasionally dabbing his eyes as he quietly cries.

June is not tough at all. This is another phenomenon I run into frequently as an interventionist. Families often overestimate how much their loved one will fight against entering treatment. Sometimes they are tough as nails, but usually they are more amendable to the idea than the families anticipate. The power of a professionally run intervention has its merits.

After all the letters, pleas, and heartfelt memories have been read, June has just one question, asked through her tears. "Am I allowed to pack first?" We all laugh in relief. It's her way of saying, "Yes, I will accept your offer of help." I love it.

"Sure, you can pack," I say. "Your friends can help you." Having shared a small amount of my own story of addiction with June during the intervention, I add, "And thank you, June, for consenting to go. I was a patient at this rehab twelve years ago; you are going to a wonderful place."

Then she asks, "Can I get a manicure and pedicure first, too?"—half joking and half hoping I would say yes.

"No, not today," I say, gently, and then with exaggerated enthusiasm, "but you can at the rehab. They have a salon bus every Thursday. Just make sure to sign up on Monday for what you want done and then hop on the bus Thursday afternoon. I went every Thursday when I was there. I swear, by the time I came home, I had no hair left!"

During my last trip upstairs to check on June's packing progress, I notice her hands shaking as she goes through her small bedroom safe, organizing her jewelry. After encouraging her to leave all expensive jewelry at home, I ask when her last drink was.

"Last night," she tells me.

"Are you physically addicted to it?" I ask.

"Yes," she answers, adding, "there's no alcohol in the house. I'll need some vodka."

Even though I let some patients drink or use during transport, it's not an easy decision for me. Some patients must have some alcohol so there is no chance of a withdrawal seizure during transport, but regulating how much is the tough part. And at this point, people are almost always less than honest with me. I am aware that June has been prescribed tranquilizers by her primary care doctor, presumably to detox off of the alcohol, and her husband has been doling them out. I have what I think is the remaining amount on me to give to the rehab center with June's other medications. June had a recent history of pill addiction, so her individual pharmacology is hard for me to determine. Later, when she is too intoxicated to hide it from me any longer, I will find out that she has pills stashed on her. This was an unforeseen complication. But I don't frisk patients before we travel, although I am rethinking my liberal policy of letting them use during transport. I must admit I'm a softie in this regard and use this privilege to entice the patient to go to treatment. Out of the hundreds of interventions I have done, it has only rarely been a problem. But when it has, it's been a whopper. There are no simple solutions to this problem.

"Okay," I say. "How much do you usually drink in a day?"

"About a pint of vodka and a bottle of white wine," she says, as her friends look on aghast.

I go downstairs and tell Joe to buy the smallest bottle of vodka he can find. I like to think that with each intervention I do, I learn something. What I learn this time is to always pack only miniatures, not half pints. That way as I drive, I can better control the amount.

When June is packed, we all assemble outside. There are hugs all around followed by encouraging words as we depart. Almost immediately, June asks, "Can I smoke?"

"Sorry, I have asthma," I tell her. "We will make a few pit stops where you can smoke," I offer, as an alternative.

"Okay," she replies, reluctantly.

We settle in for a long ride. This is usually when the patient and I are alone together for the first time, and when we get to know each other better. Without thinking much about it, I let the patient take the lead. Most people tend to talk excessively at this point. Their lives are not going well, and they seem to need to speak about it. Either that, or the opposite occurs, and they are stone quiet. Rarely is there an in-between. No matter the type, silent or chatty, they usually trash their spouse. I have even had patients who trashed their dead spouses. June is the talkative type, and yes, she has a few things to say about her husband.

She also becomes a bartender, expertly taking a can of lemonade and emptying some of it into a tall plastic drink container. Satisfied with the amount, she adds vodka. She sips and talks.

We share some substantial conversation about our children and her attempts at recovery. My gut tells me she wants to be sober. She has tried in the past and is active in recovery meetings in her neighborhood. She has a sponsor and has attempted to do the Twelve Steps. This is encouraging and opens the door for me to tell her of my struggles with sobriety and motherhood and about my personal growth in recovery.

Everything goes well for a while—until it doesn't. The last sane thing I remember June doing is putting on her makeup in the car mirror as we continue to talk, all the while sipping her drink. Maybe she has gulped it and I didn't see, but I don't think so. I will continue to look back on this day and try to figure out how it got so bad, still startled by how abruptly the day turned on me.

It's time for a pit stop. I need to use the facilities, and June wants to smoke. Stopping at a McDonald's, we both get out of the car. I leave June alone on the curb with her cigarette as I go in to use the bathroom. I leave the car unlocked because it's cold outside, but as usual I keep my car keys.

Initially June denies needing to use the restroom, but when I return she changes her mind. "I think I will go," she tells me. Steady on her feet, she goes into the McDonald's.

Back in the warm minivan, we continue our trip. Pulling out her makeup bag, she starts to apply her makeup in the visor mirror. "How old are your children again?" she wants to know.

"Twelve and eight," I say. "My eight-year-old has autism."

"Oh, I'm sorry," she says, empathetically, while reaching over to touch my hand.

"Thanks. It has been a challenge. On my worst days, I say to myself I did not sign up for this. And then on my good days, I remind myself that he is high-functioning and in a normal school. And he is Max! The little boy I love, quirks and all."

In a somewhat dreamy and distant voice, she responds simply, "Yes."

I look over at her to see what's up. She is distracted while digging around in her makeup case, intent on finding something. When she does, she declares, "I'm going to hide these little fuckers." She is talking out loud to herself more than making conversation with me. I begin to have an odd feeling. Her personality is shifting quickly and right before my eyes. One sign of alcoholism is personality change with drinking, but I have not seen her consume a large amount, and the bottle on the floor is two-thirds full. But the "little fuckers" she is hiding in a row of rubber bands wrapped around a piece of cardboard are tranquilizers.

"What are you hiding?" I ask, hoping I sound nonchalant while making a mental note to tell the people at the rehab center where the pills are hidden.

"Ativan. What's it to you?" she aggressively spits out while simultaneously pitching a few into her mouth. I suspect at this point that she consumed a few in the ladies' room at McDonald's as well. She is going down fast, the fastest I have ever seen: one minute she is fine, the next she is exceedingly impaired.

I start to drive faster, instinctively knowing I need help. We are perhaps three miles from the rehab center, but the roads are becoming narrow and steep. "Hey, sweetie, no more tranquilizers, please, okay?"

Without a direct response, she reaches over and starts to play with my hair. Oh boy, here we go. June has left the building, and crazy, addicted, alcoholic Sybil is in her place. I am toast.

"Wow, I see now how beautiful you are," she says. "Let me relax you, I know pressure points in the scalp." She starts massaging my head and finding the pressure points. Under normal circumstances, it would feel good.

"I don't need to be relaxed while driving," I say, as I gently remove her hand. Having her hand close to me or to the steering wheel makes me extremely anxious. There is no room for error on the narrow, isolated, hilly road. I drive as fast as I comfortably can, all the while trying to keep an eye on June. I am quiet, assuming the less I say the better.

I feel like I'm holding my breath as I'm driving. June is mumbling incoherently now. Again, I have never seen someone's personality switch so quickly, and I am simply afraid, intent on getting to the rehab center as quickly as I can. The only place to stop would be at a rural farmhouse or home; there are no stores or gas stations this high up in the hills.

Then, as if some strange new being has inhabited her body, she starts gently rubbing my knee with her hand and cooing "Baby, baby, baby," over and over. Gently I redirect her hand to her side of the car. But she quickly comes right back at me, higher on my leg this time, and with escalating sex talk. We continue to play this game of back-and-forth with her hand for what feels like an eternity. Her words as she attempts to touch me are becoming more and more aggressive and sexual.

"This is not appropriate, June," I say, as I attempt to reason with her.

"You bitch, you're a whore, I see it now, I know what the fuck you're up to," she screams at me. She slumps over and rests her head on her window. Good, I think, she has run out of steam. We are maybe a half mile from the rehab center.

But after a brief rest she pops back up, and with her left hand she grabs the steering wheel. As she pulls the wheel toward her, I hold tight. "Let go of the wheel, June, fucking now!" I scream, no longer able to negotiate quietly.

She laughs an evil laugh and abruptly lets go of the wheel. With her long blond hair covering her face, she looks like someone who is truly insane. As she lets go, because of my overcompensation to hold the wheel tight and steady, the car veers sharply to the left and into the lane for oncoming traffic. For a moment we zigzag back and forth as I attempt to get the car under control. Luckily, no vehicles are in the other lane.

I can now see the grounds of the rehab center ahead, and it looks like nirvana to me. As I take a breath, June is taking off her seat belt and climbing into the back of the minivan. *Dear God, don't let her strangle me from behind* is my first thought. She continues to mutter aggressive, nonsensical things to me.

Pulling into the parking lot, I turn around to take a peek at June. Before I can duck or react, she takes her fist and punches me *hard* in the right cheek.

Although I've gotten used to her hostile behavior toward me, I'm still shocked. All I manage to utter as I continue to quickly park the car is, "June?" My unspoken question hangs in the air: "Why would you do that to me?" There is no answer. There is no making sense of a brain this altered by alcohol and drugs. In simple terms, it is chemical insanity. Flashing in my mind are the physical fights that Gary, my twenty-something boyfriend, and I used to have while we were drunk. Making no sense, we would repeatedly physically abuse one another. Never holding grudges, never remembering what we fought about, we would repeat the cycle of physical abuse within days or weeks of each incident.

I hustle out of the car before June can come at me again, locking her in behind me. She becomes a raving lunatic in the locked car. I am afraid she'll break a window with her fist in her irrational rage. I run inside and breathlessly tell the receptionists at admissions that I need security *right now!* I run back to the car. June is laughing at me through the window.

Within seconds, two men are with me in the parking lot.

"What happened to your face?" My old buddy Frank asks me, with a big grin on his face. "Just another day on the job, huh, Joani?" He is a seasoned pro at the rehab business, and he knows this tiny little lunatic has punched me.

"Just help me get her out of the car," I say, smiling back, so glad not to be alone any longer.

When we open the car door, June sits up, rearranges her shirt, and exits my minivan like a queen—a very impaired queen, one who can barely walk—trying to look majestic and innocent in the presence of two big, fine-looking men. It cracks me up. I don't know if it's from the stress of the drive or the sheer relief that we have made it to the treatment facility alive, but I laugh. June is actually trying to hold her head high and pretend she has been a good girl. With a big man on each side of her holding her up by the armpit, we walk into the center.

They put her in a chair, and she immediately starts up again, talking nonsense, pleading her case as to why she does not need to be admitted. The other patient waiting to be admitted and his family are escorted to a quieter room.

As June babbles on, I am offered ice for my face, all the snacks I want for the ride home, and treatment brochures for future clients. The people at the center are not at all fazed by this out-of-control woman. Alcoholics are their business.

"Do you want to press charges?" the admissions counselor asks me. "It's your right."

I don't hesitate. "Nope, but thanks." June has been lovely—until she turned on me. As I tell the families every time, "This is about being sick, not bad." This is not to say that active alcoholics and addicts who are abusive should not be held accountable for their actions. But this is not the time for that.

With June still in the chair and the two men with her, I tell them, "I'll be right back; I need to get her bags out of the car."

Within a split second, as I walk out to the car, June leaps out of the chair, and before the men can catch her, she charges at me in the parking lot. I turn as I hear her and, just in time, jump out of the way as she lunges at my back. She ends up on the asphalt and rolls down a hill, laughing hysterically. The guys are close behind, and I let them retrieve her from the ground. Apparently she is not my biggest fan at the moment, and I'm staying as far away as possible.

After bringing her bag in, I excuse myself for a quick restroom break before my long drive home. Our time together does not end with a hug and a kiss. As I come out of the bathroom, she is sitting in the chair, flanked by the men, her head hung to her chest; mercifully, she has passed out.

I tiptoe around her chair, and the men smile at me as I slip out the door quietly, so as not to wake the sleeping beauty. I turn one last time to look at her, and in her drunken slumber she looks like an injured child. *Sleep, June, wake up and heal* is my silent prayer. I leave with no animosity. I believe what I tell the families. She is sick, not bad.

Alcohol was never my best friend but always second best to my first loves and desires—pills. Like a fair-weather friend, booze would come and go—until the day when all my old friends were no longer available. Then my new passion for the time-honored spirits took me by surprise. Looking back, I can see it was a natural transition, but I didn't know it at the time. Like most heartaches in life, it's best understood in hindsight.

Two years passed as I worked as a new RN on the GYN medical-surgical floor at a hospital in Arizona. I became savvier about stealing narcotics. The cancer patients often were admitted with their own personal supply of pain medication. The normal procedure was to send it to the lab to be relabeled. I would send it to the lab but first siphon off my own personal supply. I worked many nights under the influence of opiate narcotics. And thank God, no patient issues ever occurred. The irony in the beginning stages of addiction is that the addict operates on a normal level.

I decided it was time for a change. My plan was to relocate to Annapolis. As a kid I spent most summers on the East Coast. My mother had an identical mirror twin, meaning they were identical in every way, except my mom was left-handed and her twin was right-handed. Interestingly, my mother struggled with addictions, and her twin did not. I think my mom's left-handedness was the marker. Five percent of the population is left-handed, but 30 percent of addicts and alcoholics are lefties. I think my mom's being left-handed set her apart from her twin. It was the only difference in these two sisters, raised in the same home environment.

So every summer I stayed with my mom's right-handed twin and her family in Maryland. Those summers were the highlight of my life. Their family was stable for the most part, and the fondest memories of my childhood come from those wonderful extended summer vacations. So when I decided to relocate from Arizona, Maryland was the natural choice.

But I had a problem. I needed a lot of pills to drive across the country. I started to stockpile drugs. These were the days in hospitals when medications were not so strictly monitored and accounted for. Extra medications for a discharged patient were frequently placed in clear plastic cups, ready for the next patient. I drew from this well over and over, saving the Valium and hypnotics such as Dalmane. I diverted as many controlled opiate drugs from the locked cabinets as I comfortably could. I had many refills on my personal Ativan prescriptions. I requested all four refills—120 pills for each prescription—telling the pharmacist I was moving and needed all the pills for the transition of finding a new doctor on the East Coast. I remember his kindly face as he handed me the 480 pills and said, "Wine would be easier, you know." I did not know, but I would soon find out.

By luck or fate I found a rider to accompany me on my trip out East. He drove and I, apparently, slept. We went through some Midwestern town named Sleepy, I can't remember the state. My rider photographed me leaning up against the town sign to signify my state of consciousness during our trip together.

As I settled in with my aunt, it was time to find a job. My supply of pills was rapidly dwindling, and I did not have a plan for how to refill it. Not having a hospital job or a doctor to supply me with my drugs, I started to worry.

I interviewed at the local hospital, but the only opening for an RN was in the newborn nursery. I had never entertained the idea of neonatal nursing, but I said yes. I quickly realized there were no drugs to speak of in a newborn nursery. On my first day on the job, I went through the emergency cart. The only thing of interest to me was a prefilled syringe with ten milligrams of Valium. Taking the syringe into the bathroom, I shot the Valium into my left thigh. I remember my disappointment at feeling nothing. I was a girl with a hefty addiction to tranquilizers; ten milligrams was like spitting in the wind.

My pastime was obsessively counting out how many tranquilizers I had left. I would make up schedules of how many I could do in a day, slowly decreasing the amount each day until I had detoxed myself. I was unable to stay on schedule, though, and for the first time I sought outside help for my addictions.

I can't remember how I found the psychiatrist I sought treatment with, but I ended up in her office. Always being upfront and pragmatic, I got right to the point. "I'm addicted to Ativan," I remember telling her.

"Are you asking me for a prescription?" she asked.

"No, I want help getting off of them," I told her. "I'm tired of having to have them on me at all times."

And so it began. Over a period of perhaps sixteen weeks, she and I slowly decreased the amount of tranquilizers I was on. She would prescribe only enough for one week at a time. I was surprisingly committed to the process. She never called me a drug addict or suggested recovery on any level. I think this was completely out of my realm of thinking. She was taking me one step at a time, I believe.

I was resistant to any attempts at talk therapy. I was firm on the fact that I was there only to get off the Ativan. As much as she pushed me to open up, I would not, or could not, loosen up enough to discuss any issues in my life. I was acutely uncomfortable in her office. Looking back, I can see that my anxiety was due in large part to the detox process of getting off Ativan. But the psychiatrist helped me get through the panic of not carrying the tranquillizers with me. We made a deal one day that worked.

"Joani, I want you try something this week," she proposed.

I was immediately suspicious. "What?"

"I want you to leave the Ativan at home, just briefly at first, and see how you do."

There was a chicken restaurant I loved in Eastport, a suburb of Annapolis, that was maybe three blocks from my house. I made a contract with the psychiatrist to go get a piece of chicken without a tranquilizer in my pocket and go right back home. That was my first pill-free outing. It felt so odd, leaving my pacifier at home. For about a month, the time and distance of each venture away from home without tranquilizers in my pocket grew longer and longer.

Finally the day came when I no longer had any tranquilizers left at all! I continued seeing the doctor for perhaps three more weeks as I talked of my progress without pills. I was very proud of myself and announced to her that I no longer needed her services and that it was time to say good-bye. Her alarm was immediate and intense.

"Joani, I am so proud of the work we've done, but I really feel we have much more to explore together."

"No thanks. I'm done here. Really, thanks again." I left as abruptly as I had come.

Three months later: It was two o'clock in the morning. I had been drinking Bacardi 101 proof rum and Coke. Mad at my boyfriend, Gary, I shoved him down the staircase that led up to my apartment. After rolling and stumbling down to the bottom, he stopped momentarily to look up. He stared at me defiantly before angrily charging back up the stairs. Grabbing me by my forearm, he in turn threw me down the stairs.

Getting up, I screamed at the top of my lungs, "I will fucking kill you!" as I charged back up the stairs. A neighbor called the police. They came to my apartment once again to check on the two twenty-something hospital professionals who kept beating the shit out of each other. The next day at work, my right arm bruised from the fall down the stairs, I told my co-workers I fell while riding my bike.

Gary and I were in love. I cannot claim he abused me, because I always started the physical altercations. Our drunken fights were frequent and unpredictable. While we were driving home one night, I angrily kicked in the radio in his new car. I mangled the radio buttons as I repeatedly slammed my boot against the console. Livid, he slammed on his brakes. We were on a bridge in the wintertime. He reached over, opened my door, and shoved me out of the car. I stumbled to a friend's house, curled up on her cold front step, and slept on the doormat.

We frequently lost each another, literally. We were having dinner at a local restaurant one evening. My favorite drink was hot coffee with four different types of liquor in it. I would get drunk but remain alert—or so I thought. This night I excused myself to go to the ladies' room. On my way back to the table, the room started to spin, and I thought I might puke. Not having enough time to get back to the ladies' room, I ran out the front door to the nearest alley. I vomited all over myself. Unable to return to the restaurant like that, I started to walk.

Gary looked for me all night. Again I found the doorstep of someone I knew and curled up and slept.

I also developed the unbecoming habit of peeing outside. I remember having to urinate a lot during my years of alcohol abuse, and any place could be a toilet. These were the alcohol years. All my drugs were gone, and alcohol became the central player. Gary and I lived together for a few years, and it was chaotic, loud, and exhausting. Even when we traveled to the beach or to my mom's home in Arizona, we managed to fight. We would argue loudly in front of anyone, making spectacles of ourselves.

Much like June, I could not control my moods while drinking. My personality could shift into ugly overdrive or extreme sentimentality with crying jags. As with a flood, once my personality was off center, I couldn't contain it. For the longest time I didn't see alcohol as the problem; the problem was Gary. Like a good alcoholic, I placed the focus outside of me.

Then one day I had one of those light-bulb moments. It was a faint one, but my reality started to shift slightly. For the first time, I identified myself as someone with a substance-abuse problem.

It was a pretty fall evening. Gary and I were out walking, something we did frequently. Evening has always been my favorite time of the day. I always feel safer when the dark descends. I'm not sure why. We carried big drink cups with Bacardi and Coke in them. A brook ran along one side of the street, and I could hear it gently gurgling as we walked among the fall leaves. A few ducks milled about as we stopped to enjoy the view.

As we stood side by side, our faces flushed from the cold and alcohol, I remember thinking how odd it was that we always took our walks with alcohol. How is it, I wondered, that a familiar situation, one that has taken place many times before, can suddenly look out of place? Like a soft but significant whisper in my ear, I felt a shift in my perception as something outside of me pushed me toward the truth.

"Do you think we'll know when it's time to go to AA?" I asked Gary, seemingly out of the blue.

"Yes, we'll know," he replied. Gary continues to drink to this day, more than twenty-five years later.

The two of us hobbled along as the alcoholic couple for perhaps another year, until I put a painful end to our relationship. I sat curled on top of the warm radiator, watching the snowfall from the kitchen window. Phil Collins's *One More Night* played on the radio from the top of the refrigerator as Gary moved out. We both grieved intensely as our romantic relationship ended, but we have managed to remain good friends. To this day, I am sure there is nothing we wouldn't do for each other. Gary returned to my life to help me when my mom was dying. We were two good people, crippled by alcohol and emotional wounds. In another time we might have gone the distance.

I did not magically begin to recover from alcoholism after Gary moved out. I was twenty-five, and it would take four more years of chaotic alcohol use before I waved the white flag. Even then it was at half-staff.

When Gary had moved in, my sex drive for him went out the door, a theme that would plague me for life. My ability to be close to men, especially those who live with me, has been a challenge I have yet to overcome.

I returned to serial dating, which included larger quantities of alcohol. Men were transient in my life, and the nights became increasingly difficult, if not impossible, to recall the next day. Blackouts became the norm. Anxiety and depression were my closest companions, and the morning shakes started. Standing in the shower, I would place my face against the cold wall to try to quell the emotional pain and physical lethargy I would experience most mornings. I felt suicidal for the first time in my life, and I had no real idea what was wrong with me. That momentary glimpse that alcohol might be the problem was no longer in my thoughts. I was lonely and lost, unable to make any real connection with a man. In addition to serial one-night stands, I had serial pregnancies. Using birth control while under the influence was beyond my ability. And the pill was not an option because my blood pressure rose when I took it. My frequent trips to outpatient abortion clinics left me hormonally and emotionally fragile.

My new drink was Rémy Martin cognac. My favorite trick was to pour it into the belly button of the man of the moment, then lick and suck it out. Men loved me . . . for one night.

I needed help. Depression and anxiety, morning shakes, constant insomnia, and loneliness drove me to find a therapist. I first went to my primary care doctor for a physical. Sitting on the crinkly white paper in a hospital gown, I weighed perhaps one hundred pounds and was again severely hypertensive.

"Joani, I don't know what to tell you," the doctor said. "You are skinny, young, and apparently healthy, but your blood pressure is extremely elevated." A familiar story.

Before I had a chance to confess, he asked, "How much are you drinking?"

"I drink a lot. Party, you know," I said.

Like a windup toy, he started up. "God I hate those beer commercials they aim at you young people. They make drinking alcohol look like so much fun, no consequences to it at all as you romp along the beach playing volleyball and drinking Bud."

I wish it was as simple as watching beer commercials, I remember thinking. Sitting in a chair below me as my legs dangled from the exam table, he looked up from my chart. "Are you drinking every day?"

"Most days, yes." I started to cry.

"Wow, you nurses can drink!" he said.

Apparently beer commercials and my nursing profession were the cause of all my alcohol problems. Maybe if I stopped watching TV and got a new job, my life would straighten out.

Finally he came up with some solid advice. "Okay, Joani. I have the name of a great psychiatrist. He's helped my wife immensely. His name is Dr. James Kehler. I want you to make an appointment," he said, as he wrote down the name and number. I can still see his name on that little piece of paper.

"Okay, I will," I said, and I meant it. I was out of answers and hope. My darkest hours have always been right before the dawn, but right now I didn't know that. I was a young woman, and I was struggling with alcoholism, like my father before me.

I don't remember calling Dr. Kehler, but I do remember my first visit. It was days before my thirtieth birthday.

"I think with what you're telling me and your family's history, you should give up alcohol. As you turn thirty, I see you at a crossroads," I remember him saying.

Wow, give up drinking—it sounded so simple. Why had I not thought of this? It seemed like a revelation.

"I also think you could benefit from an antidepressant. Sounds like you've had a long history of anxiety and depression."

"What's my diagnosis?" I wanted to know, ever the nurse and pragmatist.

"Dysthymia," he said, referring to a form of low-grade depression, "and general anxiety." If he ever called me an alcoholic, I don't recall it.

After trying several antidepressants, we found one that worked for me—doxepin, which treats both depression and anxiety.

I immediately gave up alcohol and started on the antidepressants. For the first time in my life, it seemed, I could sleep. The constant anxiety and vague feelings of depression slowly lifted as I gained the courage, with Dr. Kehler's help, to explore issues in my past and present. I joined a local recovery group, Adult Children of Alcoholics. It was there that I learned I was not alone. The preamble read at the beginning of each ACA meeting, describing the characteristics of a child of an alcoholic, fit me like a glove, and I stayed in the group for years, gaining strength in that wonderful community of recovering people.

I no longer drank alcohol or took any type of drug, other than the antidepressants. I identified myself as a child of an alcoholic with a psychiatric condition. I now felt that all my years of drug use were an attempt to self-medicate for my anxiety and depression. "Alcoholic" and "addict" were labels I gave my parents, but not myself. I defined myself as a psychiatric patient who no longer drank or did drugs. I liked the label.

It turned out to be a half-truth. After five years of calm, with personal exploration in therapy and recovery groups, I experienced a level of addiction that brought me to my knees and took me to the depths of a hell that I could never have imagined.

At the time of this writing, June is still in treatment. Her therapist reports that she has been a receptive and hardworking patient. The treatment team suggested that she undergo extended, inpatient care, but she has declined. She has no memory of our drive to rehab.

CHAPTER 8

Moms Who Die

She is beautiful. She embodies the stereotypical all-American good looks and lifestyle: tall, blond and blue-eyed with a perpetual tan, an avid golfer, and a passionate mom. But her beauty is quickly overshadowed by her insecurity and her need to be liked. She seems to be missing a vital link to her personality; although sweet, she lacks authenticity when communicating. She is extremely easy to love, though, producing in me a fierce feeling of protectiveness. Her fragility and sweetness are hard to resist—until close to the end of our time together, when I will no longer be able to help her.

She always sits in the front row at Alcoholics Anonymous meetings. Most newcomers hide in the back. I'm not sure if it's because she needs room for her long legs or if it's motivation to get to know the group, but I appreciate the fact that she is front and center.

I sit opposite, facing her from my chair along the wall. We make frequent eye contact and exchange slight smiles as we acknowledge one another's presence in the room.

"Hi, my name is Joani," I say, introducing myself after a meeting. "Want to go for coffee?"

"That would be nice," she replies, in a voice that does not match her stature. It is a quiet, refined voice, more of what you would expect from a petite woman.

"First, could you meet my husband?" she asks. "He's sitting outside in his car."

"Sure, okay," I say, not certain what to expect with this curbside introduction.

As we walk down the uneven, red-brick sidewalk that is the norm in our historic town, I marvel at the fact that she's wearing high heels. They make it tough to negotiate on these streets, but I will learn that Terry is always a lady.

Walking the short distance to her husband's car, she asks me a question that usually takes people a while to get around to: "Would you be my sponsor?" A sponsor is a mentor and teacher who guides addicts through the Twelve Steps and the process of recovery. Twelve Step meetings are a place to find a sponsor. The Twelve Steps are not complicated. They are not daunting, but getting some guidance and support from another addict in recovery is essential to working through them.

I am taken by surprise. Not at being asked—I have been a sponsor before—but because she barely knows me. It's like being on a dinner date for the first time and being asked for a second date before you have had a chance to eat.

Her sense of urgency makes me curious, but it seems odd to decline the honor of being someone's sponsor, no matter how unusual the timing of the request seems to me. She has recently been discharged from rehab, and they do emphasize getting a sponsor as soon as possible. So as we walk along, I assume this must be her motivation. Soon, however, I will suspect it is something else.

As we approach her husband's car, he watches us with the window rolled down. He is lovely to look at, and the two of them make a handsome couple. He pulls his Ray-Bans down his nose to get a better look at this stranger with his wife, and we shake hands.

"Andrew, this is Joani, my new sponsor," Terry says immediately. "She was a patient at the same rehab I was at, but a long time ago. She does interventions for a living now, and she has been on *Dr. Phil.*" Repeating herself, she adds, "She agreed to be my sponsor."

"Nice to meet you," he says, politely but with a twinge of suspicion to his voice.

I think I see now. Terry seems to be using my résumé and willingness to be her sponsor to add a level of credibility to her efforts at recovery in her husband's eyes.

His voice and body language make me think he isn't buying it. As I stand by the car, with two virtual strangers, I have the odd feeling that I am smack dab in the middle of some marital drama. My thought is that this husband has been down this road before, and he does not trust his wife's efforts at getting well. This all turns out to be true. What determines her fate? His lack of faith in her ability to get well from this disease, driven by her track record, or simply her inherent inability to get well? I don't know. I do know that some alcoholics are just more fragile than others. Just as some diabetics lose their eyesight or kidneys at an early age while others live long, stable lives with their disease, some alcoholics die young, and some do not. All diseases are on a continuum of severity. Terry is a brittle alcoholic. And she is young, with two beautiful little girls, and a son on the way.

Walking down a crooked, brick-lined alley, Terry and I make our way to the back door of a local café, Chick and Ruth's. Our time together begins.

"Can you meet me once a week to work on the Steps?" I ask. This is not optional. No doubt this congenial girl has friends; she does not need another one. She needs someone to take her through the Steps. And the beauty of the program is that I *need* someone to take through the Steps, as well. As I help her, she helps me; such is the circle of recovery.

"Absolutely," she says, with no hesitation.

"Great. Do you have the Big Book?"

"I do. They gave me one in rehab."

"Okay."

It's a hopeful start. We make plans to meet the following day at Hard Bean Café in downtown Annapolis after the 7:30 a.m. AA meeting. I make a point to buy her a little Big Book, one you can stuff in your purse or pocket, a trick I learned while I was a patient at La Hacienda treatment facility. Every morning in the Big Book lecture, Chris Raymer, the teacher, would pull out of his back pocket a well-worn little Big Book. After putting on his reading glasses, he would skillfully, eloquently, and with forthright Texas style teach us the basics of recovery, as outlined in 1939 by Bill Wilson, cofounder of Alcoholics Anonymous. I got well in large part because of these lectures. Chris always carried a little Big Book, and he had recovered from a seemingly hopeless condition. So I carry one with me, too.

Terry and I meet a few times a week, sometimes at her home, and we see each other frequently at the morning AA meetings. We have young children and schools in common, as well as alcoholism. We speak of them and our marriages. Her marriage is not perfect, according to her, but most marriages are a challenge at some point. I am not making light of her struggles in her marriage, but the longer I'm married, the more I realize most of us weather some really rough patches.

Sitting on her beige sectional sofa, you can see the expansive Chesapeake Bay. Surrounded by the usual artifacts of a home with children—toys and pictures—we do Terry's Fourth and Fifth Steps. These two Steps are a housekeeping of sorts: we take a moral inventory of circumstances in our lives and deal with them. The process helps illuminate our responsibility in difficult situations that have occurred in our lives. From these Steps, another list will be created so we can make amends to those we have wronged. For those circumstances where we truly were the victim of someone else's actions, we learn to forgive. The whole process is freeing. As our minds are cleared of resentments and guilt, we start to live more responsible and less burdened lives.

Going into the kitchen to get another cup of coffee, I glance at a sonogram of Terry's baby-to-be on the refrigerator. I think back to this moment frequently. The baby is nestled in the fetal position, and you can see his little feet. Terry will never know this baby. Alcoholism will rob this child of its mother. Life is not fair, my first therapist's voice echoes in my head. "Understand this fact, Joani," she would tell me, "and your life will be easier." Life is not fair, and it can be sad.

Terry is unable to stay sober. Her pregnancy, coupled with her alcoholism, is a chaotic time for her and her family. Terry's mom is a professional woman. She is always dressed properly and sports stylishly short blond hair. Her concern for her daughter is unending, and it's hard to witness her anguish. I have so few answers for her. If I feel helpless in the tide of Terry's illness, I can only imagine the hell her family is living with.

"Joani, I can't reach her, and I'm at work. God, I'm so worried," her mother tells me on the phone one day. Terry's family members often call me with concerns about her condition,

"I'll go check on her," I tell her. "I'll call you when I see her."

I pack up Lucy and we make the forty-five-minute trip to Terry's house. It's a familiar drive. Different person, different time, different state, but the sense of urgency and purpose feels like it has been with me always. My very identity is wrapped around my ability to take care of other addicts and alcoholics. Early life skills linger. The skills I learned while watching my parents' illnesses have morphed into my life's passion. I am lucky. It's all in the balance and perspective. It could just as easily have become pathological. My own addiction teaches me that my chances of surviving and thriving with this disease are far greater if I help my fellow alcoholic. The trick is to know when to cut your losses.

As I pull into Terry's driveway, I scan the yard and landscape around the house. When I drove in during my last trip here, Terry appeared like a pale, barefoot ghost in a long, white, flowing nightgown. I watched from the car, unnoticed, initially confused about what she was doing. Terry crouched behind her neighbor's bush. With her nightgown trailing in the mud, she started digging the earth with both hands, like a dog searching for a cherished, hidden bone. The bone was a vodka bottle. Wiping the dirt away, she unscrewed the top. Standing, she took a long swig of the clear liquid. In the sunlight, I could clearly see the outline of her body through her nightgown. Seeing her beautiful and pregnant body against this desperate scene of pure addiction left me momentarily spellbound. I was motionless, with Lucy in my lap, as I witnessed Terry's personal hell. No one would choose this life. We addicts have lost the power of choice in alcohol and drugs. Taking her fill, Terry put the cap back on the bottle and reburied it.

But today she is not in the yard. Approaching the house, I can see the dogs through the side window at the front door. Terry is a dog lover. These are big dogs, but friendly. I ring and knock on the door as the animals bark and wag their tails at me through the window. I have left Lucy in the car; she is not always well behaved with other dogs.

No answer. The door is locked. Terry always locks the door. Her neighbors have a key, and before I have a chance to walk to their house, the old man is standing at the chain link fence, peering over at me. We have met before on one of these missions. As I walk toward him, he looks worried.

"She's in bad shape," he tells me, before I have a chance to ask. "We got her to go to the ER the other night. They sobered her up and sent her home the next day." The usual course of treatment for alcoholism in American emergency rooms drives me crazy. But there are no simple solutions.

Taking the key, I thank the neighbor for keeping watch on her.

The dogs go nuts when I enter the house. I have found that animals are extremely intuitive and unsettled when their owner is sick. With their loyalty and pack mentality, they seem to instinctively know when something is amiss with their beloved leader. It is both moving and remarkable to observe this trait in dogs.

I follow them down a hall, letting them lead me to Terry. They take me past the master bedroom, where I assumed she was. The animals turn right into the two little girls' room. I stop momentarily, afraid of what I might find. *Dear God, let her be alive,* I silently pray.

The dogs, having done their job of getting me to their owner, stand strangely still as I survey the room. Terry is lying on her side, her back to the door, her knees drawn up to her pregnant belly, a position eerily reminiscent of the sonogram of her unborn child on the refrigerator.

I sit at her side, and the nurse in me immediately kicks in. I feel her wrist for a pulse and gently lay my hand on her back to feel the rhythm of her breathing. She is alive, and her vital signs are stable for now. But as I watch her curled up on her children's bunk bed with a stuffed animal in her arms, I know her heart is broken—she is broken, and cannot be fixed. Her children and husband moved out weeks earlier, no longer able to witness or deal with the carnage of her unremitting alcoholism.

She responds slightly when I try to shake her awake, mumbling something incoherently. I again survey the room, looking for the bottle and perhaps a suicide note. Under the bed I find an empty half-gallon vodka bottle.

Alcohol levels in the body can continue to rise dangerously after your last drink. I have no idea how much she has drunk or in what time frame. She is about six to seven months pregnant. She and the baby need medical treatment.

I manage to get her to sit up. It is like waking a swarm of bees; she slaps at me and is generally not happy. I am beginning to believe, as her mother does, that this is suicide by drink.

"Terry, I need to get you to my car, to take you to the hospital," I say. This is like throwing gasoline on a fire.

"No, no, no," she mutters loudly, as she tries to lie back down. "Just let me sleep," I think I hear her say, as she slumps back over.

Terry is a big girl—slim, but tall and strong. I need help, so I call 911.

"Yes," I repeat to the operator, who acts as if she didn't hear or believe me the first time. "I'm with a woman who is extremely inebriated on alcohol, and she's between six and seven months pregnant."

"Is she conscious?"

"Barely. Her vital signs are stable, but I have no idea how much she has had to drink or when her last drink was. I'm an RN."

"Are you her nurse?"

"No, a friend."

"Okay, the paramedics and police will be there soon."

"Thanks."

Suddenly, with no warning, Terry is up and stumbling down the hall to the bathroom. I help steer her as she mumbles on about something I can't understand. As I hold her steady on the toilet, I can hear the sirens of the approaching ambulance and police car. The noise is way too loud. I question the need for such a blaring entrance on a rural road in the middle of a work and school day when there are virtually no cars or people to navigate around. Sirens antagonize and agitate impaired people. And Terry hears the sirens.

"What the hell," she slurs out, as the noise seems to go on unabated.

"Terry, I called the ambulance. You and the baby need medical assistance."

"No, no, no, no," she says, and she tries to stand up while still peeing. As urine splashes on the floor, I push her back down onto the toilet seat. "Finish going to the bathroom," I say, sternly.

The police and paramedics are at the door now, and the dogs are going crazy. I can't get to the door and hold Terry at the same time.

"Come in," I yell, as the doorbell continues to ring and ignite the dogs.

As if in a movie, I suddenly hear a loud bullhorn from outside the hall window. *"You must contain the dogs."*

Crap, I think. If they hadn't come barreling up like a SWAT team, everything, including the dogs, would be much calmer. I did tell the 911 operator that Terry's vital signs were stable!

"My dogs, my dogs," Terry starts to cry. My only option is to get her underpants back up and walk with her to the door. We manage to stumble down the stairs to the foyer, to the dogs, police, and paramedics.

I open the door. The dogs bark frantically, Terry screams "No!" as soon as she sees the police, and the officers are yelling at me, "Contain the dogs!"

"I can't hold the patient and the dogs," I retort loudly. "I need you to help with one or the other. The dogs are friendly!"

"Ma'am, you must contain the dogs!"

I slam the door in their faces.

"Terry, honey, just sit right here on the step, everything is okay." Thankfully, she complies. I round up the two dogs and take them to their crates in the basement. I hustle back up the stairs. Terry is slumped over her pregnant belly with her chin in her hands, as if contemplating something that we will never know.

I'm not happy with the police and paramedics outside, but I keep my mouth shut. Or more accurately, I keep my words to a minimum. It's amazing what you can express with a few words spoken with a hint of vinegar.

"Hello, boys," I say, as I open the door again. I don't know if they catch my implied disdain for their Rambo-like antics, but I feel better.

Barging through the door, they observe me and Terry, who is quiet now, after all of the drama. I tell them the history as far as I know it. I help them get Terry to the couch. The paramedics take her vital signs and do a general assessment. Terry is not saying anything. She appears to be ready to slip from consciousness again—until the paramedics tell her they will be taking her to the hospital.

"No, I am not going," she says, clearly. Terry is by far the most obstinate person I have ever dealt with. I think the mental health professionals might call it an oppositional defiant quality of her personality. She displays this trait even when sober. When she makes up her mind about something, she simply will not budge or consider alternatives to the situation. This almost pathological trait may be what contributed to her eventual death.

As the paramedics attempt to get her up and escort her to the ambulance, she starts to fight like hell. It is a full-blown temper tantrum. She hits, kicks, tries to bite, and screams at all of us. I'm thinking that the police were right about containing the dogs. They would never have tolerated seeing their master like this; they might have attacked us if they perceived us to be hurting Terry.

Finally, the two police officers have to restrain her. While one holds her down on the couch, the other cuffs her hands behind her back. Soon she quiets down; she knows she is beaten.

I say good-bye to her at the front door, kissing her lightly on her cheek. I watch from the front steps as the police escort her in her night-gown and flip-flops to the squad car. In the usual police fashion, they protect her head as they place her in the backseat. I remember her look-ing at me through the window. No smile, just a blank look. It's one of the last times I will see her alive.

I clean up the house a little, feed the dogs, and let them outside to run. The house displays the trappings of an all-American family with children. It is decorated in a light and breezy beach style. Pictures of her children adorn the walls and side tables. Toys are scattered about the house and in the playroom off the living room, where a small child's basketball hoop hangs on the wall. Baby blue skies and clouds are painted on the ceiling of the expected baby's room. Stacks of diapers and dainty nightgowns are neatly folded on the changing table. This was an intact family at some point, but now alcoholism has robbed it of all that was good and secure. As I look at the sonogram on the refrigerator again, I sense that this child will pay the highest price for his mother's alcoholism: fetal alcohol syndrome. And I will be right. Terry loves her children as much any mom, and still alcoholism is trumping that love. Again, no one would choose this tragedy. This is a powerful and baffling disease, and Terry is not to blame. She did the recovery work with me. She showed up when I asked her to. As Father Martin once told me, "Some people will simply not survive this progressive and fatal disease." He added something that day that I have never forgotten: "Joani Baloney, I have a different feeling about you." Maybe he says to this everyone, I don't know, but his words have always stayed with me, giving me hope.

Terry eventually is forced to move out of her home, based on legal action taken by her husband. The children deserve to live in a family home free of active alcoholism. She has given birth to her baby boy. After having two girls, this is her long-awaited son. Her husband comes to the hospital with legal papers and takes the baby from her while she is a patient in the maternity ward.

She moves into an apartment and becomes even more isolated in her disease. She lives in abject filth. She acquires another large dog. Because they live on the top floor of an apartment building, the dog rarely goes out. Dog filth litters the floors, and the bathroom toilet is clogged beyond comprehension. She is evicted from this apartment and moves to another down the street. She is allowed to see her children periodically, but always with supervision.

The last time I see her, four of us from my AA home group visit her. I am the first to leave, realizing I have reached the limit of what I can do for her. She has my number, but I write it down for her again anyway. Handing it to her I say, "You know where to find me, Terry," and I leave.

A few months later, as I am working out at a gym, I receive a phone call. Dr. John McClanahan, a friend to me and a therapist to Terry, gives me the news. "Terry was found dead in her apartment. Looks like she fell over and hit her head on the coffee table." A tale as old as time: drunk falls over, hits head, and dies.

Terry's two little girls walk behind her casket at her funeral in a quaint rural church. Her infant son is in her husband's arms. Alcohol has won this time.

In spite of our family's dysfunction and trials as I grew up, I always knew my mother loved me. She was my best friend and biggest fan. How I can rewrite history in my mind. I assume I'm still trying to assuage my hurt childhood feelings. The thing she said to me during childhood that I remember most is, "You can't do a goddamn thing." Instilling confidence in me was not her strong point when I was a child. It was not until years later, when it was just the two of us, that she became my biggest fan. Despite her ineffectual parenting, I was extremely attached to her as a child, almost pathologically worrying about her death. I would hide her Kent cigarettes from her. I seemed to have a premonition of things to come.

Starting when I was young, we communicated more like friends than parent and child. She held almost nothing back from me, disclosing her every heartache and grievance about my father. I was her little adult. I remember her telling me at age five that there was no Santa Claus. "I don't want you to believe in fairy tales, and I will never lie to you," she said to me one day. She then emphasized, "Don't tell any of your friends, though." I felt a strange sadness keeping my secret as my friends prepared for Christmas and Santa Claus. By third grade, my mother had described sex to me in all of its detail. My childhood was abbreviated by mom's dependence on me, and I loved her with my whole heart in return.

Mom was not a twenty-four-hour maintenance drinker—someone who needs to drink around the clock because he or she has become physically addicted to alcohol. But was she an alcoholic/addict? She drank two to three cans of Bud beer most nights and always had tranquilizers at her disposal and a bottle at the ready sitting on the kitchen counter. Frequently her personality radically changed when she drank, which is a strong indicator of alcoholism. Her demeanor would become either cantankerous and argumentative or morose, with bouts of crying, but not always. The one constant was her cigarettes. She smoked from the age of fifteen until her forties. A diagnosis of chronic obstructive pulmonary disease, which affects the lungs and makes breathing difficult, motivated her to quit the cigarette habit. Later, as the disease became worse, she gave up beer. When her belly became distended from the brew, her breathing would become labored. Ultimately it was the cigarette habit that killed her. Lung cancer came to visit. As her world came to an end, mine was turned upside down. I experienced devastating grief and huge responsibility as I helped her die over nine and a half months. It was a journey I would never want to repeat, but I would have not missed it for the world. Along with the heartbreak and bone-crushing work that comes with being a caretaker for someone who is dying, I was rewarded with belly laughs, sharing whole boxes of ice-cream sandwiches guilt free, and learning how to make peanut brittle. I was thirty-three years old, and she was fifty-nine. I had yet to establish my own family; connections with men were still beyond my emotional reach. My mom was my closest family member, and I lost her.

I was working the evening shift in the newborn nursery at the hospital in Maryland when the phone call came. It felt like years earlier, when Arizona state troopers knocked on my door to tell me of my dad's death. But this time the phone was the delivery instrument heralding untimely death to come.

"Your mom is in the hospital," her co-worker told me. "We took her from work. She suddenly could no longer type on her computer. They thought it was a stroke, but they also think it might be a brain tumor. The doctors are looking at her now."

Sitting in a chair at the nurses' station in the nursery, I listened closely, trying to absorb the words being spoken. At the same time my mind was working overtime as a nurse trying to piece together the facts that we had so far.

"Okay, I'll fly home tomorrow," I managed to say.

My colleagues—fellow nurses and an in-house pediatrician I was close to—gathered around me as I tried to hold on to my composure. I couldn't. I left work to absorb the news and to make arrangements to get to Arizona.

I drove home in a trance. Washing smeared mascara off my cheeks, I clutched a towel to my face and sobbed. Sitting on the side of the tub, I cried—howled—into the towel. I knew this was the end of my mom's life. What I had always feared, my biggest fear, really, was becoming reality, and I had no idea how I was to cope. I no longer had an arsenal of drugs at my disposal. I had been sober for four years, since seeing Dr. Kehler at age twenty-nine. I continued to identify myself as a child of alcoholics who had been self-medicating for psychiatric conditions. Half-truths. But it was working—for a time.

Flying home I read a tiny little book cover-to-cover that gave me the strength to make it to my mom's side: *When Bad Things Happen to Good People*, by Rabbi Harold Kushner. I don't recall how I came to possess this book, whether I bought it or it was a gift, but the main thing I remember learning is that the human condition here on Earth, our temporary home, is a kindergarten of sorts for spiritual people living a human existence. For God to change many of the circumstances that we grieve and labor over would remove this human condition. And then there would be no growth or lessons. And most important, I learned that God cries with us. I was not alone.

So, armed with a little dog-eared book by a Jewish man who had lost his young son, I made my way to the hospital in my rental car.

I walked into her hospital room. It sounds like a cliché, but she looked small in the bed. Her eyes were big with her glasses on and contacts out. I can still see her. The emotion on her face at that moment is indelible in my mind; she looks at me still, and forever. What a wonderful gift. Her relief that I had made it to her side registered clearly as I approached to hug her. Then, kicking my shoes off, I pushed her over so I could lounge in the bed with her. I managed not to cry, remaining matter-of-fact and pragmatic, reserving judgment about the possibilities of her diagnosis until we had the facts. That would require more tests the following day. For now she and I were content to negotiate the TV remote control and take comfort in each other's physical presence. And wait for tomorrow.

Tomorrow came, and the news was not encouraging from her new doctor, a neurosurgeon who had been called in for a consultation. Having reviewed her brain scans, he gave us his opinion. "Mary, it looks like you have a brain lesion of some sort."

She and I remained quiet, waiting for the other shoe to drop.

"We'll need to operate and do a biopsy to see what we're dealing with."

"Okay, when?" my mom asked. She trusted doctors above everyone.

"Tomorrow," he said. Then he added, "Have you ever had a history of melanoma, breast, or lung cancer?"

Bingo, there you have it, I thought to myself. He was looking for metastatic cancer, a cancer that originates in one place in the body before spreading to choke the life out of you. Most likely lung cancer in my mom's case; that was my deduction.

"No," was my mom's short answer. She seemed at a loss for words.

"Can I do a quick body and breast exam?" the surgeon asked.

Before my mom could answer, he was pulling closed the bedside curtain to examine her. Melanoma is prevalent among people living in the deserts of the Southwest. But the doctor did not find any lesions. Next he massaged her breast, feeling for lumps. Nothing.

"Okay," he said. "We'll go in tomorrow and see what's happening. We'll need to shave a small portion of your hair off, Mary. We'll do it after you're asleep. I just don't want you to be surprised when you wake up looking like I scalped you!"

It would not be the last time she lost her hair.

"Can I please have a tranquilizer?" It was her only response.

"I don't think that's a good idea, Mary. You don't want to be dependent on them," he answered, as he walked out the door. My mom didn't reply. She was of the generation that did not question a doctor's authority. I am not of that generation, and I work in a hospital as an RN. I followed close behind the doctor, approaching him at the nurses' station.

"Excuse me, doctor. My mom is dependent on tranquilizers. And this is not the time to get her off of them. Her anxiety level, considering the circumstances, is already over the top."

"I'm sorry," he said, "but I'm a Latter Day Saint, and I consider tranquilizers to be unnecessary."

I was pretty sure I was on another planet about now.

"Well, I am sorry, and with all due respect, I do not agree," I said. "She has been on Ativan for over ten years. You and I both know that we're looking at a catastrophic, life-threatening medical issue right now, and this *is not the time* to take her off tranquilizers. And by the way, I am Episcopalian, but that has nothing to do with anything right now!"

He stared long and hard at me before conceding to my wishes. "Okay," he said to the nurse standing at his side. "Give Mrs. Gammill one tablet of .5 milligram Ativan now."

"She takes one milligram," I said, "and needs it every three hours for anxiety. Please write that in your doctor's orders."

Staring at me again, he seemed to be sizing me up. I stared back. Yep, I am an assertive, knowledgeable hospital nurse, I silently transmitted to him, and I am not backing down. And more important, I love that woman passionately, and I have become her mother-bear advocate. I was already helping her die peacefully, but I did not fully realize this yet. I was beginning to do what I felt was impossible the day before, coping with the unbearable. Love is an amazing force.

Taking her chart, he scribbled away. I still believe it was the right decision.

Going back into the room, I told my mom, "Your surgeon is a Mormon."

"Well, let's hope he has God on his side," she said, chuckling.

I knew she was mocking, but I still countered, "I thought God was bullshit according to you."

"He is. If he thinks I'm going to start praying now, he's misjudged me. Hell is right here on Earth."

"If hell is here, where is heaven?" I wanted to know.

"There is no heaven."

I have heard it all before. I was in second grade and living in Lubbock, Texas. "The church and God have let me down. I am done with both of them," she said. Discouraged about life as a mother and wife to an alcoholic, she gave up the Episcopal Church and the choir that she had loved. "It's all bullshit." She never looked back.

There were no unforeseen complications to her brain surgery. I kept myself busy doing a jigsaw puzzle in the waiting room as the hospital team cut my mom's brain open. Maybe because I had been brought up by a diehard pragmatist like my mom, I had no illusions about what they were going to find as they probed her brain. But just like the day I was told, after years of searching and knowing, that my son Max had autism, when I heard the definitive diagnosis about my mom, I fell apart. Knowing and feeling are different things.

The surgeon approached me in the waiting room, with his operating-room mask casually hung around his neck. Our power struggle over Ativan from the day before felt like a century ago and insignificant to me now.

"Can I talk to you in the hall?" Silently, I followed him.

We stared at each other again, but this time there was softness in his eyes. I could see the diagnosis in his face before he opened his mouth, and he seemed to know this. He was not long-winded with fluffy words. The day before, I had showed my hand as an RN who grasped the reality of the situation, and he didn't waste my time. I appreciated his approach.

"It's over" were his first words to me as he touched my arm. "We'll wait for the biopsy, but the tumor was gray in color and mushy in texture, surely metastatic cancer. Her lung scan shows irregularities. This is lung cancer that has spread to her brain. Give her the best time she has left, but it's time to wrap it up."

"Okay," I croak out. "Any treatment at all?"

"You could radiate her brain, and that will buy her a few more months. She has maybe one year at the most, and that is optimistic. We're going to tell your mom we found a tumor, but we're not going to tell her it's cancer until the biopsy comes back. That will take three days. Each day that I see her, I will give her bits of information leading her in that direction. I'll tell her slowly. It's usually easier this way."

"Thanks, I appreciate that. Don't be surprised if she asks for it straight up. She's a direct shooter," I said, as I leaned on a wall for support. I felt like my legs might buckle.

"Okay, I'll play it by ear. I'll follow her lead."

"Fucking cigarettes," I said.

"You're right, fucking cigarettes," he replied.

I smiled. "I thought Mormons didn't swear."

"That has nothing to do with anything right now." So he *had* heard me the day before. I appreciate a man who can learn from his missteps. We became friends at that moment.

I broke down in the hallway bathroom, this time howling into a rough paper towel while I was on my knees, at the altar of anything out there that could feel my indescribable pain. I felt like a child, a scared and lonely little girl, who was about to lose the only source of real security and primary family she had left. And how my heart ached for her. This simply was not fair for either of us. I was in the darkest, most challenging place in my life to date, and I had no idea if I was up to the task of helping my mom die. It seemed I had trained for this moment my whole life—taking care of my mother was my specialty—but I felt fragile and so alone.

Leaving the hospital that night, I drove to her townhouse, my childhood home. It was early April in the desert Southwest. The orange blossoms were in bloom, and the air was filled with their fragrant sweetness. The warm, dry air kissed my face as I drove. And I started to talk to God.

"God, I can't do this. Ask anything, anything of me, but not this. *Not this, not this.* I can't say good-bye to my mom, not yet, I'm not ready. I can't help her die. I can't do it, can't do it, can't do it," I chanted over and over, holding the steering wheel tight while sitting forward, my whole body rigid with intense feeling. "Please, God, help me, you have the wrong girl. I've reached my limit of what I can handle." My tears were choking me as I hiccupped my prayer to the parting clouds ahead of me.

Just as I reached the depths of this cruel despair, I was relieved of some of my burden. Like many significant moments in my life, I never saw it coming. I have only experienced this other world a few times in my life, and this was the first.

I was approaching the intersection of Chaparral and Miller streets in Scottsdale, Arizona. I remember the light turning red. As I brought the car to a stop, I got a momentary and powerful glimpse of something I am still at a loss to describe. It was just the briefest of moments. The car was filled with a warmth that I could feel on my skin. My body was enveloped in a solar hug, and the light in the car changed. I cannot say for sure if it got lighter or darker, but the light changed, and it enveloped the interior of the car as I felt a presence near my face. I was not alone, and I knew this as surely as I know the earth is solid under my feet. I felt safe, secure, and suddenly calm. I did not hear words out loud; I heard them in my mind. I felt the truth of the message. It was a consciousness that did not use or need words, and the message was clear as it transcended my being: "Joani, you can do this. You can help your mom die, and you can say good-bye." As quickly as it came, it was gone. In its wake I was left with an unwavering faith that I could accomplish what I had felt moments before to be impossible. The unbearable task of helping my mom leave this world was within my ability to do. My grief did not subside, but my fear of being able to tolerate the grief and help Mom exit this world evaporated. God was near.

So it began. Mom accepted the softer approach from the doctor, listening each day to an increasing amount of negative news. She was eating her lunch when the surgeon came in on day three. The doctors had put her on steroids, and her appetite was voracious.

"Mary, your biopsy results are back."

She looked up from her hospital food tray, fork in midair. She just stared at him, her eyes big again with glasses on. She said nothing.

"I'm sorry, your tumor is cancer. I think it came from your lungs."

She continued to eat as the doctor stood there.

"Mary, do you have any questions for me?"

"What do I need to know?" It was a loaded question.

"It doesn't look good."

"What do I do now? What's next?"

"You can do radiation to your head to shrink the tumor. The procedure is not too tough, and it will prolong your life some."

"Okay." And she continued to eat. I sat on the side of her bed, again feeling indescribable anguish. I had no idea that pain like this existed. It enveloped me with a cruel, unrelenting intensity that took my breath away. I would not feel this pain again until my son was diagnosed with autism years later.

Mom seemed to be reacting to the news of her health from a distant place, a place of safety and denial, where the mind can rest until it is able to absorb the reality of impending death. She stayed in this place much longer than I would have anticipated, slipping in and out of recognizing the truth over the nine and a half months it took her to die. I was firmly grounded in the reality of the situation but learned to navigate around my mother's self-made cocoon. She moved to the East Coast, a decision based on both of our needs. I could continue to work at the hospital and take care of her. She would be close to her twin sister, and Maryland was her birthplace and the state she grew up in. She wanted to return to the Chesapeake Bay. Looking back, I have wondered if we should not have stayed in her home in Arizona, close to her many friends and colleagues at the insurance company where she worked. But at the time it seemed like the natural choice for us both, so we packed her up and flew east.

The months passed in a blur of doctor visits, grief, and laughter. She had the brain tumor irradiated to buy her a little bit of time, but the treatment had side effects. Her throat became sore, raw almost, and eating became difficult. And just as she got over the sore throat, her hair started to fall out.

"Joani, can you help me?" she called out from the bathroom. I peered around the door. "I think my hair is coming out," she said, as she combed through it. I could see clumps on the floor. "I don't want to make a mess." She seemed insecure about what to do as she looked to me for answers. I felt I had none, but I improvised.

"Here, Mom, let me see," I said, as I took the comb. No one prepares you for these moments. I wanted to retreat into a ball of sorrow as I realized her hair was coming out. But you have to be brave and get through each day and challenge that comes when living with the terminally ill. As I took the comb and gently ran it across her head, her hair softly fell from her scalp. "Hey, Mom, remember when I was a kid and you cut my hair on the back porch? Let's go to the back porch."

It was a late summer day. My mom and I had a passion for birds. Under an ancient dogwood that was brilliant pink every spring, we had fashioned various types of feeders. A couple of ducks even came around for our upturned garbage can lid filled with fresh water each day. As I combed through my mom's falling hair, she watched the birds. "Just let it all come out, Joani. No sense doing this slowly."

So as she chatted about the new red-winged blackbird that had found its way to our yard, I combed the hair from her scalp. All of it came out, except for a small, stubborn tuft at the very top of her forehead. For Halloween that year, she took some petroleum jelly and twisted it to a silly point. When she came out of the bathroom that fall evening, she and I laughed so hard that she peed in her pants. I still have a photo of her, the mirth in her eyes apparent. She then put on a red clown nose, and that's how she greeted trick-or-treaters at the door. She laughed until she could laugh no more.

Her pain and my fatigue marched on and increased as the cancer grew in her body. Her insurance allowed for a respite hospital stay, which meant there was no medical reason for her to be admitted to the hospital, but she and I, the caretaker, needed a break.

Many moments in the months it took my mom to die have slipped from my memory. Others are indelible. While she was hospitalized, the doctor ordered an MRI body scan to determine where the cancer had traveled. I was working in the newborn nursery the evening she was scheduled for the scan. It was convenient and comforting for both of us, I think, for me to be an employee in the same hospital where she was a patient. Telling my fellow nurses, "Hey, I'll be right back; going to see my mom's MRI test," I took the back stairs to find her. The nurses, even when extremely busy, were always accommodating to my needs when it came to my mom. Even as their pity was apparent on their faces, a constant reminder of the hell I was living through, I depended on them greatly. Their friendship and support were my breath.

Running up the back stairs, I made it to the radiology department as my mom was being wheeled into the X-ray room. Kissing her forehead, I helped the technician get her onto the table. Physical affection was not our family's strong suit, but facing the permanent loss of the love of my life, I learned quickly on my own to let my emotions show. My mom was not always comfortable with my outward show of feeling, but I didn't back down and instead teased her about it. "I'm going to hug you until you like it," I would say, as she giggled like a small child while I nuzzled her neck.

Once she was on the exam table, I secretly slipped a Snickers bar out of my uniform pocket and left it on her stretcher for her to find when she was done with the procedure. A little surprise. Looking at the lone candy bar on the stretcher, I was filled with sadness. Unable to pinpoint my sadness, I turned my attention to the X-ray tech. I joined her in the booth above the room as the MRI machine scanned my mom's body. Being a nurse and employee of the hospital, I was allowed a bird's-eye view of the test as it took place. Was this a blessing? As I watched, I wished I was a faceless family member in the waiting room, oblivious to the test other than to be told the results.

During the scan, red spots would bob and weave on a screen, appearing almost everywhere. "The red color is the cancer," the tech told me pointing to the screen. "Here in her liver and in her hip and leg bones," she said, softly and expertly.

It was like watching a monster, a monster invading my mother's cells, marching on with its army, with no regard for life or feeling. I viewed the red spots as a separate entity, one that I wanted to murder. I fumed with rage and seemingly had no outlet. I was in the middle of a bad movie, a sad, sappy, endless-tears movie. I was so tired and defeated as I watched the screen. It's amazing I was sober—at least I was while she was dying. Things fell apart soon after she left me and this world. But for the time being, when I needed to be the most responsible, I was in God's grace and drug free.

I don't remember telling my mom the results of the MRI. She liked to live in the world of denial, and I let her linger there as long as she needed to. When I think about it now, I realize that the doctor probably told her the outcome of the test, and she was keeping the news from me. She was protecting me, as I was protecting her. But nothing could protect us from the final act. Our only control was to make her death as comfortable as possible. And we were on the same page about that. Our animals in this country often die more humanely than our human loved ones. My mom would not suffer, not as long as I had a breath left in my body.

The days moved on. We had a final Thanksgiving and Christmas together. I gave her a book of poems for Christmas, marking a special one about mothers and inscribing my feelings to her inside the book's cover. She taught me to make peanut brittle that Christmas. She was adamant that I learn. She had already made me an expert fudge maker, teaching me to rely on the soft ball that the candy forms to tell you it's done, instead of depending on a candy thermometer. We almost went up in a ball of flames together that holiday season while making the peanut brittle. Wrapped in a blanket with fringe for warmth, and with oxygen flowing into her nose from nasal prongs, she maneuvered herself into the kitchen in her wheelchair to help me make the candy.

"Stir the peanuts until they smell roasted. Do you smell them yet?" she asked, while bending over the boiling pot of sugar and nuts. The heat came from an open gas flame, and her oxygen flowed all around her face as the fringe from the blanket hung loosely at her shoulders.

I heard a strange noise, a crackling at the base of the pot. The flames from the stove appeared to be licking the side of the pan, beyond the original flame.

"Oh my God, Mom." In a split second, a ball of flames shot out from under the pot. I immediately realized our error. Turning the flame off, I shoved my mom's wheelchair back. And it was over, no flash fire, and the fringe did not ignite around my mom's shoulders. How could I have been so stupid? Oxygen and open flames. My mom and I just stared at each other.

"The peanut brittle is ruined," she said.

"Yeah, but we didn't go up in a ball of flames," I replied. And then came our daily belly laugh. We laughed so hard; you know the kind—your face gets all contorted, there are tears, and you just can't stop yourself. Every time we would get control of ourselves, my mom would repeat, "Yeah, but the peanut brittle was ruined," and off we would go again, peals of uncontrollable, blessed laughter. Then we made another batch of peanut brittle, minus the oxygen, and ate it late into the night as we watched our favorite TV shows.

When the pain from the cancer came, we just could not laugh anymore. Although her existence with me had been tolerable, enjoyable at times, she had had enough. I think she made it through Christmas for me, but soon afterward she started to decline steadily.

We had a hospital bed brought to the house. She needed to sit up when she slept, as she was no longer able to breathe when lying flat. Propping pillows behind her back did not help.

"Will it be painful when I go? Will I be gasping for breath?" she asked. It was her biggest fear.

"No, Mom, you'll be comfortable, I promise."

She trusted me, just nodding her head, not needing any further clarification.

Her pain was no longer controllable with oral medication. Her physician had prescribed liquid morphine in a multiple-vial bottle, so I had a large amount from which I could draw a dose with a needle. I never thought of using it myself while she was alive, but my mindset quickly shifted when she departed.

She lost her ability to urinate and I inserted in her bladder a Foley catheter that the hospice nurse had left at the house for when we needed it.

As she slipped from this world, we watched a slide show of her life and mine that I had prepared. She enjoyed this immensely. She narrated the slides for me as they played over and over. Candles glowed softly, and Enya's *Watermark* songs played sweetly in the background. We had one last, brief laugh.

"See, Mom, in case you have trouble with your life passing before your eyes, this will help out." She smiled the old smile.

"Thanks," she said, chuckling. "Do you think that will happen?"

"I don't know, but if you get the chance, could you get back to me somehow and let me know? Nothing too scary. Just a message from beyond."

"If I sit at the end of your bed, will that scare you?"

"Yeah, that would be good. Just don't pop out from behind a curtain or anything."

She laughed her old laugh but only briefly. She did not have the strength to belly laugh, or maybe more accurately, she did not have the oxygen in her lungs. Fucking cigarettes.

"I love you, Mom."

"I know." Those were our last words to each other before she slipped into a coma for the last twenty-four hours of her life.

I have pondered why she didn't tell me she loved me back that last time. I don't know. Her strength just might not have supported three words. She certainly told me she loved me many times in those last nine and a half months. It was her last gift to me, for me to know that she felt the love I had for her.

That last night, I again shoved her over and slept by her side in the hospital bed. And I did sleep, peacefully. I would wake up periodically and feel her shallow breath. Deciding that she was comfortable, I would slip back to sleep myself. I think I accidentally pulled out her bladder catheter that night. I still hope she didn't feel like she needed to pee on her last night. Funny, the things you dwell on.

The next morning, just as she took her final breath and her heart beat for the last time, she squeezed my hand. Was this a neurological reflex? Maybe. She had not moved in twenty-four hours. But it was just her left hand that moved in mine for one last time, for just a brief second. Sometimes it's comforting not to be the pragmatic nurse. I think she squeezed my hand. It was her good-bye to me.

I still had one last good-bye to her, though, one last thing to do for her. She asked that her ashes be scattered in Chesapeake Bay. Her sense of humor always acute, she would say, chuckling, "I've eaten crabs my whole life, so it's their turn to eat me." Few laughed at her joke. At first I was not sure if she was serious. But as time progressed, she made her wishes clear to me. "I don't want an expensive funeral, Joani. I don't want a funeral at all. Use the money on something else for you. Promise me, no funeral. Cremate my body and just put me in the bay. Promise?"

"I promise, Mom," I would say, trying to hold back the tears.

On an unseasonably warm January day, after I attended St. Anne's Episcopal Church with a few close girlfriends, I planned to pick up my mom's ashes at the funeral home. Leaving the church, I shook hands with the priest at the doorway. I had not planned the exact day for this last journey with my mom. I knew I would know when it was time. And it was time.

Holding the priest's hand, I said, "I'm on my way to put my mom's ashes in the bay."

"Well, please take a liturgy book with you," he said. "You can read from the funeral passages."

"No, thank you," I replied. "My mom didn't want any formal religion messing up her passage from this world. Plus I'm pretty sure God doesn't care that much about the funeral passage words in the book. Just a hunch, but I appreciate the offer."

He looked at me benignly. I have no idea what he thought, and I did not much care.

"Would you like us to come with you to pick up the ashes?" my friend Nora asked me.

"Thanks, no, I want to do it alone," I said.

At the funeral home, the owner gave me a small black box containing her ashes (*How in the world is my mom in that little box?* I thought) and helped me place it in my backpack. As he did, he gave me instructions on where to open it. "And be gentle," he said. "Sometimes when you open it, the ashes fly around."

My car was parked on Main Street, and I had to walk a few blocks to reach it. As I walked, my mom on my back, I started to talk to her. In the last months of her life, as death approached, she became very controlling. I would frequently say, "Mom, you're always on my back about something." So as we walked, she and I shared one last joke. "Mom, you really are on my back now!" I could almost hear her laugh.

Taking a short trip over the Eastport Bridge, I went to an area of the bay called Horn Point. Sitting in the car, I gently pried the box open. Nothing flew around. The contents were less like ashes and more like chunks of small stone. I ran my hand through the stones, letting my mom drift back through my fingers over and over again, giving her a last, long hug. I did this for a few minutes before getting up the nerve to place her in the water. A part of me wanted to take her home, but I feared becoming one of those people who keeps her loved one's ashes next to her bed or on the mantel, forever mourning. And Mom wanted her ashes in the bay; I knew I must honor this last request of hers.

As the waves lapped at the beach, I took handful after handful and gently laid her down on the wet sand. The waves softly and tenderly returned over and over again to take her out into the bay. After I had placed all the ashes on the beach, I picked up a stick. In the sand I wrote: "I love you, Mom. Good-bye." I sat on a bench and watched the waves deliver my words to my mom. When all of the words were washed away from the sand, I went home. I hope it was the funeral my mom wanted. I think it was.

I have not communicated with Terry's family since the funeral. I think of her mom and children often.

My mom used to say, "I hope there are no Jesus freaks in heaven and that there's a corner where they drink Bud and play cards." Maybe my mom is busy playing bridge; I have no idea. But she has not come back to sit on the end of my bed or pop out from behind a curtain. I am still waiting.

From time to time I take my kids to the beach where I placed my mom and said good-bye. We write Grandma Mary messages in the sand and watch the waves carry away our love to her.

CHAPTER 9

OxyContin, and Coming Home to Pills . . . Again

Christine could be on a magazine cover. She is tall, model-thin, with striking, emerald-green eyes, and lashes so dark and long that they look false. She has full lips and a haunting look on her face. Even the dark circles under her eyes are attractive, as if a makeup artist painted them there to give her that fashionable hungry look. Her hunger is real, though. It is for OxyContin. She is so young, just nineteen.

She has a younger brother and is from an ethnic Italian family on the Jersey shore. I love doing interventions with families who are steeped in their ethnicity. I find the social differences and customs among families intriguing as I am allowed a brief glimpse into their lives. And they seem to feel any gathering is worthy of a fabulous feast. An interventionist's job is never boring.

Christine's mom is highly emotional and basically wrung out when it comes to her daughter. "I can't sleep, I can't eat. I am barely functioning, I'm so worried about my daughter," she tells me. Her husband is more restrained—at least until the intervention—and has taken on the role of calming down his wife. Christine's brother feels he is betraying his sister by participating in the intervention, a common state of mind for siblings.

"Look at the intervention as a gift of the truth delivered in a loving and respectful manner, with a solid plan on how your sister can live a fuller, more productive life," I tell the brother. Then I add "We're not ganging up on her. We're surrounding her with love." He seems to hear me, and his face brightens slightly. "Okay," he says. Teenage boys are usually short on words.

Christine is in bed on the morning of the intervention, not unlike most nineteen-year-olds on a Saturday. With her immediate and extended family, a few aunts and uncles, I wait in the kitchen as her dad goes to wake her. We have removed her car keys from her purse, and her parents have theirs out of Christine's reach. I always do this; I don't want anyone taking off in a huff of anger. It's easier to chase someone down by foot, and that has only happened three times in my practice. Out of those three, two still ended up in treatment.

Christine's dad tells her that her aunt and uncle have stopped by and that they want to say hello. She comes down the stairs looking like a beautiful rock star, all punked out with a few tats and a lip ring. Her makeup is fashionably smeared, and she has one hand stuck deep into her jean pocket as the other one casually holds an unlit cigarette. Her black-and-white tennis shoes are untied, and her white, V-neck T-shirt shows off her long, dark hair wonderfully. A music group I'm not familiar with is splashed across the front. She epitomizes cool, and I like her instantly, even as I immediately start subconsciously planning my strategy and perceiving that hers will not be an easy intervention. My ability to morph and adapt with each situation is a big part of my effectiveness as an interventionist. I do this without thinking about it. Actually, there is very little time to think. Good instincts are a job requirement.

"Hey, Christine, my name is Joani. I am a drug addict in recovery, and your family has asked me here because they're worried about you."

She is too cool to overreact. It is in her invisible handbook on how to behave. "Yeah, so?" she slurs out.

"This is an intervention, Christine. Have you seen interventions on TV?" I'm betting she thinks interventions are cool. Many kids do. On the way to treatment, many of my younger patients text and call their friends, proudly reporting that their family has just sprung an intervention on them. It's the surprise party of the twenty-first century. ("Yeah, that chick that goes on TV did it," Christine will boast on her cell phone on the way to treatment.)

"Yeah, I've seen them," Christine says.

"Well this is your lucky day, honey. This one is for you."

She rolls her eyes as I direct her down the hall. "Want a cup of coffee before we start?"

"Yes, and I want to smoke my fucking cigarette." The ego comes alive.

"That's cool; let's go out back," I say, casually. For today's intervention, I'm dressed in low-slung Juicy Couture pants with a short black leather jacket, in hopes that I look like a middle-aged woman who has a clue. We leave the quiet group behind as I accompany Christine out back to smoke.

I stay quiet as we sit. After taking a long drag on the cigarette and sloshing down some coffee, she's ready to talk. "Who set this up?" she wants to know. I would think that considering the group assembled it would be obvious, but she must be trying to wrap her head around what's happening.

"Your parents."

"Shit!" is her only response.

"It's not so bad. All you have to do is sit and listen to some letters everyone has written, and then you make the decision on what you want to do." No one wants to feel trapped.

I have done entire interventions on young people sitting on their beds or at a patio table. Sometimes they have no desire to hear anything anyone has prepared, especially their parents, but they're willing to go with me to rehab. If the letter-reading is a deal breaker, I have skipped that part of the intervention. As one young man naively told me as I sat cross-legged on the end of his bed, "I'll go to treatment, but I am not doing the intervention with all of *those* people." Silly boy—I was doing the intervention, not with the original players, but an intervention just the same, as I sat on his bed. Luckily he didn't know this, and off we went in my van to treatment without the formal procedure his family had planned. My sense today, though, is that Christine will listen to the letters.

"Come on. Let's go in and listen. It won't take long."

She stubs out her cigarette and reluctantly follows me inside. I put my arm around her shoulder as we walk in. "Thank you," I say. If you can bridge the gap with some physical touch, if the patient is open to it, it can work well in getting the patient to connect with you.

Christine plops down on the couch next to her brother and an aunt. As I look at her parents, it's hard to determine where Christine gets her alarming good looks. It must be a combination of genes.

Each person reads his or her letter in turn, asking Christine if she will accept the help we have found. She never verbally answers; she just keeps her eyes downcast—intently looking at something invisible on her tennis shoe, which is propped up on the coffee table—and shakes her head no. As her family reads, I watch her closely. I see sweat appear on her upper lip and forehead. It's not warm in the house. She wipes the sweat repeatedly with the back of her hand as she pushes her damp bangs off her face. Anxiety? Maybe. But before the last person has a chance to read, she suddenly declares that she needs to use the bathroom.

"Okay. We'll wait," I say, as she quickly goes into the powder room off the kitchen on the ground floor. If this were a tactic to do drugs, she would have gone to the upstairs bathroom, near her bedroom. My radar is telling me she is dope sick, or, more accurately, OxyContin sick. Her family has told me she is addicted to OxyContin, and now I sense she is undergoing narcotic withdrawal, that miserable no-man's-land that defies description.

I wait for her outside the bathroom door at a distance that I hope makes me look less concerned than I am. "I need to talk to my boyfriend," she tells me when she comes out.

"After we finish the letters, you can call him," I counter.

"No, I need to talk to him now," she says, and without waiting for me to reply, she bolts up the stairs. She needs a fix, and the boyfriend is the supplier. When someone is sick from opiate withdrawal (either heroin or prescription opiates) at an intervention, it can show itself in one of two ways: either the person is motivated to get to rehab to get detox medication and feel better, or, more commonly—especially among young people—the person refuses to go until he or she gets the drug into his or her system. Often the young patient doesn't trust that the rehab center has medication that will make him or her feel better.

After giving Christine a few moments, I climb the long stairs to her bedroom. She is texting on her phone and looking pissed.

"Hey, you okay? You sick?" I gently ask.

"Yep, and my boyfriend can't get me anything until he gets off work tonight."

"The rehab will have Suboxone waiting for you. It's the opiate they use to help with withdrawal."

"I know what Suboxone is. Fuck that," she says, while looking increasingly pale and sweaty. "I am not going anywhere feeling this way."

After some cajoling and negotiating about the wonders of detox medication and getting nowhere, I move on to plan B.

Going back down the stairs, I am greeted by eight staring adults, waiting anxiously for an update. Sometimes I feel like I'm negotiating the Middle East peace process, going back and forth between the parties. "She is sick and pacing around looking for her boyfriend to provide her with some OxyContin. It's hard to get her to focus on anything other than her immediate need to get the drug and feel better. Does anyone have any opiate drugs with them or in the house?"

Some days you just get lucky. Her uncle pipes up. "I have the old box from Uncle Joe that I told you about. You know, to show Christine what his life was reduced to before he OD'd and died," he tells me. "There are a few OxyContin in it."

I did know about the box, but I assumed it held only old parapher-nalia: crack pipe, spoon, bong. I had asked her uncle not to show it to Christine. Paraphernalia can backfire, making the addict crave. They see it as candy, not the destructive force that it represents to the nonaddict.

"Can I see the box?" I ask. Retrieving it from his car, he proudly hands it to me. I lift the lid off the ratty old shoe box and sure enough, a prescription bottle is rolling around in the carnage of a dead man's drug utensils. Lifting the bottle from its grave, I feel like I've struck gold. Shaking it out of habit, I hear the familiar tinkle, that secure sound that still says to the addict in me, "You have a few pills left, Joani, no need to worry." I can almost predict that there will be three pills in the container. My history with OxyContin runs long and hard; the memory of it is imprinted in my mind, whispering both rapturous joy and death. Such are the contrasts of this strong, addictive drug.

I place the pills in my hand. How could something so small and innocent-looking, smaller than a Tic Tac for God's sake, have caused me such inexpressible wreckage? As I gaze at the pills, I silently mock them. "Not today, old friend. Today I will *use* you to get someone help." I feel a small amount of vindication, even as I have the slightest of urges to feel its effects again. Amazing—my brain never forgets, never completely stops wanting the poison, the rapturous part of the poison. Maybe someday I will never crave, but I'm not there yet.

"Okay," I tell the group, as I slip the pills into my pocket. "I'm going to use this OxyContin to get Christine to come with me to rehab. Anyone have a problem with that?"

In unison, they all shake their heads no. Their trust in me is complete; if I had time to think about it, it could scare me. I'm just a drug addict making a living. My own insecurities rarely abate for long, even in the face of repeated success at my job.

"Hey Christine," I yell up the stairs, "could you come down here for a second?"

She comes halfway down the stairs and sits. Her chin in her hands, she stares at us silently. For a second I have a flashback of pregnant Terry sitting on the stairs with her head in her hands, and my heart goes to my stomach hoping it's not a harbinger of things to come in Christine's life.

"Sweetie, I have some OxyContin that you can take to make the ride to treatment easier," I tell her. Her head pops up. "Let me see," she says, instantly eager and suspicious of my offer at the same time. Taking two of the pills out of my pocket, I hold my hand out to show her. But only briefly, just long enough for her to verify that they are the real deal. I'm afraid she might snatch them from me. Slipping them back into my pocket, I say, "I'll give them to you when we're on the road."

It takes her less than five seconds to make up her mind. "Okay, I'll go."

The group erupts as if the Redskins have made a touchdown. Her mom rushes to get her previously packed bag, as I collect the letters. Her therapist at the rehab center will review them with her.

As soon as we get settled in the van, Christine wants her reward, and who could blame her? Maybe a person who doesn't understand addiction. For the record, opiate withdrawal is *not* just like having the flu. It is indescribable in its brutality. But I don't want to give Christine the OxyContin until we're on the interstate highway. I'm afraid she will bail on me at a red light.

"You don't trust me, do you?" she says to me.

"I like you, Christine, and I feel your pain, but no, I don't trust you. I'll give it to you soon."

When we get to the interstate, I reach down my pants pocket and fiddle around for a minute, making sure to retrieve just two pills. I'm not sure why I'm holding out on the third pill. The greedy part of my addict brain seems to be working independently of my frontal lobes. I have a slight awareness of this but no real plan as to what will happen to the lone pill. For now I ignore this, concentrating on Christine.

"Here you go, sweetie, I hope they make you feel better." She seems to be looking paler by the moment as she continues to sweat. This girl has a habit, meaning a severe physical dependence on the drug. I flash back to my husband, Brian, during the coldest February that I can remember, wrapping me in a winter bedspread twice a day, carrying me and loading me into the Honda, baby Mary in the back in her car seat. Brian would drive me to outpatient detox in Baltimore morning and night for five days. It seems like a distant nightmare, but it happened to me, to my family. I would beg and plead with Brian that I just could not do it. How he had the fortitude to handle me and an infant, I'm not sure. I think love of his family best describes his state of mind. When not in the car going to the outpatient center, I was huddled in the bedspread at home on the bed. Incomprehensible demoralization was my closest friend, and I wanted to die.

So as I hand Christine the pills that I know will release her from her hell, I am above all else compassionate with her. This is the greatest gift I give her—my understanding and knowledge born from my dark days of OxyContin dependence, allowing me to see her beyond the addiction, with no moralistic agenda attached to my image of her. I view her as one might think of any patient with any other chronic disease that threatens his or her health. I think my patients know this and feel this, and it is one of the factors in my success as an interventionist. As I love and understand them, I love myself, and, more important, in some small measure, I forgive myself. With all of my knowledge and pontificating about this disease, there is still a part of me that feels disgrace for succumbing to this malady, for letting myself and others down. It does not make sense, but there it is. Such is the case with this ugly disease of addiction. Long after the chokehold is gone, the addict can continue to feel a sense of shame. It truly is a cunning and baffling disease.

Christine has a ritual. She takes her driver's license and a dollar bill out of her back pocket. Sliding the two pills between the securely folded bill, she crushes the drug by applying thumb pressure to the driver's license. When satisfied that the pills are pulverized, she slides the powder onto the top of my client folder. Any hard surface will suffice. Rolling the dollar bill up now, she expertly and smoothly inhales the powder in one long snort up her nose. With her eyes shut, she pinches her nose closed with her fingers, preventing any of the precious dust from drifting out of her nostrils. She is quiet as she waits for the relief she seeks to descend upon her. Satisfied that her world appears better, she opens her eyes and reaches for her phone.

"Yeah, my uncle had some Oxys left over from my uncle Jack's Box of Doom," she tells her boyfriend. Replying to something I can't hear, she says, "Yeah, it was his leftover stash and shit."

Finishing up the communication, Christine almost immediately lapses into nodding, a common phenomenon that happens to opiate addicts as their consciousness wanes. Christine's head now hangs down, gently bobbing up and down with the movement of the road. She is in that dreamlike state of intoxication, a place between sleep and consciousness that some addicts aim to get to. I preferred to be more of a functioning addict, awake but blurry as I went through my day-to-day routines as a mom, wife, and nurse.

Like a homing pigeon that knows it is about to reach its destination, Christine pops up five miles or so before we reach the rehab center. Taking out a clear case from her backpack, she reapplies her dark Goth makeup, managing to look chic, even with extreme application of eyeliner and eye shadow. Natural beauty, coupled with her youth, would allow her to pull off any look, I think to myself, as I watch her with the envious heart of a middle-aged woman.

In the end, as during the drive, she is a girl of few words. But as I will later find out, she runs deep as her recovery progresses. And I will be proud.

"Bye, sweetie," I say, as I hug her tightly. "Thanks for coming with me," I add.

"Yep," she says, her last and only word to me as she walks off with the admissions counselor.

After my mom died, I howled in my grief. I watched the birds we once shared, sitting for hours, inert in a kitchen chair, unable to move as I absorbed my loss. The sun would set as the birds settled for the night, the moon would rise, and I was still in my chair. Staring at the moon, I would wonder where my beloved mom had gone, and I had no answers. As I returned to work before my three days of allotted bereavement time was up, I started thinking about her leftover narcotics.

I didn't know what to do with the drugs—a vial of liquid morphine and boxes of Percocet. Somewhere I had heard or read that there are people who read the obituaries looking for notice that someone died of cancer so they can break into the house to steal leftover drugs. This consumed my thoughts. The addiction from within was actually the biggest threat to me, but I didn't see it, as I projected my fear outward toward some unknown narcotics robber.

I decided to throw away the morphine. In the dark of night, I found a big garbage receptacle behind a grocery store. I threw the bottle high into the air like a tiny basketball, depositing it in the pile of garbage. I stood for a second, thinking maybe I should have kept it, but it was irretrievable, so I moved on to the next problem: what to do with the Percocet? Somehow I felt I could simply throw the pills away in my own garbage, but not the liquid morphine. My mind was not working correctly.

I was on the three-to-eleven p.m. shift at the hospital. For about two weeks, I had a routine. On my way to work, I would throw the boxes of Percocet into my trash can on the side of the house. I neglected, though, to put the pills into the trash when the can was curbside and ready to be picked up by the garbage haulers. Like a ghost in a white lab coat, I would return night after night after working my shift and retrieve the pills from the trash. I felt like a possum foraging around in the can. I was a nurse addict, in remission but getting closer to the edge of returning sickness. Swirling around in my grief, the perfect storm was forming.

My biological predisposition to addiction, coupled with psychological influences of extreme grief and social and professional comfort with pills, would be the cloud that broke over my head. But not yet. I had a weapon in my arsenal: I was an active member of Adult Children of Alcoholics. It was there that I told my friends of my dilemma.

"Every afternoon I throw the pills away, and every bloody night when I get home from work I fish them out," I told the group.

There was one particular rough-around-the-edges guy in the group I was fond of. His no-nonsense style of stating the obvious always appealed to me, and we were friends. He was a member of the group as someone who grew up with an alcoholic parent, but he was also in recovery for his own alcoholism.

"I tell you what you do with those little fuckers," he said. "Beat them to a pulp with a hammer, and then flush them down the toilet. That's it— they are gone, and think how good it will feel to pulverize them."

Why did I not think of that, a permanent solution?

I could not manage the task on my own though. I asked my friend and fellow nurse Nora O'Brien to help me follow through with what I knew I needed to do. So, at home, she and I emptied out dozens and dozens of Percocets onto a cookie sheet. Hesitating at first, I gazed at the sea of round, white pills, becoming increasingly intoxicated with their beauty. Before I lost my resolve, I took the hammer and repeatedly pounded them. It sounds easier than it was in reality to smash them up; they popped all over the place as I struggled to finish the job. Then I tapped all of the white powder to one side, as if I was distributing cake flour around a greased baking pan, dumped it into the toilet, and unceremoniously flushed my nemesis down the bowl. I felt relieved but regretful that they were no longer available. For the time being, I was safe.

Fast-forward four months. I bought a house with the money I inherited from my mom. The real-estate agent closed the deal with a bottle of red wine. I had not had a drink for about five years, since first seeing my psychiatrist, Dr. Kehler. I did not consider myself an alcoholic or addict. I was a psychiatric patient with general anxiety and low-grade depression. My life had greatly improved: I was a supervisor on my nursing job, I traveled, and I had a large group of friends and interests.

It was my birthday, and the bottle of red wine looked good.

Sitting in the kitchen at an antique gateleg table my aunt had given me, I took the bottle of red wine down from the 150-year-old fireplace mantle. The gas log was burning in the hearth to take off the early spring chill in the air. I had a habit of leaving the French doors to the patio and garden open, even on cool evenings. The tinkling noise from the fountain and fish pond in the background always delighted me. Gardening was my new passion, and I was happily obsessed with creating an outdoor oasis. I would spend hours poring over gardening books, taking field trips to learn all I could about perennial and water gardening. When my hands were not dirty from gardening, I was cycling with friends and a bike club. Foreign films, art museums, and plays were other favorites of mine. Out-of-town trips for professional conferences with fellow nurses were a blast. When exploring New Orleans or Coronado Island off the coast of San Diego, I was fully engaged in a life that was sober. Soon, though, all hobbies and interests would disappear into the void of addiction. But I did not know this on the evening of my birthday. An innocent glass of wine would lead me near death and steal more than a decade of my life.

I remember the fragrant smell of the wine as the cork popped out of the bottle. Pouring a glassful, I took a long, greedy sip. Almost immediately, my head was filled with a glorious warmth, that first afterglow of the effects of alcohol on the brain. I remember watching the evening birds flit about, preparing to settle for the night, and they seemed magical. *Why had I ever given up alcohol?* I wondered. I was in love once more. But I would not spend much time with alcohol. Booze was like a substitute lover I spent time with until my one true love returned to my side. My mind and soul were waiting for narcotics. I had awakened a sleeping giant with drinking, and now my brain wanted its favorite drug back.

In clinical terms, this is called cross-addiction. A less-favored substance, in my case alcohol, would lead me back to narcotics. This is why it's impossible for addicts or alcoholics to use a substance they don't consider themselves addicted to without getting addicted once again to their original love.

Months passed and I continued drinking—not daily, but alcohol became increasingly important to me. Again a perfect storm was brewing. The clouds already darkened with intense grief and loneliness over my mom's death would collide with chronic back pain and, ultimately, spinal-fusion surgery from a work injury. I was also on an emotional and pragmatic search to find a husband and father. My ovaries were running short on time, and I wanted my babies. Emotional closeness with men was still largely beyond my reach, and the intimacy that I yearned for still caused me great psychological fear. During this time, I transferred from my job in the newborn nursery to an outpatient ambulatory surgical floor. A candy store of narcotics was now at my disposal. Looking back, I can almost hear the thunder as the storm was forming. The breeding ground for addiction to manifest itself and flourish was dangerously upon me. But I didn't know this; I stumbled along each day living my life, oblivious to the fate and struggles that awaited me.

The journey back to narcotics happened with seemingly little thought process. Brian and I were living together and planning our wedding, after having met through a personal ad that I placed in our local newspaper. After a great deal of time in therapy and recovery for Adult Children of Alcoholics, I thought I was capable of getting close to a man and starting a family. I think I severely overestimated my emotional capabilities.

During our engagement, I injured my back and at times was in chronic and debilitating pain. I went through tests, steroid injections, chiropractic care, acupuncture treatment, and every sort of anti-inflammatory medication for pain, but I never requested narcotics from the doctors. I was afraid of them. I still had a working memory of my love affair with pills, so I stayed away—until I didn't.

Brian had a bottle of Percocet in the house, left over from kidney-stone pain. From time to time it called softly to me as I glanced in the bathroom cabinet. But it was never a clear option, until one day. I'm not sure why this day was any different from the others, but I decided to take two of the pills. The euphoria was immediate and complete; my brain was enveloped in a sense of well-being that could not be denied in its quest to repeat it. I became a slave on that beautiful fall day. It was not a slow burn, it was an immediate obsession. Not only was I experiencing the abnormal psychological payoff of extreme euphoria and the sense that all was right in the world—that exclusive place that only addicts seem to experience with drugs—but I was also out of physical pain for the first time in over a year. I was no longer afraid to get married. The seduction was absolute, and it would consume my life for a decade.

Christine completes her treatment. She does not resist rehab like so many young people do. I never receive any emergency calls saying she is about to leave the facility against medical advice or is being administratively discharged for unacceptable behavior. Her treatment, it seems, is as quiet as our ride together. Still waters do run deep sometimes.

I have the opportunity to speak in Christine's area of the country about two years after first meeting her. After my talk, a young person approaches me to say we have a mutual friend.

"You did her intervention. Her name is Christine."

"Yes! How is she doing?"

"She has started up the first young people's recovery group in our area. Our numbers are huge, thanks to Christine's efforts and commitment to getting this group off the ground."

I react with goose bumps and tears. I could not be more proud, as I envision my beautiful Goth girl standing tall in a home group that she organized. People do get well from this disease, even tatted, pierced rebel girls. I can see her group now—dozens of *cool* kids in a recovery meeting that she helped to start—and it gives me hope. Christine is my rock star.

After dropping Christine off at rehab that afternoon two years ago, I had driven home with the lone OxyContin pill burning a hole in my pocket. It disturbed my postintervention routine, which included drinking a cup of McDonald's coffee and playing the satellite radio loudly. Even though I didn't ingest the pill, it was stealing my usual pleasures and passions.

A good therapist resonates with a patient for years. So on that afternoon, Sunny Pawlik, my counselor while I was a patient at La Hacienda treatment center in Texas, was sitting on my shoulder, whispering her wisdom to me. She repeated a saying that I'm sure is indigenous to Texas: "That dog don't hunt here anymore."

"No, he doesn't," I said to Sunny, as I let the wind take the pill from my hand out the open van window. The coffee again tasted rich, and the music was sweet in my ear. God was near.

CHAPTER 10

Stephanie and Joani

I walk into the apartment with Stephanie to help her gather her things and get her out of the place where she's been shooting coke and dope, on a binge for days now with a middle-aged man. Stephanie is in her early twenties. I have no desire to know the arrangement between them. This is my second meeting with Stephanie, days after meeting her the first time at her friend's house. She assured me then that she would be fine. She is not fine.

While I think that Stephanie is taking off her nightgown to put on some clothes, she has another goal in mind.

"I hope this doesn't bother you," she says, as she pulls her nightgown over her head, "but I can't find a fucking vein."

Taking her breast nipple in her left hand, she squeezes until she finds a vein where the skin and areola meet. Picking up a used needle full of blood and cocaine, she pierces the tender skin, injecting the drug into her breast. Finished, she throws the needle down on the apartment floor. It comes to rest next to a bare mattress on the floor.

Suddenly, she screams, "I've gotta get out of the goddamn apartment," which is exactly what I am helping her do, but, jacked on cocaine, her agitation is over the top. She slams her fists on the kitchen wall. "This is not what my life was supposed to look like. I don't want this life," she cries, as she slumps to the floor. Holding her knees, she rocks in a self-soothing gesture, only to get right back up and start pounding the kitchen walls again.

She looks like a college student, and my heart momentarily breaks for her, until an old, intrusive memory slithers across my mind, momentarily disrupting my sense of all that is good in me. *God, why these thoughts now?* I have never shot drugs in my breast, but my fear and mother's guilt is that there were drugs in my breast as I breastfed my baby. *Go away* is always my reaction to this nagging recollection. *Not now, not now.* Sometimes maybe the truth does not set you free. I don't know, and right now I have no time to figure it out, so I push the thought back to the recesses once more. Stephanie is desperate, unhinged, and crazy on cocaine, and I need to get her out of the apartment before the man who lives here returns. I instinctively survey the room, making sure I'm aware of the exits as I hurriedly gather her things. We're on the fringe of public housing, and I sense danger.

"Where is your purse and wallet?" That's all we really need. But she has her belongings scattered everywhere.

A few days before, I had gotten a call from a concerned mom wanting my help for her babysitter. "My babysitter, the sweetest girl ever, is in trouble with drugs. I'm not sure exactly what's going on, but I understand from a friend that you sometimes facilitate getting help for girls and their drug addiction through the *Dr. Phil* show."

So it begins. The girls I have helped to get to Los Angeles and the *Dr. Phil* show always found me. The few times I have searched to find them, it has never worked out. Then when I least expect it, they appear, and for a brief period of time I get a reprieve from my own life's ups and downs as I concentrate on helping someone else in more need.

I have learned how to take advantage of the resources in L.A. to help drug addicts with little means to fund their own treatment. The story of the woeful state of adequate treatment for addicts and alcoholics in this country, with and without insurance, could take up a whole book. So whether you like or hate the shows that depict the pain and struggles associated with this disease, they provide treatment for the addicts, treatment that in most cases would have been impossible for them to access on their own. I have made lifelong friends in Dr. Phil and his wonderful staff. They provided for me and my family love, support, and the gift of truth when we needed it the most. In short, they saved our lives. For me to be able to provide that same opportunity to one of my fellow addicts brings me profound personal satisfaction.

Beyond the benefit of treatment, the shows help illuminate how intense and devastating this disease can be. For me to go back on camera and show folks that I am well, that addicts do recover and become productive once more, is the icing on the cake. My friend and teacher Chris Raymer at La Hacienda has a saying: "They saw us sick; they might as well see us well." Amen. Anonymity is a personal choice that I respect. But my personal feeling is that to hide our disease is to cloak it in shame.

So I got into my van with Lucy, my Sony camera tucked into my backpack, the extra battery charged, and plenty of tapes on hand. Having a purpose, a mission, felt great. I had spoken to Stephanie on the phone. She was sick and out of money, but still an aura of naïveté and sweetness came through to me on the phone. Sweetness is the one endearing quality of Stephanie's that has never abated. That, coupled with her intense frustration over her addictions and her difficult family history, made it easy and a pleasure to help her. I miss her as I write this.

On our first meeting, I drive to a suburban neighborhood lined with a sea of townhouses. Stephanie is staying in the end unit with a childhood friend who has given her shelter. Stephanie had been living at home with her mother, but tensions ran high, and she felt she needed to move. Tamera is letting her crash with her temporarily, even as she is at the end of her rope with her friend—or is she? Tamera's father was a fragile alcoholic, and I believe this world of helping an addict is a familiar one to Tamera. Tamera will need her own help at some point in life, and

I will have the opportunity to bring this to her attention in a gentle way in the coming weeks. As someone who grew up with an alcoholic, I can see myself in her.

As we come into the house, a cat three times Lucy's size gets one look at my little dog, hisses, and runs off to hide. Tamera and I share a laugh; the cat's reaction is so intense, while Lucy just sits there staring hopefully at her, tail in full swing, oozing "Let's be friends" from her entire body. "Give it time, Lucy," I say, as I pick her up to console her. Lucy loves cats and hates other dogs.

I find Stephanie in the bed, huddled deeply under the covers. Over her head is a wall-to-wall mural of Jimi Hendrix. *God, why him?* I wonder. Glorifying those who have died of this disease is dangerous ground for our youth.

I sit on the side of the bed and let Lucy loose to do her work. It's a wonder to watch. Having recovered from the emotional rebuff of the cat, she immediately marches her little legs up to the head of the bed. Nudging the covers back gently, she finds the face she's looking for. She licks Stephanie's cold and sweaty face as her little five-pound body shakes with all the love she possesses. It seems the sicker the patient, the more persistent and loving Lucy is. Instinctively, she seems to know when someone is down and in need of her Chihuahua love.

Lucy goes everywhere with me. We were in a Trader Joe's recently. Lucy rides on top of my backpack in the kid's seat of the grocery cart. On this particular day, the manager approached me and asked me if Lucy is a service dog. "You bet she is," I said. "People everywhere would have lost their minds without the love of this little dog." The manager looked at me suspiciously as the other customers around me laughed, some of them having gotten a dose of Lucy love themselves. "She's even been on TV," I added, hoping to not get kicked out. Without a word, the manager retreated, looking at me like I was some sort of eccentric dog owner. Which I am.

Stephanie responds as Lucy continues to wake her with her kisses.

"Who are you, little guy?" Stephanie manages to croak out, as she turns on her back. Good sign, she is out of the fetal position. Small moves can make a big difference. Sick addicts get stuck in the fetal position under pounds of bedclothes when withdrawal starts. I did. The term "going cold turkey" comes from the physical state of goose bumps and cold experienced as you withdraw from opiates. In an effort to conserve your body heat, you stay huddled in the fetal position; also, you can't think of any earthly good reason why you should get out of bed. Your mind is so devoid of the usual feel-good brain transmitters dopamine and serotonin that a profound depression sets in. A thick fog of blackness descends, and the lights go out, twisting your inner voice into knots of disillusionment about *everything*. Hence the fetal position, until your stomach declares war on you, and off to the toilet you trot. Back in bed, you huddle back down until the kicks set in. "Kicking the habit" refers to the neurological reaction that happens as withdrawal deepens. Your limbs, especially the legs, thrash out at an imaginary enemy, dumping all of the bed linens onto the floor. Shivering from sweat, you reach over to retrieve the sheets as you lie on a bare mattress; the thrashing is so intense that even the bottom sheet has ended up on the floor. And all the while you know that just one pill, one shot, will have you back in the game.

So when Lucy, with her little body and big heart, can cut through this bizarre state of being, she becomes a miracle worker. A true service dog.

"That's my dog, Lucy. She loves addicts and alcoholics," I tell Stephanie.

Sitting up now, she takes Lucy in her arms. "She's so small."

"I know. I didn't try to get such a little dog. She just never grew."

So it starts with Stephanie and me. "Can I turn my camera on?"

"Sure, I can't believe you're here. I've seen you on TV."

I am flattered. "I can. I've been waiting for you," I say, smiling at her. My heart is filled with love and hope, as it is every time I turn on my camera. And I *have* been waiting. At random times, when I'm driving down the road, caught up in my own worries and self-absorbed wants, I pray, "God, please bring someone to me, someone who needs my help." Then Lucy and I wait.

So for a brief period of time I walk with a fellow addict, chronicling his or her life with my video camera and making plans to go to Los Angeles and the *Dr. Phil* show. This is how it works. Someone who is struggling with addiction is brought to my attention by a friend or family member who knows of my work either through having seen other *Dr. Phil* shows I have done or through an acquaintance who knows of me. I videotape the person's struggle with addiction and send the tapes to the production staff in L.A. We then make plans to bring the addict to the show to meet with Dr. Phil. I love it. I feel a sense of purpose and intense good fortune to be able to give back to someone what was originally given to me. I film Stephanie, her struggles and interactions with her friend Tamera on this first day. In the days to come I will film every aspect of her life as she bravely opens up to me and my camera. While filming we are making plans to travel to L.A. and the show's studio.

Stephanie continues to hold Lucy as she stumbles out of bed. She puts on a heavy bathrobe and impossibly big fluffy pink slippers. We go into the kitchen to find her friend. Tamera, as blond as Stephanie is brunet, is standing in the kitchen making toast for lunch before her job starts on the evening shift.

"Please, Tamera, just twenty bucks for a Suboxone pill, and I swear I'll be better," Stephanie pleads. They seem to be midway into a previous conversation. Suboxone is a synthetic opiate used to detox addicts off narcotics. Initially it was marketed as a drug that had little potential for abuse. That has turned out not to be true. Addicts now readily buy it on the street, and the liquid form, buprenorphine, is what I injected into my arm for two and half years.

"You say that every time, Stephanie, and every time you start up with the heroin again," Tamera says, as her blue eyes fill with tears. She loves her childhood friend.

"I swear this will be the last time."

Lucy and I ride in the back seat of the car as Tamera takes Stephanie to buy the Suboxone from a street dealer. We are the victims of Tamera's unrelenting lead foot and jerky manual shifting of gears.

Suboxone in hand, Stephanie swears she will wean herself off heroin with this one pill and will no longer need me or my camera. And I believe in Santa Claus. But I remain positive. Hoping that I'm wrong, but knowing I'm not, I leave Stephanie with my phone number.

"Okay, sweetie. Here's my number. Call me if you need anything."

"I'll be okay. I'm done with this sickness," she says. "But thanks, and yeah, I'll call you if I need you, but I'm pretty sure I'll be all right."

Four days later, I get a frantic phone call that leads me to the apartment on the fringe of public housing. It is a gray day. Overcast and cold, it is late, late winter, a miserable time of the year on the East Coast.

"I don't know where the fuck I am," Stephanie tells me on the phone. "But I'm dying over here. I have to get out. If he comes home, I'll never leave here."

"Look for a piece of his mail," I say. "There will be an address on it."

"No fucking mail that I see."

How is that possible? She is just so fragmented. Her ability to focus is shot.

"Give me landmarks, grocery stores," I tell her.

"I don't know, I don't know," she cries. "An apartment complex close to Severna Park, I think."

"Okay, go outside and look for a street sign or the name of the apartments," I instruct her.

"It's a brick building," she says. That's not enough for me to identify her whereabouts. "Wait, I see a sign."

She gives me the name of the apartments, and I know approximately where is. It's a big complex, though. "Stay outside and look for my red van. I'll drive around the complex."

"Okay."

There she is, standing outside in a short silk nightie in the fading cold winter light, cell phone to her ear, screaming and crying. She does not seem to know we're no longer connected.

Leaving the van at a no-parking curb, I quickly escort Stephanie into the apartment. "Come on, Stephanie, get dressed," I say, as I look over and see her jabbing at her breast with the needle. At the same time, I hear the door open. *Shit,* I think, *he's home.* I scramble to stand by the sliding-glass back door in case I need to run, at the same time making sure my cell phone is accessible.

"Fuck you, George. I'm getting out of your filthy apartment," Stephanie says. My presence is giving her strength, I suppose, but I'm not feeling that strong, although I know how to bluff at this point in my career. "Hi, my name is Joani," I say to George. "I'm a friend of Stephanie's. We were just packing up."

He stares at us. He's wearing a name tag from a chain electronics store. I make a mental note never to buy anything from that store again. Silly, I know, but I'm feeling protective of Stephanie.

"Hey, my name is George. I've been in recovery for twenty years. I've been trying to help the kid." Yep, I still believe in Santa Claus.

"Great," I say. "I'll take her off your hands. I know she can be a handful."

Four days later, Stephanie and I are on a plane, headed for Los Angeles. Once again my friends at *Dr. Phil* have come through for me. The plane lands, and I feel a sense of peace and accomplishment. It feels like coming home. As Rich Whitman, chief operating officer of La Hacienda, once told me, it's like going full circle. It's the place where my recovery really solidified. A man named Phil McGraw told me the truth, and La Hacienda provided the treatment that helped save my life. As I look out the window at L.A.'s perpetual sunshine, I turn to Stephanie. "We made it, sweetheart." Help is on the way in the most unlikely of places— Paramount Studios—and I can breathe.

It was mid-fall, the most beautiful time of the year in Annapolis. The long, oppressive summer heat and humidity had finally abated, rewarding us with cool, crisp days. Our historic streets were lined with old trees with bright foliage; the brick steps were adorned with pumpkins, and the smell of wood burning in fireplaces filled the air at dusk.

The sugar maple tree just out of my infant Mary's room was a brilliant orange. As I crept again into my baby's room one night, the full moon cast a light on the tree. Mary's room was illuminated with a soft yellow glow, and I was grateful. For the fourth time that night, or maybe the fifth, I returned to her softly lit room to lay my hand gently on her chest. I was relieved to feel it rise and fall. Her little fist lay loose as she sucked tenderly in her sleep, her dark hair in contrast to her milky white skin. I could smell her baby newness in the room. I loved my Mary, named after my mother, with a fierceness and completeness that I never knew existed until her birth.

She was three months old, and I was addicted to narcotics. I awoke in a near panic, with an urgent need to check on her, after having another of my recurring nightmares. Even the obscene amount of narcotics I had consumed throughout the day and night did not keep me asleep for long. I compulsively checked on Mary, fearing sudden infant death brought on by narcotics-tainted breast milk. Yet I *could not stop the addiction.*

When I speak to various nursing organizations and recovery groups and at professional conferences and rehabs, I frequently say, "I loved my babies as much as any mom in this country; I would walk in front of a truck if it meant my life for theirs, and I still could not stop my addiction." I have had more than one person tell me they didn't understand addiction until they heard those words. My atonement will never be complete, but I take some satisfaction in educating people about addiction.

Addiction has nothing to do with love or the lack of it. It is a brain disorder. I heard an interventionist on the popular A&E network TV show *Intervention* tell a mother, "If you loved your children enough, you would not drink." I thought I might have a stroke. How about this? If you loved your children enough, you would not have breast cancer?

Before the babies' births came marriage to Brian. Six weeks after our wedding, I was a honeymooner at Father Martin's Ashley rehab center. I was a child of thirty-nine in treatment. Nightly, Gigi and I would jimmy open Father Martin's office, just off the campus chapel, with our driver's licenses. Crouched under his desk in the dark, we would take turns using his phone. Soon another patient, the chief executive officer of something, joined us, making us a trio of rebels in rehab, until I got disgusted one night and threatened to kick him out of the club. On the eve of Ash Wednesday, as he waited for his turn to use the phone, he discovered Father Martin's bowl of ashes set out for the next day. He touched the fine, dark, dusty powder with his thumb, and it flew everywhere, including onto Father Martin's beautiful white altar linens. I rushed to try to clean them up, but the harder I tried to wipe clean the ashes, the more I smudged them into the linens.

"I'm sorry. I've never seen a bowl of ashes before," he said, contritely. The next day there was a padlock on the office door. Our mischief was over.

Prior to Father Martin's Ashley, I was using an ever-increasing amount of narcotics. Having taken the Percocet that Brian had been prescribed for kidney stones, my disease was activated and in full swing. I was now requesting narcotic pain medication from the doctor who was handling my medical care prior to the spinal-fusion surgery on my lower back. I'm sure my request for narcotics seemed innocent enough. For the two and a half years that I was in chronic pain and receiving acupuncture, chiropractic care, steroid injections, and physical therapy, I never asked for or accepted any prescription for narcotics. I was simply afraid of them. Although I did not identify myself as an addict, I still had a clear working memory of the role that pills played in my life in my early twenties. But now that my brain was tweaked, it was as Father Martin often said: "One is too many, and a thousand is never enough." With my very first prescription for narcotics I called the doctor's office requesting a refill early, saying I had spilled half the bottle down the drain. This would set a pattern that would continue for the next ten years. Through spinal-fusion surgery and two C-sections, my doctor and narcotic shopping became more sophisticated with each passing year.

Another source of narcotics prior to my first treatment at Father Martin's Ashley was the outpatient ambulatory surgical floor I worked on. It was a candy store of narcotics, and I would "divert" whatever patients had not consumed after their discharge. I stole narcotics from patients. I can say with a clear conscience that I never denied a patient who needed pain relief a medication simply so I could use it. I took the leftovers, and on an ambulatory surgical floor there was plenty to go around.

I spoke not long ago at Severna Park High School in Maryland. Kids can be so honest and so brutal. They pose questions that most adults are too sensitive to ask. One teenage boy asked, "Were you sober during your pregnancies?"

"Yes, I was sober with my daughter, Mary. And no, I was not with my son, Max." I always pause at this point, contemplating my words carefully. "I was drinking wine the first five weeks of pregnancy, not a huge amount, maybe a couple glasses every few days, until I found out I was pregnant. The end of the second trimester, I started using Tylenol with codeine, daily." I pause and stare at the crowd. Will the truth set me free? I wish it would set Max free. In my mind I hear fragments from the song "Losing My Religion" by R.E.M., and I consider saying no more:

That's me in the corner
That's me in the spotlight
Losing my religion

Taking a breath, I continue, "My son has high-functioning autism." I feel as if the audience is my confessional. Kennedy Krieger Institute, associated with Johns Hopkins Hospital in Baltimore, is considered one of the best health care providers for kids with developmental disabilities. It is there that Max had his evaluation for autism. I wanted him to be seen at the best, so we waited almost nine months for his evaluation appointment. The providers there asked questions about the pregnancy and my health. I was completely honest with them. They told me they doubted that my substance use during the pregnancy caused Max's autism. As Max's mom, I will always wonder and live with guilt. Yet I believe, as Khaled Hosseini put it in *The Kite Runner,* that "true redemption is . . . when guilt leads to good."

God, I hope so.

Stephanie has had a few ups and downs in her recovery. That's a euphemism for "relapse." She continues to struggle in finding her place in this world, like many of us, I suppose. Sobriety is a process. Many times it takes more than one trip to treatment to get really well, and Stephanie is no exception.

One day I hear the "ding" of a text message on my cell phone. Oh boy, a picture. There is sweet Stephanie. Having just gotten out of four months of extended care, she has her arms up, muscles flexed, and a big smile on her face.

I call her. "Wow, great picture, sweetheart! When did you get paroled?" That's code for being released from treatment.

"Two days ago. Man, I feel good."

"You look good." Then a call beeps in. It is work. "Shit, I have to take this, Steph. Work. I love you."

"I love you more."

CHAPTER 11

Doctor Shopping

Kathy is a professional doctor shopper as a way to get narcotics. Her husband, Todd, has suspected for some time that she is addicted to hydrocodone but is unaware of how deep her problem runs until the day before he calls me.

The usual introduction takes place. "Hi, my name is Todd. How are you? I got your name from a rehab."

"Oh, I'm okay, at the gym, all sweaty, and my kids are out of school early today, but good . . . really good," I say, sort of out of breath in the locker room, straddling the workout bench, water bottle in hand. Yes, my style is very informal. Some say my boundaries with people are questionable. I prefer to think I'm approachable and human with my less structured style of communication. It puts people at ease, I think, and lets them see I'm a real person—a working mom and wife with lots of demands, just like them.

Todd chuckles. "We have three little kids. I get it." We're off to a good start.

"So who's having a problem?" I ask gently, but directly.

"My wife, Kathy. I knew she was taking a lot of pain pills, but I got a disturbing phone call last night from a friend of ours, a neighbor."

"Hmm, tell me," I softly encourage.

"Our friend is a doctor in the community. Kathy doesn't see him as a physician, but he told me she came by his house and asked him for a prescription for narcotics."

(That was a familiar trick of mine, and I lost a friend in the process. It still makes me sad. Some bridges are never repaired even when amends are made. Again, addiction is a thief.)

"Oh, my," I reply.

"Yeah, it gets worse. Apparently he was discussing the situation with a couple of his buddy doctors. You know, getting their opinion on how to handle her. I guess this isn't the first time she's asked him for a prescription. When he mentioned her name, the two doctors felt certain she was a patient of theirs, getting prescriptions for narcotics for fibromyalgia. I never knew she had fibromyalgia."

"Wow," I say, although I'm not surprised. Doctor shopping is not new, and it happens frequently among prescription narcotic addicts. I have a PhD in it. What does surprise me is that in the course of discussing this situation with *two* doctor buddies, this neighbor physician finds them both to be prescribing for her. *The lady must really get around,* I think. How many more doctors are out there prescribing medication for her?

"I'm sorry, Todd, this must be difficult for you."

"Thanks. Yep, shocked is the best way to describe how I feel. So, I went through the insurance information. She does the bills, so I had to rummage through her desk. I found six specialists that she's seen for the fibromyalgia. I never heard her mention this condition to me."

"There might be more, Todd. At some point you need to stop using the insurance or they'll tip off the doctors."

"Oh, there's more. I found receipts for urgent care centers she's visited, too. She didn't use insurance with these visits; looks like she paid cash. Then I did a search on the computer for frequent sites visited, and it looks like she's getting drugs off the Internet as well." With this his voice starts to crack.

"I know, Todd, it must feel like she's somebody you suddenly don't know."

"Exactly. Who is this woman?"

"She is a sick woman, Todd. She's a drug addict. Don't take any of this personally, as much as you feel deceived and violated by her lack of truthfulness. Try to remember the wife and mom you have loved in the past before the addiction. She's still in there. What you're seeing is the addiction taking over her mind and personality." As I talk to him, I talk to myself, always deep inside trying to assuage my old guilt. "And Todd, I was right where Kathy is. I did all of these things in my disease. Does she carry any X-rays around in her car, in case she happens to see an urgent care center?" I ask with a slight chuckle and in self-deprecating style. "They could have put a bumper sticker on my car: 'Caution, Brakes for Urgent Care Centers.'"

"God, I don't know. I'll have to check the trunk," he says, with a chuckle back.

I'm not trying to make light of the problem his family is facing. My goal is for him to identify with me. In doing so I think I give him hope that his wife can get well and also alleviate his natural tendency to vilify her for her actions. Her behavior is not uncommon. Prescription drug dependence has reached epidemic proportion in the United States, and the means addicts resort to in order to acquire drugs can be very similar and at the same time unique. And at times even laughable. But not until the family is well and there is some distance from the active addiction is there much humor in it. Still, I try to lighten the mood with new patients when I can. It helps the process of intervention.

Serious now, I ask, "Have you approached her about all of this?"

"Yep, and a huge fight went down. She screamed, 'You spied on me!' That type of thing, turning it around on me, like it was my fault—that the reason she needs drugs is because I'm so controlling that she's going crazy."

Of course, I have no idea what type of husband he is; he could be overcontrolling. A lot of spouses are. But most spouses, male and female, don't addictively use narcotics to deal with marital discord. Her deflecting the blame for using narcotics is also not uncommon. By the time an interventionist is needed, the addicted person will almost always have something or someone to blame for his or her condition. I hear "controlling" as the complaint and cause so often that I think it's the usual way the nonaddicted partner copes. As things are spiraling out of control with the family or relationship, the nonaddicted person tries to manage the situation with increasingly controlling behavior.

This is where Al-Anon comes in: getting significant others to embrace recovery for their side of the problem can be tougher than getting an addict into treatment. All good rehab centers have family programs that address this issue. But a good interventionist should plant the seeds of family recovery with education during the preintervention process. What I say to family members about getting involved in recovery for their own benefit goes something like this: "If you get into treatment— get active in a recovery program of your own like Al-Anon—the odds of your loved one's getting well and staying well go up exponentially." Codependents are so wrapped up in the other person that if you tell them to get involved in Al-Anon for their loved one's sake, they will go. They live to take care of someone else, so if going to Al-Anon means helping the other person, they are all for that. It's a bit of a con, because once they get to Al-Anon, they are taught to take care of and focus on themselves. But when they throw the controlling away, everybody wins. The addict feels the control go away and can then take responsibility for his or her own life.

But it's not time to talk to Todd about Al-Anon yet.

"So," I say, "she's resistant to treatment, I assume."

He laughs. "She doesn't have a problem, Joani, so why would she go to treatment?"

"Because they have great food, yoga, a golfing range, gym, salon on Thursdays, and personal therapy," I say. "I have my ways of getting her

there. She could probably use a break, and I'll emphasize that: revitaliza-
tion, rest, and relaxation. When she tells me she doesn't have a problem,
I'll agree with her, sort of. I'll say something like, 'I don't know if you
have a problem or not. I just know that the people who love you most in
this world feel that prescription drugs might be causing you problems.
Your family and friends are just asking you to go to this rehab for an
evaluation.'

"My job is just to get her to rehab, where professionals weave their
magic, getting her to identify with other patients and to engage in the
treatment process. Before this point of discussing the logistics of going
to treatment, you will have all read to her letters of love, with memories
and examples of how you feel the prescription drugs are out of control.
I will sprinkle in my own experience with addiction and, being a mom,
tell her that getting sober was the best gift I ever gave my kids. The intervention is as much for you and the kids as is it for her. If she refuses
treatment, we go on to the consequences. What are you not willing to
live with any longer? I help you to frame those boundaries with her in a
respectful and loving manner. I'm not a hard-line interventionist. I find
that love and respect go much farther in getting someone to the point of
accepting help. I rarely need consequences. Honestly, many times they
don't work. Or if you are successful with consequences, the addicts are
so pissed off that once they get to treatment they spend an inordinate
amount of time being so mad about the intervention that they don't
get the real work done. Having said all that, I must add that each case is
individual, and I play hardball when I have to and when harm to others
is imminent. I need to know where you stand if she refuses to go for
help. But my gut tells me that love will get this mom to go to treatment."

And so we begin to plan the intervention. All interventions are
highly charged situations. You can feel the emotional electricity in the
air, as friends and family come together with old and new memories.
Thoughts and feelings collide, making the atmosphere intense. Bringing young children into this climate gives me pause. The younger the

children, the less they can understand what is happening.

The three children in this family are too young to be involved in the process, but Kathy's parents and a sister live close by, and all are willing to participate. The neighbor physician and his wife are also willing to be part of the intervention, and I am overcome with gratitude. It would be easier for him not to involve himself. Because he is not her primary physician, there is no violation of privacy. I don't even approach the other two physicians who said they thought they were treating Kathy. Federal privacy laws prohibit them from disclosing any knowledge of her case to me.

Todd is a tough husband and dad. Actually, he's what I imagine a federal prosecutor might be like. Even worse for Kathy, he's an IT guy, and the Internet is his specialty. He has amassed a pile of evidence as proof of Kathy's addiction, and he brings it with him to the preintervention. As he hands me a huge pile of papers, I have to contain my laughter. We addicts think we are so slick, but in today's electronic age, you can track just about anything.

"Wow, well we certainly have the proof that she's done her due diligence in acquiring narcotics," I say, as I scan the papers. "But believe it or not, she may still deny everything, even in the face of such an abundant amount of substantiation."

I don't want to start off the intervention with guns a-blazing, with a pile of paper to convict Kathy with. Love is always the card I play first. My goal with Todd is to keep his anger in check. Anger is always a secondary emotion, usually being driven by hurt and fear.

"Did you bring the photographs?" I ask.

"Yes," he says, his face visibly softening as he pulls out a packet of pictures.

Todd and I sit side by side on a couch in a hotel room that could be anywhere in the country—the rooms are all starting to look the same to me—and we take a tour of happier times. Weddings, babies being born, birthdays celebrated. Even as the hotel rooms blur together, I am always entranced by these family photographs. They represent something so worth saving and working for. They give me strength to perform my job, even as they lighten the anger of the main people in the family who have been hurt by this complicated disease of addiction.

"Good job, Todd. These are great. I'm going to spread these out on the table in front of Kathy. As you read your letters, she'll be able to see the pictures."

"Okay," he says, as he busily arranges them on the table to see what formation works best. Yep, he's a controller, but he's also just showing the man side of him. I love it. Most men like something tangible to work with as a task. He's doing what I've asked of him—he wants to fix his family. It's not all codependency, and I'm happy that the focus is off the evidence of Kathy's addiction.

But Kathy has a surprise for us the following day at the intervention, and all our efforts and preparation are not needed. Her actions for a few brief and comical moments make me reevaluate my intervention style.

The hard part is getting Kathy away from her three young children so we can do the intervention without them present. The only logical way is for her sister, Sally, to offer to take the children for an outing so Todd and Kathy can have some alone time. It's not unusual for Sally to take the children, so it seems natural, but it means Sally cannot be at the intervention. I have the letter she has written to her sister, and I plan to read it for her. But again, all of our efforts are barely needed.

The neighbor physician has written the most loving and respectful letter to Kathy, expressing how her requests for narcotics put him in an awkward position and stating that he cares deeply for her family and her health. Wow, I think, how much easier it would have been for this doctor to just give her a prescription and be done with it. Instead, he takes the high road, talking with her husband and following through with the hard work of an intervention.

We all assemble at Kathy's parents' house for what is supposed to be brunch. The room designated for the meeting is an added-on sunroom.

A ceiling fan quietly hums from high above. Summer is in full bloom, and the garden out back is bountiful with black-eyed Susans and baby-blue hydrangeas. My gaze always moves to the outdoors just before the patient enters the room. I suspect I'm looking for my own inner peace before the hard work in front of me begins.

Kathy walks in.

"Hi, Kathy, my name is Joani. I am—" and before I can finish my usual self-introduction, she blurts out, "Oh my God, you're Joani from the *Dr. Phil* show!"

I always leave *Dr. Phil* out of my interventions unless the family brings it up. I am easy to Google and my website has some *Dr. Phil* material on it, so I don't keep it a secret. But this is *their* intervention, not my life.

Kathy throws her arms around my neck, hugging me tight. "Is Dr. Phil here? I can't believe you're here. I've seen all your stuff on TV." I can't get a word in. "Really, is he here?" I almost hate to break the news to her.

"No, Kathy. I do private interventions for a living. That's what this is."

She looks at me suspiciously.

"I swear, Kathy, Dr. Phil is not going to pop out of the closet, no cameras or anything, just me and this wonderful family that loves you. Come sit down; they have some letters to read to you," I say, trying to get things on track.

In a daze, she sits on the couch. She sees the pictures, but she is still focused on me and the *Dr. Phil* show.

"I can't believe you're here," she repeats. "I really respect all the things I've seen on TV with you and the show."

Her mom chimes in, getting to the punch line much earlier than I had intended. "So you'll go to rehab with her, then?"

With a nanosecond of hesitation, she quietly says, "Yes, I will," as she covers her face and drowns herself in tears. It is the easiest intervention I have ever done. *Maybe I should start all of my interventions with the Dr. Phil thing—skip all the usual stuff, maybe show a clip or two with me on the show,* I think comically to myself. Part of me feels Kathy is slightly captivated by my presence, having seen me so much on TV, and that is part of her willingness to accept the intervention and go to treatment. But I take whatever I can get when it comes to getting someone to rehab.

We do go through the process, though, reading the letters and looking at the photographs. Not only is there a lot of love in the room, there is a mild acceptance on Kathy's part that she does have a problem, and that's a good start. Todd's letter touches briefly on her behavior to acquire narcotics, but we never need the pounds of paper evidence, and Todd loses his need to indict her with it. It is a wonderfully smooth intervention—until the reality of leaving her children sets in.

Kathy's bag, packed prior to the intervention, is in the trunk of my rental car. I am to go with her to the treatment facility, and we have a flight to catch. "What about my kids?" she asks, with a sudden panicked look on her face, as the realization of leaving them starts to sink in.

I have flashbacks of hugging Max good-bye, of him crying, barely understanding why I was leaving (these memories haunt my heart still). Mary walked me down the long hallway of the hotel after Dr. Phil's intervention, holding my hand tightly as I prepared to leave for treatment.

"I'll be back," I told my children. They were four and six years old at the time. "I'm going to a spiritual retreat, sort of like when you go to camp!" I said, trying to sound normal. They knew that what was happening was not normal.

"But why can't we go with you?" my little Mary wanted to know. Max was in preschool at St. Anne's Episcopal Church; Mary was in second grade at St. Mary's Catholic Church, both in Annapolis.

"This is a camp for moms who have lost God's love in their hearts. I'm going to find God's love, and then I'll be right back home," I said, through too many tears. I wished I could be calmer for their sakes, but I couldn't.

It took everything I had in me to walk away from my children. I thought the pain of my mother's death would be hardest thing I would deal with. I was wrong. So whether or not my clients should say good-bye to their children always weighs heavily on my heart. I don't like making this important decision in other people's lives, but it's part of the job. It's not cut-and-dried. I have had a few moms nearly back out of their decision to enter treatment when they see their little ones. On the other hand, Mommy or Daddy may suddenly be gone, with no good-bye. If not being able to say good-bye is a deal breaker, I always take the chance and accompany them as they say their farewells, but I'm never completely confident in my decision. I temper my own regret over the fact that parent and child have not had one last hug by reminding myself that the children are far healthier and safer when the addicted parent is getting the needed help in rehab.

"Hey, sweetie," I say to Kathy, "is it okay if we call them later from the phone? Saying good-bye could be too intense for them and you. In my experience, it's better to have the family explain where you are in terms they can maybe understand. Then they can all visit Sunday after next."

Kathy looks at me silently, and the anguish on her face is so palpable, I can feel it in my gut. Lending her my courage and experience (I will go full circle with my own maternal pain; again my darkest past is my greatest asset), I quickly add, "Almost every day that I was in treatment, I would send my kids cards and little gifts, gum, small candies from the store they had at the rehab. They still have every card I sent them, in the 'Mom's rehab' bag! When the van at La Hacienda would take us patients to outside recovery meetings as part of the treatment process, I would dash into the 7-Eleven and look for little things to send them. I don't know how much I spent on stamps and envelopes during my time in Texas. But I know I felt better sending them those little tokens—the connection kept me going, imagining their little faces at the mailbox, looking for a card and a Tootsie Roll or two. When the moon was full, I would make a point to call my daughter, Mary. 'Look at the moon tonight at eight before you go night-night,' I would tell her. 'I'll be looking at it at the same time and blowing you a kiss that will bounce off the moon to your face.'"

Kathy starts to cry but is still standing. When the patient sits down, I get nervous. Taking her hand, I quietly say, "You can do this. This is the greatest gift you will ever give your babies." *This is the greatest gift you have ever given your children, Joani* echoes in my ear like a soft whisper from some other place. Distracted, I pause to listen to the murmur. Is it from close or far? I can't tell.

The moment over, Kathy nods her head in agreement to depart and gives hugs to everyone present as we prepare to leave in the rental car.

We spend a long time at the airport that day. Our flight is delayed. A torrential summer storm has blown up, so we wait nearly six hours for the next departure. Kathy has enough pills on her to keep withdrawal at bay, and this is fine with me. We talk a lot about the *Dr. Phil* show as we watch buckets of rain fall from the sky when thunderclouds burst. Because she is a fan, I think it's fun for her to hear the inside story about the show. It distracts her from her own reality, if only for a brief period. Then, like old friends, we lapse into a comfortable silence. At one point her head slumps to the side and she naps on my shoulder. Addict to addict, mom to mom, we wait for our flight.

After I was discharged from my first rehab center, Father Martin's Ashley, I still lived in the shadow of chronic back pain. Spinal-fusion surgery, two C-section deliveries, and elective plastic surgery were to come. I call it my decade of narcotics. It was also my decade of treatment. I was like a revolving door—in and out of every sort of medical care for addiction as my disease flared up, over and over again.

My doctor shopping for narcotics became a full-time occupation; like a trade worker, I honed my skills, year by year. In the spring of 2010, I spoke at the annual Tuerk Conference for addiction-rehab professionals in Baltimore, Maryland. The title of the symposium was "Prescription Drug Abuse: The New Epidemic." In preparing for my talk, I was reluctant to share doctor-shopping tactics; a lingering shame persisted, I suppose. But a physician who was speaking with me in the afternoon at two adjunct workshops about chronic pain and the narcotic addict encouraged me to talk about the doctor shopping. She pointed out that it was important for health care professionals to be aware of the ways addicts manipulate the system to acquire controlled drugs. My husband, Brian, helped me prepare my PowerPoint presentation. I think it gave him a measure of satisfaction to see me put into print my conniving ways. He titled the presentation "Confessions of a Narcotics Shopper," citing my examples of how I acquired narcotics as "Creative Cons."

Early on, with a spine that looked like mine on MRIs and X-rays, it was easy to play the chronic-pain card and get narcotics. In reality, prior to my surgery, the drug Toradol, an oral anti-inflammatory, worked great for the pain. But after taking those first Percocet pills of Brian's that were stored in our house for his kidney-stone pain, I was off to the races. My mind was immediately hijacked, and I started requesting narcotics for my back pain.

After my spinal fusion, I continued to hound my surgeons for more and more narcotics. In an attempt to determine why I had not received some degree of relief following my surgery, they put me through numerous pointless tests to determine why I was having pain despite what appeared to be a successful spinal fusion. I willingly subjected myself to more radiation in my quest for the magic pills. Finally the day came when I showed my hand, and the doctors would no longer prescribe narcotics for me. The surgeons had begun to tightly ration the amount of pain medication I could receive. When I requested another early refill, they prescribed only eight pills. Hell, I would consume eight pills before I finished breakfast. I needed a solution. So I altered a prescription for the first time. By adding a zero to the number 8 and adding a *y* to the word *eight,* I instantly transformed a prescription of eight pills into eighty. The pharmacist readily filled the prescription, and I was feeling rather clever—for a few days.

Sitting on my couch, happily stoned, watching TV, and wearing a back brace, I got a phone call.

"Hello, Joani, this is Betsy from Dr. Sanders's office. Can you please hold for Dr. Sanders?"

"Sure," I said. Not suspecting the ire that was about to be unleashed, I munched on a piece of candy—opiates gave me an insatiable craving for sweets, a common phenomenon among opiate addicts—as I waited for him to come on the line.

He had a slight southern accent. He started out calmly, but his voice and emotions escalated as he spoke.

"Joani, we got an interesting phone call from the insurance company, concerning the amount of narcotics I am prescribing to you. They told me I was overprescribing. I have a copy of your last prescription. It was for eight pills, *not* eighty!" he screamed into the phone. "Do you have a problem?" he bellowed.

"Yes, I do. I altered the prescription," I responded immediately. I was too caught off guard to contemplate denying and lying about it. The conversation went downhill from there. He sounded as if he were foaming at the mouth, clearly very upset, saying he had his practice to defend. "I don't need the authorities on my tail," he raged. And I was fired as a patient. I was no longer welcome in his office. And I was not offered help.

Hanging up the phone, I felt and learned a few things. At first I had a deep feeling of shame that was quickly obliterated by fear—fear of not knowing how I was going to get my pills from then on. It would take me years of recovery, education, and being in the field myself as a professional to question why my surgeon did not give me resources for getting help for my addiction. If I had manifested symptoms of any other type of medical disease while under his care, I assume I would be given the names of other doctors who could treat that particular illness. Whether I was ready to accept the help or not I don't know, but I deeply believe the medical community has an obligation to offer assistance to addicts when it is discovered they are under the spell of this disease, not just cut them loose with a tirade and shame. Having said that, I recognize that addicts are a difficult population to treat and that we may have just burned out the health care community with our lies and manipulation. There are always at least two sides to every story.

What I learned from that experience was to be careful of insurance companies. My rule of thumb was not to use them at all if possible, to rotate pharmacies and pay cash for prescriptions. I learned to use independent pharmacies if I could. There I faced fewer questions than at corporate pharmacies. The independent pharmacy owners are on the premises and have greater financial motivation to look the other way. I would make friends with the owner of the pharmacy if possible, and that helped tremendously.

Before finding new ways to acquire the drugs, I went through a private detox with a primary care doctor, the same woman who would prescribe liquid narcotics to me in the coming years. I really can't remember how long I stayed sober before the game was back on. My recollection of time is obscured by being impaired on and off for so many years.

After that detox, I started up again playing my chronic-pain card over and over in many different doctors' offices. Some of the physicians would prescribe narcotics for a while before getting rid of me; some put me on written contracts that clearly spelled out the conditions I must adhere to if they prescribed narcotics for me; and others denied me narcotics from the beginning, no doubt having seen my sport before. So I moved on to the yellow pages, making cold calls on the weekend. I would tell the doctor on call that his or her partner was treating me for some fictitious medical problem—kidney stones was my favorite—and I had had a flare-up of pain and needed pills. Most would not prescribe for me, but as with sales cold calls, it is a matter of quantity: if you call enough people, sooner or later someone will take the bait.

Urgent care centers were another favorite target of mine. This worked particularly well when I was out of town with Brian on vacation or on a business trip of his. I would tell the medical people that I had left home without my usual medications. I would include other uncontrolled medicines to make it seem more plausible, and, of course, I had an out-of-state driver's license to verify that I was indeed far from home. The long scar on my back supported my story of chronic pain. Once my daughter was born, I believe having an infant with me was helpful. People just tend to trust moms more, but you always get caught sooner or later.

Once on an island off Seattle, Washington, I was discovered to be a fraud at a clinic affiliated with a hospital I had visited the day before in downtown Seattle. My computerized medical trail had followed me. I was thrown out on my ear, with no empathy, as I recall. The female physician's reaction was similar to my neurosurgeon's response. I have often day-dreamed about that experience, wondering whether, if she had mentioned a wonderful rehab facility they had on the Pacific coast, I would have taken her up on it. Probably not—maybe I was not approachable—but if she had touched my hand and softly said, "Consider help," I would have felt her words. Many times in my practice today as an interventionist, the words and empathy I needed but did not receive as an addict active in her disease are woven into my approach with patients. Some good has come from those tough times.

I also took advantage of my own asthma and my daughter's respiratory infections. Tussionex HC was the elixir I loved, a medicine for colds with the narcotic hydrocodone mixed in. Tussionex helped my asthma by loosening respiratory secretions and quelling the cough. The hydrocodone in it was the icing on the cake for me. But Tussionex HC was too strong to be prescribed to children, so I would request the cough medicine Phenergan with codeine for Mary. Pediatricians prescribe Phenergan with codeine for children with coughs and stuffiness because it helps dry them up so they don't get ear infections. More than once, I told the pharmacist that I had knocked over the bottle while giving it to Mary and needed a refill. By the third bottle I claimed to have spilled, I got an icy "No more refills" response from the pharmacist.

I had the opportunity to apologize to that pharmacist shortly after returning from La Hacienda, the rehab center Dr. Phil had sent me to. My sponsor, Jill, advised against approaching pharmacies to make amends (too many legal issues could pop up, including arrest, I suppose), but I liked this particular female pharmacist. I think her name was Noelle. When I saw her one day behind the pharmacy counter, she appeared overworked as usual, while phones rang and she answered questions and instructed pharmacy technicians on this and that. As I watched her busily at work, I experienced a sense of responsibility for having taken up her time with my fabricated stories about spilled bottles of narcotic cough syrup.

In an unplanned moment, I approached her somewhat timidly and said, "Hi, my name is Joani. I wanted—" Then I stopped, not sure what to say or how to start. She just stood quietly looking at me. Then I took a deep breath and, like jumping into a pool of cold water, plunged right in. "I want to apologize. I don't know if you remember me, but I was the one who kept spilling the bottle of narcotic cough medicine and requesting refills, until you cut me off. I'm sorry. That was wrong of me," I said, with DJ's voice echoing in my head. DJ was a counselor at La Hacienda. He and I once had a conversation about making amends. I was confused. I'm not sure now how you can be confused about saying you were wrong about something, but emotional maturity seems to be a component lacking in many of us in rehab. DJ Shay suggested saying more than just "I apologize."

"Take responsibility, Joani," he said. "Say you were wrong."

Noelle continued to stand quietly for a second; it was her turn to be at a loss for words. Bailing her out, I went on. "I'm recently home from rehab. I was there for narcotic addiction. And really, you're always so busy and nice, I'm sorry I took up your time with my crap."

We are taught that with amends, the job is done when we clear our side of the street with a heartfelt, sincere apology, taking responsibility for our actions. Whether or not the other person accepts our apology is not as important as taking honest ownership of our behavior. But you always hope to get a positive response.

"Well, thank you for that," Noelle said politely. "I'm glad you got help."

"Yep, things are better," I said. "So you remember me?"

She chuckled. "I wish you were the only one who pulled some sort of stunt for drugs. But honestly, we get so many charades for narcotics that I can't remember you specifically."

As I looked somewhat crestfallen, she added, "But I'll remember you now. No one has ever apologized, until now."

"Yeah, our lawyers and sponsors discourage us from approaching pharmacies," I said, with a slight laugh.

She laughed back. "Your secret is safe with me."

"Thanks, but it's not much of a secret. I've been making amends all over town. I stomped around like an entitled bitch for quite a while." I left out the part about being the subject of a prime-time TV special.

Now she had that look on her face, like my boundaries were getting way too blurry. Too much information.

"Okay, then, I'll go now," I said. "But again, sorry, and thank you."

"You bet."

And the sunlight of the spirit in me is brighter for taking responsibility for my actions with this person. The trick is to take the lessons you learn in rehab and apply them at home. This is where meetings and sponsors are of crucial importance.

Honestly, just when I think I remember every way I obtained narcotics by nefarious means, another little weed pops up. After each of my babies was born, mastitis, a breast infection, would suddenly strike. On many Fridays after my ob/gyn's office was closed, I would come down with a fictitious fever and extreme breast pain. First I would call to see what doctor was on call. I needed to rotate my mastitis story among the physicians in the large practice. I did this often. They likely suspected my game, but only one physician in the practice ever gave me a hard time about it. So, checking the call schedule, I never approached that doctor again.

Undergoing unneeded root canals was another desperate way I obtained narcotics. Can you imagine having a root canal you don't need? Well, I had a few until I stole a prescription pad from a dentist's office, giving me a steady source of drugs for a while. This dental practice had a prescription pad with the narcotic Vicodin already filled in and signed by the doctor. All the receptionist needed to do was fill in the patient's name. I remember seeing the pad and realizing this. My heart started to beat wildly as my mind reacted to the opportune moment. As the receptionist turned to speak on the phone, I gently and quickly reached over the counter and stole the pad, seemingly with no thought process or hesitation involved.

I used these prescriptions until I had a premonition that I was about to be caught. I would fill in different people's names while trying to alter my handwriting. As my fear of getting caught for using these illegal prescriptions mounted, coming up with names that did not ring false to me became increasingly difficult. At this point I had to travel far and wide to distribute these prescriptions to various pharmacies. Sitting in strange parking lots in neighboring counties, I would ponder what name to fill in as Mary sucked on her pacifier in her car seat. My greatest fear was that I would be arrested on the spot and baby Mary, who was months old at the time, would be taken from me.

One day, I targeted a large chain grocery store, just south of Annapolis, that had a pharmacy service. I handed in the prescription and answered the usual questions.

"Have you filled prescriptions with us before?" the technician asked.

"No, I haven't. I usually use another pharmacy, but I think this might be more convenient. I can shop while it's filled," I said, hoping I sounded casual as I rested my hand on the grocery cart where Mary was sitting and happily chewing her hands. Even that hand placement, close to my baby, was contrived. Mary was my prop: her presence gave me a sense of legitimacy, because moms aren't drug addicts or con artists, right?

"Yes, it is convenient. Will you be using your insurance?" she asked, smiling at Mary as she talked.

"No, my plan doesn't have a prescription option."

"Okay, what is your name?"

"Sally Werner," I said clearly, as sweat formed on my upper lip. Most of the names I used were somehow related to someone I knew in the past. I'm not sure why.

"Okay, this shouldn't take too long, about fifteen minutes." Handing me a small piece of paper, she said, "Look for your number on the overhead board. When it lights up, your prescription is ready for pickup."

"Thanks," I said, as I wheeled Mary back into the grocery aisle.

I kept wheeling Mary around, putting this and that into the grocery cart, all the while keeping an eye out for my number to appear on the large board suspended from the ceiling.

But too much time passed—maybe forty-five minutes and still no light. I was afraid to approach the pharmacy about it. I had a bad feeling in the pit of my stomach. One hour and still nothing. Then I heard my name.

"Will customer Werner please come to the pharmacy?"

Not on your life. Cautiously, I emerged from the dairy aisle so I could momentarily glance over at the pharmacy. Seeing a man in a suit behind the counter, I hurriedly took Mary from the grocery cart. Holding her carrier tightly, I walked as quickly as I could, without looking suspicious, to the sliding-glass doors. Fumbling for my keys, I got us into the car. I was sweating profusely as I started it. Once I was on the highway, I flung the remaining prescriptions out the car window.

I don't know what happened that day. It just did not unfold the way it usually did, and the man behind the counter looked oddly out of place. What does Oprah say? Always follow your instincts? I looked over my shoulder in the car and saw my baby Mary, so unsuspecting of the drama and danger in my life, and I was filled with both intense love and regret. A visceral feeling transcended my being; I was not sure I would live to see her grown, and yet the addiction marched on, despite my love for my baby. I cannot say it enough: addiction trumps everything.

Scared that day, I did clean up for a while, doing another short-term detox and treatment. And then I met one of the most addictive narcotic pain pills on the market, OxyContin. While doing an outpatient stint at the local Annapolis Pathways rehab center, Alex, a fellow patient, and I compared notes. She was much like me—a mom, a nurse, and a prescription drug addict. She was also very personable and easy to like. We became close almost immediately.

"Honey," she said, "why are you doing all that Vicodin and Percocet? The Tylenol in it will kill your liver. Find OxyContin—*no* Tylenol, pure opiate. It has a time-release coating on the outside. You just chew right through it; tastes like crap, but it gets you downtown."

She went on to give me the name of a new female pain specialist south of Annapolis. "She gives Oxys out so easy." Needless to say, she and I were just watching the clock while in this rehab. Note comparing is always a risk with patients, but there is no way around it.

I'm not sure how long I was home before I made an appointment with the new doctor. It was just as Alex had promised: getting Oxy was easy. I had Mary with me for the appointment. The physician was young and single with hopes of marriage and family. We spoke about this at length. At this point in my life, the survival of the prescription drug addiction depended on my being a consummate con artist. I would find the person's soft spot and focus on that, deflecting attention away from myself and getting the person to engage in something important to him or her.

OxyContin grabs your soul, through the trick of illusion. It's the size of a Tic Tac, but depending on the strength, each little pill can potentially contain the same amount of narcotic as sixteen Percocet tablets. Given that it's so tiny in size, it's hard to conceptualize the sheer amount of drug you're consuming until you're so physically addicted to a huge amount of oxycodone, the narcotic in OxyContin, that you want to die when you run out. I got to the point where I was as sick on it as I was off it. I was at the jumping-off spot that the Big Book talks about: "He cannot picture life without alcohol. Some day he will be unable to imagine life either with alcohol or without it. Then he will know loneliness such as few do. He will be at the jumping-off place. He will wish for the end." I could not live with the narcotic, and I could not live without it. Love of my baby Mary was the only thing that kept my head above water, so again I tried to get sober, at an inner-city outpatient detox center in Baltimore. Twice a day, Brian would pick me up from our bed wrapped in the bedspread, put me into the car, and drive the three of us—baby Mary in the backseat, me in the front seat with the back all the way down, huddled and freezing—to Baltimore.

With my hair a tangled, sweaty mess, not having showered or brushed my teeth in days, I would beg Brian as he put a cup of water to my lips, imploring me to take liquids, "I can't do this. I need the OxyContin."

Brian gave me quiet encouragement. "You can do this. I know you can, Joani. Please do it."

"Where is the fucking OxyContin? I know you have it."

Brian was silent as he carried me to the car and took me to Baltimore, where they gave me detox meds that did not seem to touch my misery.

On day four, my seemingly intolerable state of being seemed to shift. I started to feel slightly better. Again my sobriety didn't last. I could get sober, I just couldn't *stay* sober, as I heard actor Robert Downey Jr. say one time. In a matter of a week—or was it a month? I don't know—I was back at the doctor's office. This time I requested fentanyl patches, telling her I had no control over the OxyContin. This was a slight but very important shift in the way I was relating to a doctor. *I admitted I had a problem.*

Fentanyl is a strong narcotic, approximately one hundred times more potent than morphine, and the patches release the drug over time. I thought this could be the answer to my problems. At some point in the active disease state, every alcoholic/addict ends up trying to bargain with the disease, coming up with myriad ways to try to control it: "I'll only drink on the weekends. I'll only drink wine. I'll only smoke pot. I'll only use narcotic patches." On the excuses go, and they never work for long. I didn't get enough bang out of the prescribed amount of narcotic skin patch. I felt nothing. I put the patches all over my body and still nothing. Finally I cut them open and sucked the clear gel out of the packets. Still I didn't feel enough. The next morning, with Brian gone and Mary napping, I came up with a new plan.

I squeezed the gel onto a spoon. Fishing around in the silverware drawer, I found the lighter we used for birthday cakes. With it I heated the gel from underneath the spoon and inhaled the fumes. This worked. And once again, I lost complete control over my addiction. Another brutal detox followed before I went back to the same doctor.

"Let's try methadone maintenance," she offered.

"Okay," I replied, weakly.

So she prescribed the methadone for me in twenty-milligram pills. I was to take four pills a day. Of course, it's only maintenance if you *maintain* that amount every day. This physician was so sweet, but I think she lacked some knowledge of addiction. There was no way I could control the amount of pills I consumed.

I filled the prescription and left the pills on the shelf in the kitchen. I was clean, and the thought of another detox scared the hell out of me. But there I sat, staring at the bottle, weighing what options I'm not sure. Finally, panicked, I picked up Mary and ran from the house straight to a women's AA meeting I had been attending on and off. There I bawled like a small, scared child as I told the group my dilemma. I was only being partially truthful. I told the group I needed the narcotics for chronic pain but could not control my intake. Jill, my sponsor, spoke up. "Joani, I'll keep them for you, and when you need one, come find me," she said.

I chased that poor woman all over town for those pills. I drove her nuts, no doubt. This was just another attempt on my part to bargain with my addiction. It didn't last. Before long, I asked her to give me the whole bottle back, only to end up trying it again with my friend Meg. I gave her the methadone and then chased *her* all over town. And on and on it went.

There were shorter cons as well, like the time Brian had a vasectomy. Let me say that I did not suggest Brian have a vasectomy so I could mooch his narcotics. But a successful prescription drug addict is always an opportunist. So I accompanied him to the surgeon's office prior to the procedure. He was given a prescription for Percocet to be filled prior to the surgery. I had it filled and then took it all. On the day of the procedure, I told the office we had lost it. After the vasectomy we got another prescription for Percocet, went home—and I gobbled that one down, too. That afternoon I called the doctor's office and said that Brian appeared to me to be allergic to the Percocet. We got a new prescription for an alternative drug, Demerol, and, yes, I took that as well. I don't recall if Brian ever got to take any of the narcotics for pain following his surgery. And I don't really want to ask him.

And then there was the source common to every prescription drug addict: other people's medicine cabinets. A patient once told me that she frequented open houses on the weekends just so she could raid medicine cabinets.

For my entire life, my jaw popped whenever I chewed or yawned. Apparently I suffered from temporomandibular joint (TMJ) disorder, a jaw-joint dysfunction. One time when I was pregnant with Mary and driving, one side of my jaw popped out and stayed out, a very unusual feeling. Days later, the other side popped out. I never experienced any pain, but given that I was an addict, I thought it might be time to investigate my jaw issues. I found a specialist and played the pain card again. He tolerated me for a period of time, prescribing a boatload of narcotics and then suddenly stopped taking my calls. I was irate that he would not speak with me, and I vaguely remember visiting his office. The memory sits just outside my mind, but I recall being asked to leave the office, and that is all I remember.

Following the TMJ disorder episode there was an elective plastic surgery that went horribly wrong. At this point my primary care doctor prescribed the liquid narcotic buprenorphine for me. For two and a half years I needed no more cons: she supplied all I needed, as I learned to shoot it directly into my veins.

But the buprenorphine made me extremely sleepy all the time. This presented a problem at one particular traffic signal on the way to and from the grocery store: the red light was too long, and I would drift off to sleep while waiting for it to turn green. More than once, the van crept forward as my foot let up off the brake, and I jerked awake. With Mary in the back seat of the van, I was nervous about getting into an accident. My first solution was to put the van in park at all red lights, so if a nap came over me, the kids were safe. But I was still not satisfied with the chronic fatigue that the drug caused me. I needed another solution—that is, a different narcotic.

Hallelujah—I finally discovered the "cause" of all my problems: I had had attention-deficit/hyperactivity disorder (ADHD) all these years. To prove it, I found a new psychiatrist, a co-pay shrink in a big practice. Sitting with a book about adult ADHD on my lap, I enlightened the doctor concerning my condition. He agreed with me. I suggested he put me on Adderall, a strong amphetamine. The doctor initially steered me away from the wildly popular stimulant by suggesting nonstimulant options, but after I complained that they were not effective, he prescribed Adderall on my third visit. I was persistent and patient in my pursuit of the drug as I groomed my new psychiatrist.

This was a shift for me away from narcotic pain killers, and in the end it was my undoing—and my salvation. Near death is very motivating. An Adderall overdose caused my coronary incident, and that prompted me to look for an antidote to the amphetamine. Thus, I added one more drug to my arsenal, the benzodiazepine tranquilizer Klonopin, which could reverse the effects of the Adderall. The doctor who had prescribed the liquid narcotic buprenorphine prescribed the Klonopin at my request.

My days and nights blurred together. I was a rat on a wheel, spinning round and round, unable to jump off the train wreck that was certainly my future. And I knew it. I could taste death; the thought and the terror of it was my constant companion. The fear wasn't for myself—at times the idea of death seemed comforting—but for my children. It was the awareness that they would live life without their mom that filled me with the most fear and an indescribable heartache. In short, the love of my children saved my life. My story is not unique. There are many examples, crossing all cultural lines, of the power of a mother's love.

After shooting the buprenorphine and taking the Adderall all day, I would top it off with Klonopin for safe measure, all the while carrying with me nitroglycerin tabs and the respiratory inhaler albuterol in case I needed to save my own life. I was the mother of two little ones, a wife, and an RN at an inpatient alcohol and drug rehab center on the weekends. The irony of taking care of patients recuperating from the same disease I was dying of was lost on me. I was just trying to survive and get through the day. Any extra energy I had was consumed by worry for my children, especially my little boy, Max. My concerns for Max ultimately led me to Dr. Phil on that bizarre and fateful night when I reached out with a letter of concern and desperation.

Kathy got clean and has stayed clean. She sends me an e-mail every week or so. She has me on her automated list, and I must admit I rarely have time to read her notes. But just getting them is a comforting connection. From time to time I see her picture on Facebook. Her mom, without fail, sends me a Christmas card every year with a handwritten note of gratitude. It's all good.

Jill, the sponsor I chased around town for the methadone, died quickly and unexpectedly in 2004 after a long international flight. She was a loving, patient, and insightful sponsor to many women. I miss her still.

CHAPTER 12

Needles for All

Every summer we pack up the kids and head to Ocean City, New Jersey. Having spent the happiest times of my youth there with my aunt Margaret and her family, it is a welcoming retreat. Our home there is not elaborate or fancy, but it sits on the beach about a half mile from the boardwalk and has large floor-to-ceiling windows that frame the ocean.

The day we arrive, I open the windows and let in the moist summer air. The room is like a vacuum sucking in long-awaited oxygen. The aroma of the sea is intoxicating as it heralds the sweet season to come. Brian unpacks the car while the kids and I run around uncovering the furniture with flare and gusto from its winter slumber under protective sheets. As we get reacquainted with our beach house, I begin to look forward to seeing my summertime friends. There is an old shack of a coffee shop inland to my house. In the back of the shop, with its requisite old chairs, my recovery friends congregate for meetings. We seasonal folks are welcomed back each year by the locals like long lost friends.

The next morning, I dust off my beach bike and with our dog, Lucy, tucked into a bicycle bag clipped on the handlebars, her eyes bright and nose working overtime with all the early summer smells in the air, I head toward the coffee shop. With the wind blowing Lucy's ears back, you can almost hear the song *Born to Be Wild* as you look at her excited little face.

Although the roads are flat in this beach town, the never-ending wind keeps me pedaling hard. Easily remembering our route from years past, I see the tiny side street that signals that I am close to the coffee shop. It is tucked back on a road that most tourists don't know about. Squeezed between old homes and a small gathering of shops I see a heavily shingled building that is home to Bevin's Beans and Bakery. "We are home for the summer," I say to Lucy as I wave to my old friend Bevin, who is waiting at the window inside. She and I have been close since our kids were in strollers. We met at the kiddy arcade on the board-walk and bonded immediately as moms do when their kids are the same age. She does not hold seasonal citizenship against me. She is a rare native of Ocean City, New Jersey, and we swap stories of her beloved beach town and my historic hometown of Annapolis. How am I to know that as I stop to catch up the past few months with Bevin that one of the most meaningful connections of my life will begin?

Bevin does not wait for me to stop gulping from my water bottle before giving me a long hug. Just as quick as she came in for the hug she is bustling back toward the service counter. "Hey, I have something I want you to see," she says as she starts rummaging around the kitchen looking for a newspaper. "I think I found your next girl for you," she yells from the other room.

"Oh God, no, I'm still exhausted from the last one," I reply, having just wrapped up filming for the A&E show *Intervention* before leaving Annapolis.

Then I see the paper. On the front page is a picture of a girl. Even in silhouette, you can see how waiflike she is as she sits leaning against a headstone in a graveyard. Her hair is dark and long, like my young daughter's. She is addicted to heroin and cocaine. A police officer is quoted as saying, "I don't think she will survive the summer."

My immediate thought is, *How is that possible? She's a drug addict wandering this wealthy seaside town. How can we let her die?* The fatigue I was feeling moments before suddenly lifts as I turn my attention to finding "Anne." Anne is the name the paper has given her. I will soon discover that her real name is Crystal. I bike around town for about two weeks looking for her, which is ironic, because it will turn out that she has been walking the streets near my beach house all that time.

For a fee, I enlist the help of a homeless man I know named Scott, whom I frequently see at AA meetings, to help me with my search. Scott is a great guy, a young man from New York City who periodically shows up in this beach town. When he is in town, living at the local homeless shelter, he is my babysitter, which is a sign of how well I know and trust him. I have not seen him for a while now.

Scott tells me we need to sit on the steps of the local Baptist church around four o'clock.

"Really? The steps of the church? Why?"

"I don't know, just have a feeling, and we can see the hood from here. Sadly, even summer towns have drug dens. Her connection for 'H' is across the street. Plus, don't you know anything, Joani? Addicts don't get rolling until later in the afternoon."

"I'm an addict, idiot," I comfortably retort.

"Yeah, but you live in a nice house, with a sweet, hardworking husband. You're a privileged drug addict."

"Fuck you."

"Love you too."

We smile at each other as we wait on the stone steps of the church. I am still amazed as I recall the afternoon. We have barely sat down when Scott declares, "There she is."

Like an apparition, she appears. Within three minutes of my sitting on the church steps, she has materialized. I'm a practical person with a firm belief in coincidence, but I must admit that when I think of that afternoon, I think our meeting, which came about as I sat on God's step, was preordained.

Relieved to have finally found her, I am nevertheless taken aback by her appearance. She looks wild. Her hair is a mass of tangles framing her beautiful face, which is marred with tiny scabs from obsessively picking at her skin. The place in the brain where cocaine hits activates repetitive movements, so many cocaine addicts need to obsessively and compulsively repeat an activity—sometimes purposelessly picking at the face. On many days that summer, my mantra with Crystal is, "Crystal! Stop picking your face. You'll regret it someday."

As Crystal approaches us, she is carrying a plastic bag filled with something that looks heavy. I stand and approach her. "Hi, my name is Joani. I read about you in the paper, and I was wondering if we could talk. I might be able to help you."

She looks at me suspiciously, but then, taking a chance, she says, "Can you help me get to a Coinstar? I have a bag of a change I need to make into dollars." I correctly assume that drug dealers don't take change. This money has come from a customer of hers, a vending-machine worker who has paid her in coins for sexual services rendered. As Crystal and I become friends that summer, we will refer to him as "The Candy Man."

"OK," I say. "Let's go to Safeway. My car is just around the corner." Saying good-bye to Scott, we make our way there.

We're quiet during the ride to the grocery store. She is dope sick, in heroin withdrawal, and needs a fix. Her only focus is to get the coins turned into dollar bills so she can buy heroin. I am just a means to that goal; she makes no effort to get to know me. But I'm personally knowledgeable about the hell of opiate withdrawal, so I leave her to her inner world of survival.

It's amazing how quickly I feel protective of her. When we walk into the Safeway, everyone looks at her, many with disdain. She's filthy and disheveled, but, for God's sake, she's a girl, somebody's baby at some point in her life. I want to shout out to everyone, "She could be your baby!" And of course, she *is* someone's child. Eventually I learn that her parents are divorced, but she has a wonderful mom who loves her fiercely.

It is a myth that all drug addicts who turn to prostitution to support their habits come from homes where they were abused and molested. This simply is not the case with Crystal. She's suffering from the medical disease of addiction, which has brought her down physically, emotionally, and spiritually.

Bills now in hand, we leave Safeway.

"Where do you need to go now?" I ask.

"Back to Bay Street to make a buy," she says, still sick, and short on words.

Driving back up Coastal Highway, I pull into a gas station, a convenient place to drop her off without driving her directly into the dangerous neighborhood where street drugs are sold. "OK, I'll wait here for you," I tell her.

Crystal's response forever seals my heart to hers. A simple reply, and I fall in love, commanding all of my resources—emotional and material—to better her life. "You won't leave me, will you?" she quietly asks, looking me in the eye for the first time.

"No, I won't leave you. I'll be right here." And I wait. I will wait a lot that summer, and I will worry, chase, yell, film, love, and laugh with her. My whole family will. In the first few days of our friendship, Crystal will walk the streets all night, hooking and scoring drugs. One day she will tell me, "When I glanced down the street last night and saw your van, I felt safe." This is an affirmation to me that I am doing my job, helping my sister addict, deepening our bond. My hope is that she will trust me and follow me to get help.

Now I wait anxiously as she goes to score heroin. I will become more comfortable with the area as our time progresses—too comfortable in the coming years when a relapse of my own will draw me there for my own needs for the first time. Taking the leap from prescription drugs to street drugs, I will venture back on my own to buy heroin. But for today, and this summer, I am stable.

Sprinting across the street, dodging traffic, Crystal is momentarily energized now that she has the heroin and relief is in sight. After she jumps into the van, I suggest we go to my beach house. I have a sense of urgency about keeping us safe. My family is at a water park, and we will have the house to ourselves.

Entering my beach house, Crystal asks, "Are you sure I can do this in here?"

"My bathroom is not immune to needles," I say. "I had a needle habit for two and a half years." I roll up my sleeves to show her the track marks on my arms that have never completely gone away.

Looking at my arms, she says nothing. Her singular and urgent need is to get the heroin into her body. She enters the bathroom, sits on the floor, and takes the drug. It is hard for her to find a vein. Being homeless on the street with little intake of fluids, Crystal is dehydrated. The dehydration lowers the serum level in her blood, making it much harder to hit a vein with a needle. Imagine a picture on a wall of two rivers, one wide and full of water, the other dried up and skinny. Which one could you hit more easily with a dart? The fat and full one, and such is the case with veins. But find a vein she does. I watch her with the needle; I see the blood seep into the syringe, signaling that she has hit the vein, and I'm happy for her because she does not need to keep sticking herself. I feel no sense of nostalgia for the needle. For now, I am insulated from craving: when people need me the most, when I am working my program, I am the most safe.

Done, she comes out and sits on the ottoman. My children and Brian return from the water park. The kids approach her cautiously, aware that her appearance is not completely normal.

"Hi, are you the girl in the paper?" Mary asks, as Max shyly peers at her. "My mom has been looking for you."

"Yeah, hey, how are you?" Crystal replies.

"We hope you get better," Mary offers. Max immediately goes to the snack drawer, gets out a pair of Little Debbie cupcakes, and silently offers them to Crystal. In Max's world, there is nothing that a cupcake can't fix.

Taking the cupcakes from Max, Crystal looks up. "Thanks, buddy." Throughout the summer, when Crystal is crashed on the floor in my makeshift office on an exercise mat with sheets and a pillow, having been up for days on the streets doing drugs, Max will leave cupcakes at her head.

Because of his autism, Max is a boy of few words. But he speaks volumes as he silently leaves Crystal treats while she sleeps. The whole family cheers Crystal on that summer as I use film to document her struggles for a documentary on drug addiction. On the nights she is with us, asleep when we go to bed, we will thank God that she is safe. When she is out on the street, we pray for him to bring her safely back to us. She is such a gift to our family that summer.

Leaving Brian and the kids behind, I take Crystal out for a meal. Sitting on a veranda at a local hotel, we order lunch. She eagerly drinks down a frozen coffee as we wait for our sandwiches. She tells me it's her first meal in weeks. At our beach house that summer, when she is around for dinner, she more often than not will take her plate of food outside to Max's tent. Eating outside in solitude seems more natural to her, I suppose.

We talk during that first lunch, and I listen to her story. She is not unlike many other homeless, drug-addict kids on the streets. Home life was good enough, but having become addicted and getting deeply into the lifestyle, she left home to support her habit. And now she's trapped in a cycle of severe addiction, living a dangerous lifestyle to support her dependence on heroin and cocaine.

She eats slowly that day, her body not used to whole meals. Finishing up lunch, she is ready to shoot the rest of the dope she bought. She has purchased three ten-dollar bags of heroin, called dime bags, and has shot only one. "Can I do the rest of my stuff in your van?"

"Yep," I say. Some people would criticize me for allowing Crystal to use drugs in my home and van. But I have a goal in mind—getting Crystal big-league help for her addiction. Alone, I would be unable to change the course of her life or disease. My only objective for now is to keep her alive and as safe as possible until I can summon the help she needs. Having

her shoot up in my home or van means she is far safer than her alternatives: the streets, public bathrooms, or johns' houses, cars, or boats.

But someone does not share my point of view, and one day a county
social worker shows up at our door. "We understand you are sheltering a
drug addict and prostitute in your home," the social worker says at my
front door.

What son of a bitch sent the state of New Jersey to my door? I think in
anger, but what I say is, "Yes, we have a young woman with us named
Crystal. We are helping her until I can get her help for her drug addiction."

"Can I come in?" this stranger with a social services badge wants to
know.

I have nothing to hide, and she is just doing her job, protecting kids, I
think to myself, even as I am annoyed. "Sure, come on in."

"How are your kids with her? Do they know she is a drug addict and a
prostitute?"

"They know that she struggles with drug addiction, and they know
nothing of the prostitution."

"Do your children see her do drugs?"

The question is so preposterous that I do not immediately answer,
even as I ponder the irony.

Max was about a year and a half old, a cute little toddler with a head
full of curly blond hair and blue eyes that still take me by surprise. We
were standing just outside a bathroom stall at an upscale garden center
in Maryland. "I will be right out, sweetie," I told him. "Mommy needs to
go potty. Wait here." I entered a stall. Quickly, and with a precision
honed by needle addiction, I took a rubber tourniquet out of my backpack and tied off my arm. Finding a vein, I drew up the liquid narcotic
into the syringe. Just as I inserted the needle into my arm, little Max
crawled under the stall door.

"Mommy?"

Did he see what was happening? Probably. Did he understand? No.
But he felt my anxiety, I am sure, as I scrambled to release the tourniquet

and hide the carnage of my addiction. "Hey, sweetie, come on, let's go," I said, as I shoved all the paraphernalia back into my backpack. I do not remember when I finished that shot. That is all I remember of that day.

"No, my kids have never seen Crystal do drugs," I respond truthfully. The woman from social services says she needs to interview our children.

"Mary, tell me, who is Crystal that is staying with you?" the social worker asks.

Mary, who is eight years old, replies, "We love Crystal. Don't send her to jail. She needs my mom's help, and that's what my mom does."

When Max is asked the same question, he just stares at the woman. At just five years old and with autism, as well as auditory-comprehension and verbal difficulties, he beckons the social worker to Crystal's bed, showing her the mat and clean sheets and pillow that make up her room in my office.

It does not take social services long to finish its investigation. We receive a letter of commendation, thanking us all, Mary and Max included, for helping Crystal.

On that first day of meeting Crystal, I know I have an ethical responsibility for her health. I do not yet have anywhere to take her for long-term care. It is summer and the television shows that can help get her help are on hiatus. I use a video camera to document Crystal's situation hoping that as fall approaches I will be able to contact one of these television shows and get her the help she needs. She has already used her one-time state-allocated funding for treatment. Even if I got her to a detox center, it just wouldn't take, and I know it. Detox alone rarely works. Inpatient or intensive outpatient treatment is almost always needed to make detoxification a success. We are in a holding pattern.

What I can do is take her in for a physical. So after she shoots the rest of her dope, I take her to a local urgent care in the center of town.

Parking the car and looking over at Crystal, I see for the first time what we will come to call the "rubber band dance." Crystal has the amazing ability to stay awake after shooting a load of heroin. Her head bobs and weaves in an attempt to stay conscious. It can be quite bizarre to witness, and my kids will often say, "Mom, Crystal is doing the rubber band dance again."

"OK, I'll be right there to put her to bed," is my usual response. You have to force her to lie down and just sleep, then stay by her side to make sure she is not overdosing. When Crystal is sleeping in my office, I work at my desk or in the kitchen. It becomes second nature to feel her pulse and check her breathing as the summer passes. When she is staying with us, the last thing I do before going to bed each night is check her vital signs. The nurse in me never sleeps. If she is out, the porch light is on. The rule is that I lock the door at 10:00 p.m. Many mornings I wake to find her sleeping on the porch, on a mat placed there just for these occasions. Like a cat left out at night, we bring her back into the house in the morning.

We get out of the car, and I hold Crystal under her armpit as we limp into the urgent-care center. Placing her in a chair, I explain to the receptionist why we are here.

"Hi, I have a girl named Crystal with me. She is a drug addict on the street. I need someone to examine her to check the sores on her face and body. Also, her left eye is weeping pus constantly."

The receptionist looks at me like I am insane. It reminds me of the time I took a stray cat to the veterinarian. It was an old, broken-down cat, and the vet's receptionist had that same look on her face. The vet recommended euthanasia for the cat. Joking to myself, I hope Crystal is not in the same category. She is by far the sickest addict I have ever seen.

Carl is the physician assistant on duty that day. Crystal is doing the rubber band dance when he comes into the exam room. Silently, he stares at the young women before him. "She just shot two bags of heroin," I say, by way of explaining her bizarre movements.

"OK, let's get her on the exam table," he says. As soon as Crystal lies down, she passes out, her head gently lolling to the left. Carl and I just look at her, both of us silent in our thoughts of regret over the girl's mind-boggling physical condition. As Carl places the blood-pressure cuff on her arm, I tell him as much of Crystal's history as I know. Her blood-pressure reading is perfect: 115 over 70. Taking his stethoscope from around his neck, he listens to her heart and lungs.

"I don't know if this is good news or bad news," he says. "Her heart and lungs sound great." Crystal appears so hopeless in her physical state that most people's immediate thought is that she would be better off dead.

Looking now at her face and arms, Carl examines all of the dark scabs. "She is infected with impetigo," he says, "a bacterial infection from picking at her skin. I'll give you an antibiotic for it."

Next he peels off her socks, which are stuck to her skin. "She has track marks in her feet and ankles that appear infected," he says. "I can give you a broad-spectrum antibiotic that hopefully will rid her of the infection."

Then Carl examines her eyes. Placing drops in them, he explains that the liquid will allow him to examine her with an infrared light to help him determine what sort of infection is causing the pus.

Satisfied with the examination, he looks at me and says, "I've done two tours in Afghanistan as a medic, and I have never seen anything this severe over there."

"Wow." It's all I can say. I don't feel that Crystal's situation is hopeless. Against all the empirical data before my eyes, I have been confident from the beginning that this girl could get well. My thoughts and convictions defy the reality of the situation, and I'm not sure why.

Carl hands me the oral antibiotics and eye drops, and I ask him where we can get HIV and hepatitis C tests and a gynecological exam. He gives me the phone number for the public health clinic and says, "Good luck."

"Yep, thanks," I manage to say, as I navigate Crystal back to the van.

Crystal barely rouses as I get her into the van. I put the headrest back, letting her recline, and fasten her seat belt so she can sleep in safety. *What do I do with her now?* I think, as I start the van. When in doubt, get a cup of coffee. So I take Crystal to Bevin's coffee shop. She never wakes up. I put the windows down in the van and just let her sleep. It is like the movie *Weekend at Bernie's,* in which two men try to make it appear as if their dead boss is still alive.

Crystal comes to at some point, and my next goal is to get her a shower. I don't like the idea of her being in my shower that first day. That will change as the summer progresses, although I am always careful not to use the same razor she does.

It is Father's Day, a Sunday, and I am sure my gym will be empty, so I take her to Mid Atlantic Athletic Club for a scrub down. We enter the club with no resistance.

"This is great," Crystal purrs from the shower stall. I look at her wet feet from under the stall door. Like a mom who likes to see her kids get cleaned up, I feel a sense of satisfaction as I watch the water circle the drain.

It's time for my workout, so I take Crystal upstairs to the machines that I prefer. And in a small gesture, she again steals my heart.

"You want to watch TV while I exercise?" I ask.

"Sure."

I channel surf, asking her what she wants to see. "Cartoons," she says. Not CNN or *Seinfeld* reruns or sports, but cartoons. Then, lying on her stomach, her chin in her hand, she watches cartoons and chuckles. I turn off my iPod, the music to my ears being Crystal's giggles as she watches the animation on her belly, her legs up and crossed in the back. She looks like a young child, and I love her with my whole heart. As our summer together progresses, I will learn that she has a wonderful sense of humor. We share many belly laughs, the lose-your-breath-almost-pee-your-pants kind of laughs. I also learn that she is a voracious reader. Once, in a bookstore, she picks up a fairly complex novel and reads to me from the jacket. "It sounds really good," she says, as I stare in open admiration. She's a reader!

That Friday evening, after sharing a piece of cheesecake with me, she leaves to walk the streets, making the money she needs to supply her drug habit. But each day she shares with me glimpses of the girl behind the addiction and the prostitution. To many she is just another faceless girl of the streets. To me she is Crystal, a complex, fragile, bright, and lovely girl who has lost her way in the maze of this devastating disease, addiction.

Within a few days of meeting Crystal, I discover—to my delight or horror, I am not sure which, initially—that she has a sister named Jane who is also a drug addict and lives on the streets.

The next time I see Crystal, I ask, "Crystal, do you have a sister?"

"Yes, Jane. She's in jail, county lock-up, I think," she says, with a far-away look in her eyes. "She was picked up a few months back. I miss her. I don't feel safe without her with me."

So a new, simultaneous mission begins: find Jane.

Jane is in the local county jail, arrested on drug charges. She has been there about three months when I first learn about her. After finding out the visiting days, I prepare to go see her, something I have never before done with anyone in jail. As I pull up to the facility, I am impressed with the neatness of the grounds. A few girls in orange jumpsuits are milling around outside doing yard work. Inside, I am told to lock my belongings, including my keys, in the lockers provided and then sign in. I am careful to follow all of the instructions; the imposing building, incarcerating so many people, seems to curb my natural inclination to break the rules.

I know Crystal and Jane are sisters but nothing could have prepared me for this first meeting. As I wait for Jane to join me on the other side of a glass partition, I start up a conversation with an older man in the cubicle next to mine who is waiting for his daughter. As I sympathetically listen to him relate the familiar, heartbreaking story of addiction within his family, I am momentarily distracted and no longer looking at the glass partition in front of me. Jane comes in and picks up the phone.

As I turn to the glass divider, there she is, standing, silently staring at me, with the phone in midair. I stare back speechless; her appearance is arresting. She looks *so much* like Crystal, but healthy! Her skin is clear, her eyes bright. She weighs maybe fifteen pounds more than Crystal, giving her the overall appearance of physical well-being. Our mutual silence turns to tears for both of us. *But why is she crying?* I think. *She has no idea who I am.* I pick up the receiver.

"Hi, my name is Joani. I've become friends with your sister, Crystal," I say.

"You are my first visitor since I got here three months ago," she says, tears still in her eyes. She initially seems less interested in why I have come to see her and more moved by the fact that someone had shown up on visiting day. Crystal and Jane's mom, Susan, has rightfully reached the limits of her emotional and financial ability to support the girls. After meeting her for the first time, I have never doubted her intense love for the girls and the efforts she has gone to on their behalf, and it is obvious that she has suffered as much as her daughters. I believe her brave stance of detaching with love is a major factor in the girls accepting the help I have offered. Their mother is no longer there to bail them out, and they know it. They have worn her out. The first day I met Susan, she showed me the girls' photo albums, filled with hundreds of sweet pictures of their childhood. Pointing to the pictures, taking me on a tour of their lives, she softly cried. This close family of three has been torn apart by the disease of addiction.

I explain to Jane how I have come to know her sister, and that I am seeking help for her through one of the documentary television shows on addiction.

"Would you like to be included in getting help, if I can get you out of jail?"

"Yeah!" is her immediate response. Her initial trust in me surprises me to this day.

"OK, let's do it then," I say, with a big smile, hoping I am exhibiting more confidence than I feel about getting her out of jail.

We talk specifics about court dates coming up. "Do you have a lawyer?"

"I requested a public defender, but I haven't met with anybody yet."

I need a lawyer, a good lawyer. I know a man, Patrick Jones. He is a well-respected criminal defense attorney. He's also just a good guy, known to help those in need. I give him a call. "Patrick, I have these two girls."

Crystal, though not in jail, has legal issues as well. She is on supervised probation for prior prostitution and drug charges, so she can't leave the state without court permission. I tell Patrick the whole story, and without hesitating, he takes over legally for Crystal, Jane, and me. It is an amazing gift for Patrick to give us. The amount of hours he puts in, the many court appearances, his professional expertise, never asking for payment—it is all truly inspiring and instrumental in my ability to get the girls the help they will need.

Then it happens. After holding my breath, hoping, and sending my tape of the girls to several different shows, a documentary program on a popular cable channel picks us up.

I eagerly anticipate the day the plane will leave with us on it. It has been a long summer and I need to pack up the family to return home to Annapolis and at the same time prepare to take Crystal and Jane to Chicago to finish filming the documentary.

And then Crystal is arrested.

A week or so before our scheduled departure, I get a call from an Ocean City Police officer named Betty Ashcroft. Officer Ashcroft is the unofficial den mother for the girls on the street and under the board-walk. She does what she can to keep them safe, frequently stopping her patrol car to talk to them and offer them food.

"Joani, it's Betty," she says. "Crystal has been arrested."

I let fly a string of obscenities.

We have just gotten Jane out of jail. She has been living with her mom waiting to leave for Chicago, and now Crystal is in jail. I feel like I am stuck in a chess game, and the pieces keep moving just when I have them all lined up to win.

"Where is she?" I ask.

"District court for arraignment. I assume she is going to jail, since she is still on probation."

Patrick had gotten her probation changed from supervised to unsupervised, with permission to leave the state for treatment. Now everything is in jeopardy.

"You can probably see her down at the courthouse before they take her in."

I hustle down, arriving even before the squad car shows up, calling Patrick at the same time and telling him about the new obstacle in our attempt to get the girls help. There is little I can do for Crystal without his legal aid, but at this point I'm attached to her and feel the need to see her. I know her biggest fear will be detoxing in jail. Not fun.

I am allowed a brief visit with her before she is taken to the detention center. With her hands cuffed behind her, all she can do is put her head on my shoulder and sob like a small, sick child as I hold her.

"I'm sorry, Joani, I'm sorry," she wails.

"Don't worry, sweetie, it will be okay," I coo into her ear as my tears fall on her beautiful dark hair. I have no idea if it's going to be okay, but I bluff to ease her fear. My heart aches for her as I think of a jail detox. If tough detoxes worked, we would not need rehab centers, treatment, or recovery. Brutal withdrawals serve no purpose. They do not keep people sober. But Crystal is on her own with this one. There is nothing I can do for her.

On day three of her jail stay, Crystal is brought to court. She is wearing prison scrubs and is cuffed and shackled like a serial killer. Her hair is down and disheveled in her face. Her mom is at my side, crying quietly as she looks at her daughter, who appears to be intensely ill and frightened. *How many times has this mom been through this?* I wonder.

Patrick once again weaves his legal magic, and Crystal is free to go to Chicago. But we still have five days to go, and Crystal, despite three clean days while in jail, is still deep into her addiction. It takes much more than three days to break the cycle of addiction, and Crystal scores heroin within one hour of being released from jail. The only things to do are lecture her constantly (mostly about not getting caught, because I know she won't stop), pray, and flag down every cop I know and beg them to let her be so I can get her out of the state.

I know there are probably normal, nonaddicted people reading this who are thinking, *Just put down the drugs for five days, Crystal, so you can get out of town with no more complications.* Well, it doesn't work like that when you are intensely addicted. Being a drug addict myself, I know all too well the reality of the situation, so I hold my breath those last five days.

It's the morning of the day we are to leave for Chicago. We have a long drive before flying out of Dulles Airport in Virginia, the closest airport that will give us a nonstop flight to the Midwest. I never like stops when traveling with addicts. Crystal is packed, and we are waiting for the car to take us to the airport. Her mom and Jane are on their way over to my house. It is a crazy morning to start with. As I prepare to leave with the girls, Brian is closing up the summer house and getting the kids back home to Annapolis. And then it gets crazier.

"I need one last hit of crack," Crystal tells me. "Just one."

"*No!*"

I turn around and she is gone. The town car is now waiting to take us to the airport, Jane and her mom have arrived, and Crystal is missing. As I prepare to scour the neighborhood looking for her, I get a call from a familiar voice, Officer Ashcroft. I can barely breathe as I wait for her to tell me Crystal has been arrested again.

"Joani, Crystal is over here behind the Mission Shelter. Looks like she's trying to make a buy. I thought she was leaving with you?"

"She is, but it's like herding a wild horse," I say. Crystal is cocaine crazed. I hate cocaine.

"OK," Ashcroft says, "we'll track her while you get over here." Thank you, Ocean City Police.

When I arrive, I find that Crystal has been stalking a house. Apparently she gave a dealer twenty dollars for a hit. The dealer took her money, went into the house, and never came back out with the crack.

"Crystal, get in the van, we need to get to the airport," I say out the car window.

"No, she ripped me off and I want my stuff!"

"Crystal, get in the fucking van, we do not have time for this, and the chick is not coming out." We have been down this road before; being ripped off is common.

"*I want my fucking crack!*" she screams at a window with thick curtains covering it.

"Crystal, now. Get in this van *now!*"

She and I scream back and forth for about five minutes. My heart is pounding. I have no idea if she might just run at this point. This moment has been in the making for three months, and she is frantic for the beast cocaine.

"*Get in the van now. The car and plane will not wait for you, Crystal!* You are about to blow everything we have worked toward all summer!"

Bent over with her hands on her knees, she lets out a primal scream, a noise I did not think she was capable of making from her run-down, addicted little body. Then she walks to the van and reluctantly gets in. She is silent and pissed off. I still fear that her need for cocaine will outweigh her willingness to go to Chicago.

When we reach the house, the town car is at the curb. Susan and Jane are anxiously waiting for us to return, and two squad cars are present as well. Someday I will joke with Crystal, "You actually had a police escort out of town." Because she does. I think the presence of the police this day motivates Crystal to give up the cocaine obsession and get into the car so we can make our plane to Chicago. The police are a very clear and obvious reminder of what her life will become if she does not seek the help we have planned for all summer. But Crystal is not done putting me through hell.

She is in a bad mood and insists that the driver stop so she can smoke a cigarette. The two girls are on the side of the road in the bushes, smoking, but I don't think it is cigarettes. Susan has had enough; she gets out and does the yelling-mom thing, and they get back into the car.

Dulles Airport is in Virginia, close to Washington, D.C., and security there is extremely tight. Dogs can frequently be seen sniffing about.

"Crystal, do not attempt to get through security with drugs," I say, at the curb. "If you are holding, dump it out. If you get arrested here in Virginia, you are fucked. I cannot help you. This is not your hometown, where we have been given every bit of latitude possible under the law. Patrick does not have a license in this state to practice law. I mean it Crystal, go in clean."

"I don't have anything, Joani, I swear," Crystal says. I believe her. I can be so trusting sometimes.

We approach the security line. Crystal saunters through, no problem— yet. I go through and am busted for cuticle cream that I had forgotten to place in the correct size bag. This results in a complete inspection of my bags and a body scan. Crystal just grins at me from the other side of the line.

I start to breathe easier after all of us—including Susan, who is going with us—finally make it through the security process. Then Crystal says she needs to use the restroom. Restrooms and addicts make me nervous, so I follow her in. While I am washing my hands, I smell smoke, the familiar odor of crack cocaine residue. Shit. The lady at the next sink asks, "Do you smell smoke?"

"No, I don't," I say, lying as I try to look casual while making a beeline for the now-empty stall next to Crystal's. Standing on the toilet, I look down over the divider to see Crystal smoking from her crack pipe.

"Fuck, Crystal, put that out now, *fucking now*," I hiss, sternly but quietly. "You'll be arrested in an airport; do you know what that means?" I don't, but I think it sounds good at the time.

"It's only residue that's left in the pipe," she retorts.

"Crystal, it doesn't matter. Smoking anything, even getting a lighter through security, is against the law."

"You are so dramatic," she tells me.

"I am going to fucking kill you," I say, as I prepare to crawl under the stall.

"Okay, Okay," she says.

"Throw the pipe in the tampon receptacle," I tell her. She throws the pipe in. "The lighter too." She hesitates, then the lighter follows the pipe into the disgusting, bloody trash bin. *A perfect place for it,* I think to myself. And I got busted for cuticle cream.

As we leave the restroom, a homeland security officer enters. I hear her say to a lady standing by the sink, "There's a report of smoking in this bathroom."

"Walk fast, Crystal," I say, my heart beating wildly. We hustle away, and that is the end of the drama. *I just lost five years off my life,* I think in that moment, yet I doubt that Crystal, even today, remembers the horror of it. Being impaired has its benefits.

The rest of the trip to Chicago is uneventful. I am delighted at times as I watch Crystal and Jane together. The two of them have a comfortable compatibility. They crack each other up, and each one has an incredible sense of humor that complements the other's. Their belly laughs are contagious. I love seeing them together. They fight as well, but they seem to know how to work it out. I am hoping their mom is finally feeling some peace as we make our way west.

Handing the girls off to the capable hands of the production staff at the show is a great relief. I have achieved the near impossible—getting these two precious, pain-in-the-ass girls the help they need. Where did these girls come from? I feel so attached to them both. Maybe my mom brought those girls into my life from another world. Maybe someday it will be revealed, perhaps the day my mom comes back to me and sits at the end of my bed.

My own days of needle narcotic addiction seem like a distant dream. Pills were always my first and abiding love. I could have never predicted that I would have a needle habit for two and a half years. I still have those two visible track marks; they remain like small, dark tattoos in the crook of each arm. I like having them. I can never forget as I look at them every day. And the kids I do interventions on respond well to them; letting them see that I'm the real deal helps them to trust me.

Lucy has never completely forgotten, either. With her old habit of licking the remnants of blood indelible in her little doggie brain, she will sometimes sniff around the track marks and take a little lick to see if there has been a reappearance of the old fluid. Lucy the carnivore.

Following spinal fusion to my back (a seven-hour surgery during which twelve pieces of hardware were placed in my lower spine), two C-sections, and elective plastic surgery, I was given a prescription for narcotics. Each time, my addict brain grabbed on to the narcotics and wouldn't let go, resulting in many trips to inpatient rehab and outpatient detox and treatment, and endless doctor shopping. I have lost track of how many I did, but I believe it was around fourteen. Before the *Dr. Phil* show and subsequent treatment at La Hacienda, the rehabs included Father Martin's Ashley, a local Pathways facility, an outpatient clinic in Baltimore, an addiction psychiatrist, and methadone maintenance by a pain-specialist doctor. My primary care doctor also supervised several of my detoxes.

I would have periods of sobriety during which I would attend recovery meetings. Months of sobriety would go by, even a year at one point, and then I would relapse. The surgeries that led to my being placed on liquid narcotics—a breast reduction and tummy tuck—were elective. Looking back, I don't think it was wise to have had the operations. But my breasts were so large, and because of my history of back surgery, the insurance company agreed it was noncosmetic and paid for the procedure in full.

A series of complications followed the surgeries, including a pulled stitch that led to uncontrolled, profuse bleeding; anemia from the blood loss; an infection in the area of the tummy tuck; and black, floating spots in my vision. It was all hell, and I was on narcotics during the entire ordeal. Following my last hospitalization, with my wristband ID still on, I went directly to my primary care physician to tell her I was physically addicted to narcotics again. She started me on liquid buprenorphine. Why? She had always used the under-the-tongue pill form before and only for short periods of time for detox. But this was new—using the liquid, more potent form of the drug, which required me to use needles to administer. No detox was mentioned. I was to stay on the liquid drug indefinitely. I don't know why she prescribed IV drugs for me, or maybe it's more accurate to say I don't want to know why. She was my doctor, and she was supposed to have my best interests at heart. I was to inject the drug into my leg twice a day, deep into the calf muscle, but this would not last long; I soon started to inject it into my veins.

Besides her primary care office, my doctor had a high-end, medical-skin-care salon. It was there that I received my refills for the narcotic. I would go in for laser and Botox treatments, and while I was there I would request refills. On Botox night I would bring in my friends and neighbors, frequently recommending her services to people I knew.

During a visit for some sort of facial treatment, I remember her telling me, "If you inject the buprenorphine into your vein, it has been reported it feels like morphine." This is true. Maybe she was benignly sharing medical knowledge. Whatever her intent, the seed was planted, and within days I was shooting the drug intravenously. I was a known drug addict, I had a clearly documented history of severe addiction, and she had handed me a loaded gun. I had asked her to help me detox. Why was she continuing to prescribe the liquid form of a drug for me? I certainly played my part in acquiring narcotics from her. Addicts are so smart and manipulative that we make our insanity sound good. But I was the sick one; it was the doctor's job and responsibility to help me, not enable me, for whatever reason.

Also while she was my doctor, she was performing random drug screens on me for the Maryland Board of Nursing. As a nurse with a history of drug addiction, I was being closely monitored by the board's rehabilitation committee. Having satisfied the committee's requirements, I was released from the committee's oversight while under this doctor's care. Every urine screen she performed on me, even while I was using buprenorphine, was reported as negative for narcotics.

I do not remember the specifics of the day that I first injected the drug into my veins. I vaguely remember being in the downstairs bathroom of my house. I don't know what I used for my first tourniquet. It was not well thought out, and I find it curious that I can't recall the details of that first time. Was my anxiety high surrounding this leap into intravenous drug addiction, making my recollection fuzzy? Or maybe it was the drug itself—perhaps with that first intense hit, my memory was erased, or I suffered a blackout. I simply can't remember.

My last shot was more memorable. It was in the green room of the *Dr. Phil* show before the taping of the yearly special *Escaping Addiction*. Dr. Phil was not happy about it, and I was not happy with Dr. Phil. Remember—as I tell families of addicts I help today through the interventions I facilitate—the addiction will always fight to survive. My addiction fought hard, and Dr. Phil fought back. It had finally met its match, and because of him the needles were finally gone.

Crystal is going on four years of sobriety; Jane, three and a half. They are both in college, having obtained student loans to pay for their education. I have goose bumps as I write this. It is a cliché to say, but I could not be more proud of the two girls. They are the light in my heart that gives me daily hope that people do recover from this illness. Thank you, Crystal and Jane.

CHAPTER 13

Two Parents, Two Sons, Two Illnesses

"My son is terminal." They are the first words out of Izzy's mouth as I take my seat at the kitchen table. Thanksgiving is a month away, and I can smell the delightful aroma of apples and spice coming from somewhere in the house. As I mentally register Izzy's words, I glance to the great room and admire the fireplace that is encased in an expansive two-story brick wall that reaches to the height of a loft space above. A clear fall light infuses the room with a welcome glow.

I am confused by this dad's words. Addiction can be fatal, but it is not considered terminal. I must look puzzled because before I can clarify, Izzy continues, "My son Nick has cystic fibrosis." As he speaks, his voice is thick with emotion, and his eyes fill with tears that take me by surprise. Izzy is not tall, but he is dark and handsome, with the muscular build of a workman. With tan work boots on, he has the appearance of a tough guy. I will learn quickly that Izzy rarely bullshits; he is a straight shooter who gets right to the point. He is a self-made wealthy man who, after working hard for a large air conditioning and heating company, started his own business. He has been extremely successful. As he tells me, "I have been broke, and I have had millions. It's just money, and money is not the real stuff that life is made up of." I like him immediately. He seems to speak from a place of experience, experience that comes with the heartache of having not just one son, but two with cystic fibrosis.

"I'm sorry," I say quietly.

"Yeah, thanks," he says, while still standing at the kitchen table with his hands propping him up. "He was also arrested for taking the rear door off of a parked car while a lady was getting her baby out of the back car seat. I'm afraid he's really going to hurt somebody or himself. If he gets into an accident with one of my work trucks, the company could be liable."

"Here, sit down," I say, pushing out another chair. By offering the seat, I'm trying to communicate silently, *Let me take care of you, even for this brief moment in time.*

Izzy seems grateful as he sits. "Nick's deal is with prescription pain pills, and on top of that he has cystic fibrosis. His CF is pretty stable now, but the more he gets into the drugs, the less he takes care of himself. I'm afraid he's not taking his usual medications."

I don't know much about cystic fibrosis, other than that it's a genetically inherited disease of the lungs that causes excess mucus to accumulate in the respiratory tract, so I ask Izzy questions about his prognosis.

"Well, as a little kid, the prognosis was very dim when it came to surviving into adulthood. But with new treatments and medicine, the outlook has changed dramatically and continues to change and improve as time goes on."

"Does your heart ever stop aching for your kids?" I want to know. I have a personal stake in the question. "I have a son Max, with autism, and the hurt I feel for him can be overwhelming."

"It is not like a fresh cut every day anymore. It was in the beginning. You can't function with that kind of pain all the time. Do you have a picture of Max?" he asks, generously.

"Yep," I say, as I eagerly retrieve my cell phone to pull up some shots.

So the two of us—side by side, both with sons with diagnoses we never imagined we would have to cope with—beam with pride as we share photos with each other.

Then, like most men, Izzy abruptly reins in his emotions. He slaps his money down on the table. I like it when people pay me in a timely fashion.

"Okay, how do we get started with this intervention?"

And it begins. This is an independent referral, meaning it was not generated from an intake department of a rehab center, but instead was given to me by a family therapist who works both privately and for our local school system in Annapolis.

Independent referrals are fun for me, allowing me to showcase the handful of rehab centers I work with and trust, pointing out their individual strengths, specialties, and prices with insurance options. When I meet with Izzy, I have literature and brochures from all the centers. It is a daunting task for families under stress to choose a treatment facility. It is the job of the interventionist to help them make a decision by going beyond the glossy brochures and refined websites to illuminate the pluses and minuses of each center, taking into account each family's individual needs.

Also, as I meet with Izzy, I try to get a better picture of Nick's addiction. There are high bottoms and low bottoms in addiction, meaning some addicts are sicker than others when they come in from the rain and decide to get well, either on their own, by the court system, or through an intervention. Nick's bottom, with the preexisting condition of cystic fibrosis, will be reached faster, addiction being inherently more detrimental to him because his physical condition is already compromised.

"Is Nick physically addicted to the narcotics?" I want to know.

"I don't think so. He binges on and off with them. He might have been physically addicted in the past, but I think he's between prescriptions right now," Izzy tells me with such sadness in his brown eyes. Izzy is short for the Italian name Isadora.

I'm relieved that this young man does not have a *habit*. On the other hand he could use this information to his advantage during the intervention, telling us he is "not that sick." We will have to wait and see.

This will be my first and (to date) only all-male intervention. Izzy is divorced from Nick's mom, and she is not part of the intervention. Besides

Izzy, the group will consist of Nick's boss, a few co-workers, and Nick's younger brother, Anthony. Nick is twenty-three; Anthony, twenty-one.

They are not a sophisticated group, but what they lack in polish they make up for in sentiment. Contrary to my usual procedure, none of them e-mails me the letter he will read to Nick at the intervention beforehand. Instead, the letters are all written on miscellaneous pieces of wrinkled paper that they retrieve from their pockets at the gathering.

Izzy is finishing his letter on a writing pad when I arrive. It is clear and true to his straightforward and simple style: "(1) I love you more than life itself; (2) Your drug use is out of control and you know it; (3) If you do not go to treatment I am firing you from my company and taking the truck; (4) Your choice, make it."

Anthony's letter is sweet but has a "man-up" theme to it: "Go to treatment, bro. We cannot afford any more physical problems." Like his father, he is short on words but long on emotion when it is needed the most.

Everyone assembles in the great room on a fall morning as we wait for Nick. A scarecrow on the door heralds Halloween to come. One by one the guys show up in their trucks, with work boots on. Gathered together around the unlit fireplace, we wait for Nick. As I survey the group, I'm inspired by these tough men, bravely taking part in this intervention.

My usual warning of blocking the exits is lost on Izzy. Most people don't run, but I always like to have the nearest exit route covered in case I have a bolter. Giving me a few seconds of time to soothingly explain the situation to a person who is prevented from running has made all the difference in a few interventions. But Izzy sets me straight this morning. "He won't run. When I tell him to sit down, he'll sit and listen." I love it. A kid who listens to his dad—pretty rare in my line of work.

When Nick enters the front door, I immediately go to him, take his hand, and explain who I am. He cocks his head to the right in resignation as he sees his buddies, dad, and brother. "Oh, man" is all he says as I usher him to his place on the sofa, between Izzy and Anthony.

At first the group is stoic as one of Nick's co-workers reads his letter. But as soon as Izzy opens his mouth, the tears flow and Nick breaks down as his dad puts down his letter and takes his son in his arms. We all cry. I am so moved by the honesty and the openness and the emotion these men allow themselves to express. It is a privilege to witness.

It is a quick intervention. Nick readily agrees to treatment. I don't think Izzy needed me in the traditional sense that an interventionist is called for, meaning to motivate a very treatment-resistant patient to go to rehab. Instead I was needed to help these guys, in a unified manner, express their feelings, hopes, and expectations.

Anthony has already packed Nick's bag with some clothes—T-shirts, jeans—and a few basic toiletries. As we are saying our good-byes, Nick looks down at his feet. "Hey, I don't have any shoes other than these work boots. I'll look like a weirdo hanging out in rehab with work boots on."

We all laugh. After the intensity of the intervention, we all relish the comic moment. "Yeah, I can see it now," Anthony says, "you sitting around in one of those group sessions, all in a circle, getting enlightened and stuff with your big ol' dirty work boots sticking out. They'll think you're the maintenance guy."

"Hey, maybe it could be part of my breakout outfit," Nick counters. We all crack up, and then I suggest we stop and buy a pair of tennis shoes on our way to treatment. Izzy hands me the cash to make this happen while informing Nick that he doesn't need a pair of two-hundred-dollar shoes.

Nick and I are treated to colorful fall foliage as we drive up into the foothills of Pennsylvania. We could not have planned a nicer October day to drive north. I have my tried-and-true pit stops at this point in my career as an interventionist on the road. Shrewsbury, Pennsylvania, is one of them. I like McDonald's: clean bathrooms, good cheap coffee, oatmeal, and salads that will do in a pinch. The kids always appreciate a Big Mac and fries before checking into rehab. And as luck would have it, the strip mall across the parking lot has a few possibilities for tennis shoes. Finding the shoes is harder than I anticipated—Nick is picky. This is my first time shopping with a twenty-three-year-old for shoes, and it's not so easy. I have the pleasant feeling that I will be doing this soon with my own children. Finally, at the third store, we find a pair that Nick approves of.

With food and shoes on board, we continue our ascent up "Magic Mountain," the nickname given to this particular rehab center in the hills of Pennsylvania. A love song of sorts by Fleetwood Mac comes on the radio. Nick reaches over to turn up the music. "I like this song; the Dixie Chicks' version is even better," he tells me.

"Awww, you have a girlfriend?"

"Well," he says, hesitating. He looks at his watch and playfully adds, "I did until about three hours ago. She might be a bit pissed that I just fell off the face of the earth." We both giggle. My assumption, that the relationship must not be too serious if he can make light of the situation, is correct. "We've only been out a couple times; she'll get over it."

Something more serious is on my mind, and I'm not sure how to broach it. It may be a projection on my part, but I have been pondering how I would react if I were addicted to opiates and was facing the intensely life-threatening diagnosis of cystic fibrosis. My inclination would be to say the hell with it. I could die young, so party on.

"Tell me about your diagnosis of cystic fibrosis," I say, diving right in, thinking that with a dad like Izzy, Nick is used to people getting to the heart of the matter. "Is your medical condition stable?"

"Yeah, it's good," he replies. "I don't smoke and try to remember to take my meds."

"Have you ever smoked?"

"Nah, never, not even pot, just not an option."

"Very good. Do you worry about what the future holds for you?"

"No, I figure as I get older they'll find bigger and better ways to deal with my CF. I rarely think about it."

Nick is authentically casual about his disease. After our time together,

I think differently about my assumption that having CF would color his world, affecting his motivation to get off drugs. He seems genuinely optimistic about his future and new medical research and treatments yet to be developed for the disease. I sense that Izzy deserves some credit for his son's positive outlook.

The last thing I do for Nick before leaving him in the capable hands of the rehab staff is to show him to the small kitchen off the reception area that's stocked with sandwiches and snacks for incoming patients and families. I always squirrel away a few snacks from the kitchen for the drive back down the mountain, knowing my favorites at each rehab center I visit (perks of the job!). Nick is watching me as I stuff a few bags of white cheddar popcorn into my backpack. "Hey, it's a long ride home," I say, defensively. "No," Nick clarifies, "I was just thinking. Thanks for today."

"You're welcome, buddy," I reply. "How do the tennis shoes feel?"

"They feel surprisingly good for new shoes. How do they look?"

"Great; must be a good omen. Tennis shoes fit, good rehab experience, or something like that."

We are smiling at each other now, and I know I have made a friend. "Okay, buddy, time for me to go. Can I have a hug?"

"Sure," he says. He has a strong, youthful embrace. As I drive down the mountain, taking in the Pennsylvania fall foliage again, I ponder his prognosis of getting well, not knowing that we will meet again soon.

Our family was in survival mode as the chaos of my drug addiction swirled around us. I was extremely sick, addicted to the narcotic buprenorphine, the amphetamine Adderall, and the tranquilizer Klonopin. Our finances were suffering right along with the family. If I wasn't doctor shopping for drugs, I bought them online. My ability to moderate my spending, just like stealing, was null and void. I would get on the Internet late at night, and in my altered state of euphoria and hell I would order away. Big and small items would arrive at my door, and I had little memory of purchasing them. Brian was like a rat on a wheel, trying to keep up with the bills while continuing to work in the competitive field of computer-software sales and taking care of two little kids and a very sick wife; he had little time left to figure out how to save his family.

I would approach Brian crying, "I'm dying. I'm ruining the kids, and doing the same shit I grew up with, but even worse, it's happening in this house, and I don't know what's wrong with Max." I would implore him, haunted by the fact that I was re-creating my original family and that surely my death would duplicate my parents' early deaths. Brian would look at me with a blank stare; he was out of ideas. He had taken me to about every treatment facility within our driving range and then some. When I look back now, I think he was suffering from post-traumatic stress disorder. He had been beaten to hell over the past ten years, and we were simply out of options. With our finances a mess, we were dependent on my weekend salary as an RN at the rehab center where I worked, and we could not finance another treatment for me. We had health insurance, but the coverage, like that of most Americans, was woefully lacking when it came to comprehensive addiction services.

In the middle of all of this, I continued to worry about Max. I had nagging concerns that something was amiss with him, but I couldn't identify my concerns. Then his preschool teacher approached me at the school's annual Thanksgiving buffet, and my world was turned even more upside down.

Max was in the three-year-old class. His teacher, Sandy, was a seasoned professional and had taught my daughter, Mary, two years earlier, so she was able to compare my children. But it was not this comparison that concerned me the most; it was the comment she made to me about the dissimilarities between Max and his current peers.

Standing in the buffet line with Sandy, scooping mashed potatoes made by three-year-olds onto my plate, I casually asked, "How is Max doing?" I knew he could be a handful—his hyperactivity was evident from the moment he could crawl, and his ability to focus was hugely lacking, even for a three-year-old. I knew the teachers at St. Anne's Episcopal Church preschool were patient with him, but I was also aware that Sandy had a difficult time coping with Max at times.

Sandy replied, "Joani, I'm not sure what's up with Max, but he's not like his peers." My heart went to my stomach. That single comment intensified my concern for Max. Sandy had been teaching a long time, and I respected her opinion implicitly. "What do you mean, Sandy?" I felt like I was holding my breath as I waited for her answer. Everything else in the room dimmed as I focused on her reply.

"I'm not sure what it is, Joani. He's just different than the other children."

"Sandy, you've been teaching for a long time. Do you have an educated guess of what's happening with him?" I was sure she knew what Max's problem could be and was trying to be gentle with me, possibly holding out on me.

"Really, I can't say. He is definitely hyperactive, but it's more than that."

My worry went into overdrive. Then a comment by another mom a few days later brought me a glimmer of hope. Chrissy's son, Ben, and Max were in the same preschool class. One day on the playground at pickup time, Chrissy approached me.

"Hey, Joani, I observed something with Max today that I wanted to share. I've been helping out in the classroom lately, and I've noticed Max might have some sensory issues."

"What do you mean sensory issues?"

"Well, when the teacher asked the group to all get their coats on, Max ignored her request. He got in trouble for it and was made to sit and wait until everyone left to get his coat. He looked hurt and confused. I don't think he understood the direction; it did not appear he was being defiant."

My heart ached instantly for my little guy; the thought of him looking hurt and confused with a consequence he did not deserve or understand was difficult for me to hear. Despite my ongoing drug addiction, I was starting to catalog these comments, trying to fit the pieces of the puzzle together for Max.

Chrissy continued. "He seemed so distracted by all of the sensory stimulation around him, the noise, perhaps the light, all the activity and commotion of so many little kids, that he couldn't comprehend what was being said to him. My older son has had sensory-processing issues. I took him to a therapist who works with these sensory problems. She's great. Here, I wrote her name down for you."

Thank God for other moms like Chrissy. My journey with Max started with this sensory-processing therapist, Debra.

Before our first appointment, Brian and I had to fill out an extensive questionnaire. We finished it and anxiously waited for the first visit. Max was put through a number of tests, and it was determined that he did indeed have some sensory deficits that qualified for the diagnosis of sensory-processing disorder. He also tested high on the scale for attention-deficit/hyperactivity disorder, or ADHD. He was three years old, and his verbal language skills were delayed. He did speak, but not as well as our daughter, Mary, had at the same age. We had chalked it up to the difference between a boy's and a girl's verbal development.

Max started therapy with Debra a few times a week, taking part in many physical and cognitive activities aimed at helping to both stimulate him and moderate his reactions to stimulation. Then Debra told me something else that got my engine in overdrive with concern for Max.

"Joani, Max is possibly one of the most oppositional/defiant kids I have worked with. He's very resistant to suggestions."

"Resistant, or does he not understand what is expected of him?" I wanted to know.

"Even when I'm sure he understands, he will refuse many times to participate."

Again, my heart went to my stomach. Here was a seasoned child therapist saying Max was a tough kid to work with. At least that meant that at home, Brian and I were not just imagining that Max was a challenge.

"I think," Debra continued, "it would be wise to have him evaluated by a child psychiatrist."

Oh my God, I thought, *a child psychiatrist.* I felt as if I were standing in quicksand. I was struggling with my own day-to-day existence as a fragile drug addict. My ability to cope with Max and what he needed were just more than I felt I could handle. How much more could this family endure before it broke?

When I was pregnant with Max, I knew he was a boy before the amniocentesis was completed. In contrast, with Mary I had no intuitive feeling about her sex. But I wanted a girl desperately to name after my mom and to fill the void of my lost relationship with her. The day I found out Mary was a girl was one of the most special days of my life.

With Max, I had the enduring knowledge that I was carrying a boy, though I would have been happy with either a boy or a girl. When the call came from the doctor's office, it confirmed what I already knew in my soul. I was connected to this boy in a way that took me by surprise. During the pregnancy I attended a meeting of Adult Children of Alcoholics, where my recovery from living with alcoholic and otherwise addicted parents had started years earlier.

I clearly remember this particular meeting. "There is something about this baby. He is coming to me for a reason," I told the group, as my deep intuition about the pregnancy continued.

I was sober when I got pregnant with Max. I had been off methadone for about three months before I conceived, and I was forty-three years old—short straw for addiction, long straw for fertility, I tell people. Shortly after I conceived, Brian, baby Mary, and I went on a three-week trip to Europe, a business trip of Brian's paid for by the company. I was miserable: my energy was at an all-time low. I couldn't eat the food, and I generally felt as if I might be dying. Looking out a window in

Switzerland, I gazed at a beautiful lake, and my only thought was that I had to get home and figure out what was wrong with me. Perhaps it was cancer. I was consumed with the thought that something was extremely wrong and that I might die.

Three months off methadone is not a long time. It's a tough drug to get off of, largely because it takes a long time to leave the body. I was beaten up from all the past addictions and detoxes, and now I was pregnant and didn't know it. I was still breast-feeding Mary periodically at the age of two when I conceived Max.

So the combination of past drug addiction, pregnancy, breast-feeding, age, and overseas travel came together to produce a state of extreme physical exhaustion. While we were in Europe, I started to drink alcohol for the first time in years. I needed relief and had the warped sense that it might make me feel better. Plus, drinking wine in France seemed natural. On an Air France flight from Germany, everyone received a small bottle of red wine with the meal. And the wine did make me feel better. I recall drinking it and feeling instant relief from my fatigue, general malaise, and depression. If Brian had a reaction to my drinking, he never voiced it and I never perceived it. He was a very good codependent, in that he had a habit of looking away from my addictions. I continued to drink alcohol daily on the trip until I returned home.

Once home, I thought casually to myself that I should take a pregnancy test before going to the doctor. I felt it was more of a formality, as a way to rule out a distant possibility. Since giving birth to Mary, I had had only about three menstrual cycles, which led me to think it was highly unlikely I was pregnant. When the little strip came back positive, confirming I was pregnant, I was in shock. It was the last thing I expected. I was also relieved that I was not dying and genuinely excited to welcome another baby into our family. I stopped the daily drinking immediately.

It was not an easy pregnancy. Physically Max was fine, but my stomach was upset most of the time, and I was constantly exhausted. Mary was in diapers and an active toddler, and I continued to work every weekend at the state rehab center. I was sober from six weeks of pregnancy to the end of the second trimester. I am not sure what my thought process was at this time, but I returned to the female pain specialist that I had seen previously and told her I was having recurring back discomfort because of the pregnancy, and requested Tylenol number 3 with codeine for pain. After checking with my obstetrician, she prescribed the narcotic for me. But I was not in pain; my addiction was flaring up, again. Throughout the rest of the pregnancy, I took two to four Tylenol-with-codeine pills daily.

Max was born on a clear February day. He weighed nine pounds ten ounces and was breech. Although I had a C-section, he was still a challenge for the doctors to maneuver out of me. The scores of his Apgar test—which is done shortly after birth and measures heart rate, breathing, reflex, muscle tone, and skin-color appearance—were on the low side, as I recall. But once he was freed from me, he was robust and crying. My big, blue-eyed, fair-haired boy was so different from Mary, my dark-eyed, dark-haired beauty. I felt like a lucky mom: a boy and a girl, fair and dark, brought to me in my forties.

I took Debra's advice and made an appointment for Max with a respected child psychiatrist. Max was just shy of his fourth birthday. I had been in the hospital two months prior to this appointment with the overdose of the amphetamine Adderall, which resulted in the cardiac incident and my missing Max's preschool play. Life was tough and felt so tenuous to me, but I continued to search for answers for Max.

We entered a well-outfitted reception area. As we sat on an expensive-looking brown leather sofa waiting for the doctor, Max slipped his little hand into mine. A moment of clarity was about to descend on me—some might call it a light-bulb moment, others a spiritual experience. Whatever it was, whatever it is called, it was the impetus that ultimately led me to Dr. Phil.

Days before our appointment with the child psychiatrist, I had stolen

Dr. Phil's book *Family First* from my friend Gary's book and coffee shop, Hard Bean. (I later made amends to Gary, giving him the twenty bucks for the book. He likes to remind me that I still owe him for the tax.) I already had a collection of child-development books that I was reading in my attempts to figure out what was up with Max, but something in the beginning of Dr. Phil's book struck a nerve. I paraphrase, but the meaning was that for every small child dragged to a psychotherapist, there is invariably a sick parent behind him or her.

As Max and I sat on the couch that morning, his precious baby hand in mine, I knew without a shadow of a doubt that I was putting the horse before the cart. I was the sick one, and I was making Max the problem in order to force the focus away from me. Growing up, I was an anxious, hypertensive child, which allowed my parents, who needed help, to force the focus away from them.

I felt guilty and responsible for Max's difficulties. As we waited for the doctor, Max seemed to sense my emotion and nervousness, and clutched at my hand harder. As my hand enveloped his, covering his little fingers, I felt I was protecting him. But what was I protecting him from? It was me he needed the most protection from—I knew it, and I ached with this knowledge. As an indescribable pain filled my soul, it was mixed with worry and hopelessness, and I had no idea how I was going to get my family out of this mess. *God help me, please, please help me. If not for me, for my Max,* I silently prayed. Again I looked down at Max's little hand in mine, and it was one of those rare moments in my life that, in looking back, gave me the courage to find a solution to my problem. This seemingly casual exchange between mother and son, sitting on a couch waiting to see the child psychiatrist, was the start of something big to come. I did not know it, but I was filled with the power of a mother's love, the strongest love on earth, and God was near.

The doctor introduced himself and started Max's evaluation. Part of it involved observing Max as he played. To this end, the doctor had a sandbox with a few toys in it. I was asked to join the two of them, the doctor and Max. Did the doctor want to observe me with my son? Probably. I sat on the floor next to the sandbox as Max played with a truck in the sand. The doctor sat above us on a desk chair that swiveled so he could be part of our little group.

As the doctor made general comments to me about Max, I interrupted him with a wordless and telling gesture that was not premeditated. For the first time, I exposed my secret; my reality and world was shifting. Holding out my arm, I silently rolled up my sleeve—the long sleeves that I always wore to hide my needle addiction—revealing for the doctor the fresh red track mark from my morning injection of narcotics. The psychiatrist looked at me, silent for a second as he took in the sight of my arm. Then, looking at my face again, he said, "I see. There is more to this story."

"Yes, there is. I'm a drug addict." The physician was silent, waiting for my next words or actions.

Picking Max up out of the sandbox, I said, "Come on, buddy. Let's go home." I turned to the doctor. "We'll never figure out what's happening with him until I get well."

"I agree," the doctor said. Knowing this man had no answers or solutions for me or Max at this point in our lives, I thanked him and we left.

Late that night I settled in to read my books on child development to try to understand Max. All the while I kept the nitro tabs and respiratory inhaler close by in a red makeup bag in case I experienced another cardiac incident as a result of too many drugs. It was close to midnight, and I was sitting on a beautiful yellow chair. On the ottoman in front of me was my entire collection of child-development books, with such titles as *Sensory Processing Disorder, The Spirited Child, ADHD and Your Child*, and so on.

I had put Dr. Phil's *Family First* in the armoire where I kept my books. The remark about a sick parent being behind a young child with problems disturbed me to the point that I shoved it to the rear where I couldn't see it. But on this night, after our appointment with the child psychiatrist, I wanted to see the quote again. After digging the book out, it took me a few minutes to find the phrase that had struck such a nerve in me. But I did find it, on page 5: "No matter what maladaptive behaviors a child is exhibiting, I can guarantee you that the problem is almost certainly with the entire family, and most often the child is just the sacrificial lamb dragged to the altar of the counselor because he or she happens to be making the most noise and has the least amount of power or ability to shift the focus to someone else."

Max was the sacrificial lamb. I was the primary problem in the family, and I knew it. My denial of the situation was suddenly and completely nonexistent. A gift, I suppose, from someplace that I cannot identify. But there it was, my reality was before me, and I was uncomfortable. So what was I to do? I went on the *Dr. Phil* show's website at midnight, jacked on prescription drugs, to ask for Dr. Phil's advice. This was a first for me. I had never consulted anyone on the Internet for help. I had never seen the *Dr. Phil* show, and based on what I had seen of Dr. Phil on Oprah Winfrey's program, I did not particularly care for him.

Finding the show's website, I searched all over for a place to leave my question: was my addiction causing Max's difficulties? I couldn't find a place to submit my question, but what I did discover troubled me. There was an enormous notice that the show was seeking "Middle-class moms addicted to prescription drugs, *Joani*." Of course, it did not say "Joani," but it might as well have—it was my life's story! I definitely did not want to ask my question at this place on the website. Remember, the addiction will always fight to survive, and this was getting too close for comfort. But I couldn't find anywhere else to leave my question, so I jumped in and wrote the following letter:

Dear Dr. Phil:

*I started reading your book **Family First** but have been unable to get past the first chapter or so. I lost both my parents to alcoholism and addiction at fairly young ages. After years of therapy and ACOA* *meetings, I managed to connect with a great guy that I actively sought through various dating services. I met Brian through the local newspaper.*

When we became engaged I started using Percocet. I was thirty-eight years old at the time and had made the decision years earlier not to drink or drug due to my family's background. I am an RN and feel strongly that addiction is inherited as well as a psycho-social disease. I currently work at a drug and alcohol rehab and teach classes, etc. When I have a break I shoot up legally prescribed drugs into my arms. Our clients are uninsured, lots of street people from Baltimore. My classes bring tears to their eyes and applause. I speak from conviction and experience.

I write this not because I want to be on your show, it is more of a way of trying to convince myself to get help. I have two beautiful children, a six-year-old girl and a four-year-old boy. I was blessed with the two of them in my early- and mid-forties after a few trips to alcohol and drug rehabs, including Father Martin's.

*My motivation and question is this. My son is having all sorts of trouble and he is just four years old. He looks just like me and has inherited many of my traits. Your remark in the **Family First** book, that every child that is dragged to the altar of the therapist more than likely has a sick family behind him, struck a chord in me. (So much so that I put the book far back on the shelf and out of my sight for many months until tonight.)*

As I write, I am surrounded by your book and many others about family and children. Recently I went to a conference on SPD, sensory processing disorder. My son has been diagnosed with sensory integration issues and sees an occupational therapist weekly. The therapist told me in all her years working as an OT she feels Max is in the top scale for oppositional defiant behavior. She strongly suggested we take him to a psychologist.

We love him dearly. Am I causing him to have these problems? I seem to be reproducing my first family and I cannot stop. I have been to almost ten rehabs.

I have been telling my husband for months that Max will not get better until I do. I think the little guy knows that I am sick. My daughter seems less affected at this point, but her friends call her a Mama's girl because she is so stuck on me, both figuratively and literally. Again it hit home when in your book you write that this gig could go up in flames at any moment. I feel my daughter's reluctance to leave my side is reflective of this statement. Mom could die at any moment, she seems to be saying with her clinging behavior.

I was in the hospital for a week before Christmas. I underwent a cardiac catheterization and numerous other studies. The tests were done to try and determine why I had a near heart attack and abnormal EKG readings. . . . I knew what it was; it was an overdose of Adderall that gave me crushing chest pain and an abnormal reading on the EKG.

As a health care provider I know all the tricks. When I was admitted to the coronary care unit at the hospital, I explained that the track marks in my arms . . . were a result of a latex allergy that occurred while donating blood. My knowledge is killing me.

I take Adderall to wake up, buprenorphine to mellow out, Klonopin when I have taken too much Adderall. I am prescribed beta blockers for the shakiness from Lexapro, or so my health care providers think. I really need it so that if I get into trouble again with an overdose I can medicate myself. I now carry around a kit in a Lancome makeup bag with nitro tabs, Klonopin, and beta blockers so I can save my own life. This is after years of therapy on my own screwed-up family!

I overspend due to lack of inhibition, and our finances are a mess. My husband just stares at me when I tell him this is all due to my addiction illness—total denial.

My little Max is why I am writing. I do believe he has sensory issues; I probably had them when I was young as well and they just were not addressed as such in the early 1960s. I ended up with debilitating anxiety at an early age and was started on Valium at the age of fifteen. I was already hypertensive at this young age. Nobody ever said, "So what is going on at home?"

I feel like a shit, I love the kids so much and every fucking day is the same as the last. I will probably die young like my parents and leave my kids with this legacy. I would like to turn it around but I am stuck. Thanks for listening. I am crying now and I am so tired.

Joani

I pushed the send button and went to bed.

Just as I had described in my letter to Dr. Phil, the next day started out like all the others: I had my morning shot of buprenorphine while washing down amphetamine pills with coffee and getting Mary off to school. Max was spending the day with me. He was in preschool just three days a week, and this was one of his days home with mom. The only difference on this morning was a little nagging thought in the back of my mind. My intuition was telling me that the *Dr. Phil* show was going to call—I just felt it—as I went about my usual activities.

Following his peanut-butter-and-jelly-sandwich lunch, Max napped on the couch in the living room. I had Mozart playing softly on the kitchen stereo. I felt the music might help his little brain with whatever it was that was amiss. I curled back up in the yellow chair from the night before, needing a nap myself. Drug addiction is exhausting, and I always needed sleep to keep up my morning-to-night routine of drug consumption. Just as I started to doze, listening to Mozart, the phone rang. I knew it was the show; it was as if I had been waiting for their call all day.

An annoyingly perky young woman on the other end started in, "Hi, my name is Stephanie Granader from the *Dr. Phil* show. How are you?"

"Well, you got my letter, right? Not so good. Hold on, I have to turn down Mozart. I play it thinking it will help my little guy's brain." I like to think that at this moment, Stephanie thought of me as a mom who, although struggling with a huge drug problem, was still trying to do right by her child.

When I got back on the line, Stephanie, who had identified herself as a producer for the show, continued, "I read your letter this morning, and we would love to help save your life."

"I don't really want to do a show. I just wanted to ask Dr. Phil a question," I replied.

And then she said something that changed my attitude about going on the show—which ultimately had a monumental effect on my life. "I did not want to produce this show, either, but my therapist told me I should do it." With a touch of sadness to her voice, she added, "I lost my mom to drugs when I was seven years old, and you are going to help me forgive my mom."

Shit, who is this girl, this stranger from L.A.? I thought. Her genuine spirit and honesty rang so true through the phone lines with three thousand miles separating us. Silent at first and trying to buy some time, I said, "I'll be right back." Laying the phone receiver down on the kitchen countertop, I stood perfectly still and pondered the situation. While looking at Max sleeping so sweetly on the sofa, his blond baby curls having slipped down on his forehead, two thoughts went through my mind. Actually, one of them was a soft voice that felt both distant and near, whispering to me. Father Martin was calling.

Father Martin would say the most inspirational and funny things to all of us patients at Father Martin's Ashley. I am not Catholic, and I had no idea a priest could be so funny one moment and utterly inspirational the next. He passed in March 2009, but so much of what he taught me lingers in my mind and in the words I pass on to others.

A big portion of my stay at Father Martin's Ashley was covered by a scholarship from the center. On day three of my projected twenty-eight-day stay there, I was told that my insurance company would not pay for more treatment. Newly married, Brian and I did not have the money to pay for it. My scholarship covered 50 percent of the cost, and we paid the rest with my 401(k) retirement funds. The scholarship allowed me to finish the treatment, but it came with strings attached. I good-naturedly refer to it as Catholic guilt at its finest.

While I was walking the grounds one day on my way to dinner, Father Martin approached me. "Joani Baloney, hi there," he called, using his nickname for me. "I understand you're staying with us for the whole enchilada," he said, cheerfully.

"Yep, it was a stretch for us, but the scholarship you guys gave us really helped. Thank you."

"You bet, but you know what I would like to see in return for that scholarship, Joani Baloney?"

I felt like I had entered the secret rehab mafia. "What?" I replied suspiciously.

"We need more recovering nurses and doctors to work in the field of chemical dependency. I would like to see you, a seasoned nurse, work in this field after you get well."

I went on to work seven years in my job at the state alcohol and drug rehab center, after having worked my entire career in hospital nursing, primarily newborn and maternity services. I earned a fraction of what hospital nurses do, and it was Father Martin who inspired me to do so. Catholic guilt has its place.

As I walked away, Father Martin called out to me again. "And don't forget. When you are called in this life, step up to the plate, Joani Baloney."

So on this day, with the phone lying on the kitchen counter, with perky Stephanie from the *Dr. Phil* show waiting for my reply to the help offered, it was Father Martin's voice I was hearing in my ear: "When you are called, step up to the plate." And then a second thought crossed my mind: maybe my prayers were being answered in a way I never, ever imagined.

"Okay, I'm in," was my concise response when I returned to the phone with Stephanie. And the process that began with the *Dr. Phil* show is one I have been fortunate to share with and pass on to seven young women and one young man to date. My three months in treatment following the show were the hardest—and most illuminating—time in my life.

On a hot July day, Brian picked me up at the airport after my three months in treatment. I was excited to be home prior to Mary's seventh birthday. I was also very scared: a life sober after severe addiction can be daunting, but I had no idea my fear would escalate so quickly upon my return home.

"Let me drive," I told Brian in the airport parking lot. I had not driven my van in so long. That simple act was a treat, with an exhilarating feeling of freedom, home from rehab. While physical freedom was sweet, it was sweeter still to be home and not be addicted and to know the truth about myself in my mind and, more important, in my heart: I was a drug addict. Brian met me with a dozen yellow roses, my favorite. I was excited that I would be able to see and hold my babies again.

During the short drive home, Brian said casually, "They think Max has autism." My heart fluttered, and I felt the blood drain from my face. Then I felt intense anger. *God, how can you do this to me and Max? No more, I can take no more, no more, no more, no more. Do you hear me, God? Fuck you.* I had no idea how I was to cope. *Newly sober in the car on the ride home from rehab—is this a joke, God?*

I rushed to Max. Mary was in school at St. Mary's, and I wanted her to finish out her usual day. Max was staying with my angel nanny, Colleen. She loved my kids when I was too sick to, when I was away from them for so long. I climbed the stairs at her house. Max had just woken from a nap in the upstairs bedroom, and Colleen held him on her hip. He was holding his "mommy shirt"—an old shirt of mine that he carried with him everywhere and that he slept with next to his face as he sucked his thumb.

His face had that sleepy-baby four-year-old look to it and then he saw me. He brightened up with acknowledgment that his mommy had returned. As he reached his arms out to me, I took him from Colleen. I snuggled his neck and inhaled the smell of my baby boy as my eyes filled with tears.

Autism and addiction. How would I do it? I had never been so scared in my life as I held Max close to my heart.

Nick did his first thirty days in Pennsylvania and then transferred to Austin, Texas, for three months of extended care.

While in Texas on a networking business trip, visiting a few different rehab centers, I popped in on Nick as he was making lunch with a couple of his buddies. I was rewarded with a huge grin and a bear hug. My heart sang to see him doing so well. It was a wonderful moment for me.

Nick returned home and did well for a time. Then I got a phone call from his dad. "Nick has relapsed. I fired him, took his truck, and he's going to a state rehab, not a high-end one like before." Izzy knows how to do the hard work with his son. I remember well the tears in his eyes as he told me about his boy with cystic fibrosis and addiction. "Then he'll live in a sober-living halfway house. I think he needs about two years there before he can work for me again." Izzy could give Nick everything, but instead he is in the process of taking away the opportunities he has provided for him, primarily his vehicle and the job that gives him the money to live and buy his drugs. I know this is not easy for Izzy, but it could be the medicine that saves his son's life.

CHAPTER 14

Making Friends in the Bible Belt

I hear a solid knock at my hotel door. I open without checking the peephole. I am expecting CJ, but I am not expecting her to bring a big bag of her belongings with her. It looks as if she plans to stay with me for the long weekend, which she does. I find that I enjoy her company and her immediate trust in me very much, even as I recognize that her instant attachment to me is not completely normal. But in my world, the word "normal" is rarely used in describing me or others.

CJ's big brown eyes and long blond hair vaguely remind me of myself in my twenties, and I feel protective of her quickly. This phenomenon of feeling connected and protective of those I work with happens to me frequently. But just as I can be open-minded when it comes to addicts and alcoholics, I am also predisposed to a few ingrained prejudices.

I have not always felt warm and fuzzy when it comes to conservative Christians, and CJ is from Oklahoma, in the heart of the Bible Belt. But once in a while, if you're lucky enough and open-minded enough, those walls, usually built on misconception, can come down. And they tumble as I get to know CJ and her mom and dad, Paula and Jim.

Paula finds me through a mutual friend of a friend. Our connection makes it from Oregon to Oklahoma to me in Maryland. That original friend who contacts me is gay. It's amazing how theologies, lifestyles, orientations, and politics are transcended to try to get CJ the help she needs. Love and concern for our fellow human beings really can transform our differences into mutual concern.

Paula's gut pain for her daughter is palpable over e-mail and by phone. Having exhausted their financial resources on getting their daughter the help she needs, the family is now requesting help from the *Dr. Phil* show. I don't work for the show, but I am passionate about giving back the opportunity, help, and wisdom that I received. I obtained help for my disease of chemical dependency through the *Dr. Phil* show by having my life and story of addiction documented for a prime-time TV special called *Escaping Addiction.* I now do the same for others who are struggling. I tape addicts and contact the show, ultimately taking them to Los Angeles to receive the same help from Dr. Phil that I received. After listening to her story, I tell Paula I will do what I can.

Paula is a rare survivor of stage 2C ovarian cancer. Her disease hit the family when CJ was the last child at home, and it rocked CJ's world. Paula was fighting for her life as CJ was coming of age. Paula survived her cancer, but CJ languished into a world of drug addiction, becoming a lost child quickly, after having had a life of school and social success.

Paula picks me up at the airport in Oklahoma City. I am taken aback; her appearance is so pleasing, with a pretty face, an easy smile, and quick laughter. I feel comfortable with her immediately as we embrace at the baggage claim area. I have my video camera ready, as I always do when filming for the *Dr. Phil* show. Dr. Phil always gets to the heart of the matter quickly with the struggling people I bring to him, providing relatives and viewers valuable information on how to navigate successfully within their families and society. Funny, most folks feel intimidated at the thought of my camera, until I turn it on. They soon seem to forget they are being recorded. But I need at least a few minutes to get to know them before I take the camera out of my backpack.

Just as Paula's laughter comes easily, so do her tears. During our drive to my hotel, as she recalls CJ's struggles with her life and addiction, Paula cannot contain her emotions. I quietly take out my camera and start to chronicle her family's troubles.

Together with her intense love for CJ and concerns about her addictions is an underlying guilt about the occurrence of her own ovarian cancer, which seems to make Paula feel responsible for her daughter's difficulties. A mother's guilt often defies logic. Also peppered into our initial conversation is her devotion to and belief in Jesus and the Christian faith. I cannot help but think that her survival of severe ovarian cancer may have something to do with her faith. It is such a natural part of her as it mixes in with the grief over her daughter that my negative convictions about the religious right are rapidly shifting.

As Paula drops me off at my hotel, we make plans to have dinner at the family home with her, Jim, CJ, and CJ's older brother, Tony. CJ knows that her family sought me out to try to get help for her through the *Dr. Phil* show and has expressed eagerness to participate in the process. I am not sure what CJ's motives were to participate in the show. In retrospect I think it was as much to please her parents as it was the desire to get well, but it didn't really matter to me. It was a way to get her some help. One of CJ's friends is to bring her to my hotel, and I will bring CJ with me to dinner. CJ no longer lives with her parents, and, because of repeated problems with drugs and various petty theft issues, she is not welcome in the house when no one is home. They also no longer allow CJ to drive the car they had given her, and they are uncomfortable with the caliber of her acquaintances.

As I open the door for CJ, she exudes a casual teenage air in her communication, even though she is in her early twenties. "Hey," she says, with a twinge of a Southern accent. As she slings her bag onto the hotel floor, her hair falls forward, momentarily obscuring her face. Taking her hair in both hands, she deftly twists it into a knot that lies fashionably at the base of her neck. She looks instantly beautiful. "Damn, it's hot outside."

"It is. Is it always this hot out here?"

"Yep, the summers are long."

Looking at all of her belongings on the floor, I say, "You can stay with me for the weekend if you want." Flopping down on the bed, she replies, "Yeah, that would be fun." I will soon come to realize that CJ's options for lodging are diminishing.

CJ is very open with me from the beginning. She could be categorized as a "garbage head," meaning she will consume almost anything that is mind-altering, although she prefers the tranquilizer Xanax, calling them "bars," like many kids do. The Xanax pill is shaped like an elongated brick, hence "zany bars" is the street lingo used when referring to them. CJ would buy them from an elderly woman in her boyfriend's apartment building. This is not the first time I have heard of older Americans supplementing their income by selling their prescription drugs to others.

I tell CJ I am just along for the ride and that she should just go about her normal activities while I trail alongside with my camera. It is never ethical or appropriate to encourage drug use just for the camera's sake, but for most active drug addicts, it doesn't take long before their activities turn to feeding the monster.

And feed it she does. First we meet a drug dealer on a corner behind a gas station. I stay a respectful distance behind as she buys morphine pills. Despite her drug addiction, CJ is a cautious girl when it comes to the drugs she acquires on the street. When we return to the hotel, she uses the computer in the lobby to look up the pills she bought at a website called Pillfinder.com. You key in things like the shape, color, and any numbers on the pill, and it will show the name of the drug. In most cases, it will also show the number of milligrams, which helps determine the dosage strength of the pill. CJ has never bought morphine pills before, and she wants reassurance about what she is consuming. I appreciate her caution and think it would be a leap for this girl to start buying heroin, because you never know what you're getting and there's no way to look up the drug's quality on a website.

Feeling confident that the pills she has purchased are real, she crushes them into a fine powder. First she places them on the dresser and pushes down hard on them with her driver's license. Then, like someone finely chopping onions with a knife, she uses the edge of her license to render the pill into the desired powder texture, perfect for snorting up her nose.

CJ stays awake briefly after doing the morphine, but like most opiate addicts, she needs a nap after a while. On the extra bed, curled up with her knees pulled to her chest and her blond hair spread out on the pillow, she looks more like a child than a street-smart drug addict.

Her parents call to firm up plans for dinner. I cannot help but tell them how sweet their child looks. And I think I want them to know that I looked beyond her drug addiction and saw the girl, their beloved youngest child, who is so much more than her addiction. Again my work is my own salvation. Yes, the disease manifests itself in all sorts of ugly ways, but the behavior is the by-product of the disease. Hopefully in recovery, by working the Steps, we right the wrongs of that behavior so that those who love us will forgive the behavior and the healing can begin.

"CJ is curled up on the bed. She looks like a sweet little girl sleeping," I tell her parents on the phone.

"Can we come see her?" Paula asks. "Don't wake her; we just want a quick look at her."

"Please come over. I'll leave the door open; just tiptoe in."

Leaving the door ajar, I wait quietly for Paula and Jim. Gently, they open the door, and in a gesture that reminds me of two parents checking on a newborn, they quietly creep to the side of the bed. As they gaze at their sleeping daughter, tears come easily to both of them.

Whether it's time for CJ's nap to be over or she senses the presence of her parents as she sleeps I don't know, but her eyes flutter open to see them peering down at her. In a gesture that is pure love possibly mixed with the old fear of losing her mom to ovarian cancer, she reaches up to Paula and embraces her around the neck. CJ then breaks into a sob, and a deep, gut-level howl explodes uncontrollably from her young body as her mother rocks her in her arms, whispering reassurance to CJ of her love and presence as her dad wipes her bangs from her face. I cry as I watch the three of them, feeling like a voyeur to a powerful exchange between them, and my whole heart aches for them all and hopes that CJ will soon get well.

As CJ's crying abates, through hiccups she asks for forgiveness for her addiction problems. Paula and Jim reassure her, cooing softly their unconditional love for their daughter. It is Paula's birthday, and my hope is that this emotional exchange is an unexpected gift for her. Our conversation moves on to neutral territory: dinner plans. Paula and Jim leave the two of us to get ready. It's our job to get a surprise birthday cake. CJ knows her mom's favorite is an ice-cream cake from a local store. But before we go on the birthday-cake trek, we dress and, like girls everywhere, do our hair.

Seeing my flat iron, CJ perks up. "Hey, can you do my hair with your iron?" I am happy to: my little girl, Mary, is at the age when she will not allow me to fuss over her hair. "Sure," I say, with the exaggerated enthusiasm of a mom just waiting for the opportunity to do a young girl's hair. I take a section at a time of her long hair and run the flat iron down on it, turning her already beautiful hair into sleek and smooth strands that gracefully fall to halfway down her back.

Perfectly coiffed for Paula's birthday dinner, we pick up a cake, then make it to the family home, which is filled with country and Midwestern charm. It is small but has an open first floor. Paula tells me that the pool table in the dining room is used more for folding clothes than for entertainment.

I can't remember the main dish at dinner that night, but I will never forget Paula's corn-pudding casserole. Later she gives me the recipe, but as hard as I try, I cannot duplicate it. Before dinner we all bow our heads and, with Jim saying grace, we give "thanks to Jesus our Lord." I feel secure and comfortable with them as we're gathered around their small kitchen table. A Bible is casually placed on a side table, and their conversation is peppered with phrases about their church life and ministries. I am falling in love with this family, and they are conservative Christians. What a glorious feeling it is to have a prejudice melt away. My mind and my heart open up to this brave family that has let me into their lives during such a challenging time for them.

I spend a few more days in Oklahoma trailing CJ. She goes about her life as a drug addict in ways that I don't find shocking. In our short time together, she drinks cough medicine laced with codeine, smokes marijuana, and snorts morphine and Xanax pills. She also enjoys a cold, tall beer that she drinks standing on one leg and leaning over the hood of my rental car. With her long hair, jeans, and flip-flops, she could be in a Budweiser commercial.

Having filmed what I came for, I say good-bye to Paula, Jim, and CJ. I'm pretty worn out from our long weekend together. It's tough to keep up with a twenty-something on drugs.

"Okay, sweetie. See you in L.A.," I say to CJ.

"Yep, see you there, I hope," she replies, giving me a hug at the car.

For all of CJ's hugs, honesty, and at times sweetness, I feel there is something missing in her. I search for this indefinable quality when thinking about the young woman I have just spent the weekend with. There is a hollowness to her persona. Is this a sign of deep grief left over from Paula's cancer? Or maybe something other than addiction is brewing, a personality disorder perhaps. Either way, I like her, but I am frightened for her future.

My religious experiences growing up were eclectic. I was baptized as an Episcopalian as a baby and attended church with my mom and her parents as a very young child. When my mom announced, "The church can go to hell; God has never done anything for me," I was eight years old and living in Lubbock, Texas. At that point we stopped attending church. My mom's attitude about God and religion never changed. My father was raised a Baptist in the South. The one thing he hated passionately was evangelical preachers. He thought the tent revivals of his youth in Arkansas were nothing more than theatrics. "A circus creating fear and taking your money," he said as he clicked the TV off one Sunday morning while I watched in fascination as the emotion erupted from a preacher's mouth. I remember asking my dad, during my teenage years in the seventies, shortly before he died at the wheel of his car, if he believed in Jesus Christ. He replied, "Without a doubt." But in his usual closed-off, noncommunicative style, he never elaborated on his statement. After he died, I was relieved that he had at least voiced his spiritual belief to me; it gave me a small measure of comfort, even as my own beliefs were somewhere in limbo.

By the time I was ten or so, I had started attending church with a family that lived kitty-corner from us in northern California. In my short life, we had moved from Maryland, to Washington D.C., to Virginia, to Texas, and then to Walnut Creek, California. Later we moved again, to Arizona. Each move left me feeling more insecure than before, a by-product, I suspect, of living with such an emotionally barren family. The void was filled by other families that would adopt me into their homes, if only briefly every Sunday. I attended church with these families, and it was a pleasure and a comfort for me. So at age ten, my new faith became Catholicism.

Every Sunday I had a routine with my Catholic neighbors that I looked forward to all week. After services, we would go to a Baskin-Robbins ice cream parlor. Having guiltily held back a quarter from the tithing plate, I would get a double dip of Jamoca almond fudge. The mom of the family was always first to finish her frozen treat, and with the tiny bit of cone she had left she would beg us all for an extra little scoop of ours. Without fail, her husband would make loving fun of her as she went through her weekly habit. Because my parents rarely spoke to each other, I found this exchange between husband and wife both endearing and foreign. We would all giggle and argue about who would give up a smidgen of their ice cream.

During this time, I started to exhibit anxiety symptoms in the form of not being able to swallow food. I feared choking and dying. I became preoccupied with the thought of my death and my mother's death. In my nervous mind, my death would be caused by a piece of food stuck in my throat, and my mom would die in any number of ways. But cigarette smoking was at the top of that list (which ultimately turned out to be true). To ease my anxiety, I would pace outside, obsessively stepping on every crack I saw: in my head, I *had* to step on every crack I saw. Because I felt self-conscious about not being able to swallow the ice cream on Sundays after church with my Catholic friends, I moved on to a new family. Since then, anxiety has been an intermittent companion all through my life, sparking off my first addiction to tranquilizers. Mary frequently asks me, "But Mom, how can you go on TV, with panic attacks and an anxiety disorder?" Mary started suffering panic reactions at age eight, and I was determined that she would get the help I had not received as a child. I always give her the same answer: "Prayer and Lexapro" (the latter is an antidepressant that works well on general anxiety and panic disorder), adding, "God gave us medicine and science."

I missed church and the family atmosphere with my Catholic neighbors, so I started tagging along to a Lutheran church with my friend Laurie and her family. Her family was not as warm and cozy as my Catholic friends; her father had an air of sternness that reminded me too much of my own father, and I did not attend services for very long with them.

Finally, I found a family and church whose strong memories resonate with me to this day. I attached myself to them every Sunday and Monday— Monday evening being family-home night. I stayed close with them for a few years. I was a seeker as a young girl, and I think I was searching for a family and love as much as for a church and spiritual experiences. The spiritual experiences came later and had no affiliation with any particular religion.

This last family I attached myself to was a large Mormon family that moved in next door to us when we lived in California. They told me fascinating stories of how their lineage could be traced back to the wagon trains of the early western journey that the Mormons endured, as they moved on from religious persecution. I not only attended church but took classes during the week and graduated from what they called their primary Mormon education classes. It wasn't the faith specifically that drew me in; I think it was their love and acceptance of me. Also, their strong family togetherness was like a long drink of cool water for a very thirsty little girl. I was devastated to move to Arizona and leave this family behind, and within months I again attached myself to new neighbors. This time, the next-door neighbor was a pedophile.

In the beginning of the process of going to the *Dr. Phil* show and later when he sent me to rehab, I was not looking for God. I was looking for peace, answers about my son, and a way to extend my life past the expiration date of my parents. So far my way was not working; the chaos and near-fatal overdose on Adderall gave me the courage to say yes to Stephanie Granader, the producer, that morning on the phone. That and that strange, soft whisper in my ear from Father Martin: "Step up to the plate, Joani Baloney."

God, I think, comes to us in many different ways and through the voices and interactions with people in our lives. Shelly Heesacker, field producer for the *Dr. Phil* show and now my sweet, wise friend, showed up at my door, a complete stranger at the time from Portland, Oregon, and gave me the courage to come out of the closet with my addiction. God was near.

After I agreed with Stephanie to do the *Dr. Phil* show, Brian came home from work. I clearly remember him standing at the base of the stairs with his suit on, holding his PC bag. I said, "Honey, you know the *Dr. Phil* show? Well, they've agreed to help us out."

Remember, I was not a big fan of the show. I knew very little about him, the program had never been on in our house, and I had never made reference to him previously to Brian.

Brian looked at me like I had finally gone insane. "What?"

"Yeah, I was on the computer last night, and I sent Dr. Phil a letter, and they want us to do a show. I think they mentioned the yearly prime-time special."

"What?"

"Yeah, I know. Crazy, huh? I asked them a lot of questions about Max and then told them about my drug addiction."

Brian continued to look at me as if I were having delusions. It was one thing to have a drug-addict wife, but now she had had a complete and total break with reality—that's what the expression on his face seemed to be saying.

"I'm not kidding," I continued. "I was on the computer last night and asked them a question about something I had read in Dr. Phil's book *Family First*, and this producer Stephanie called today and said they would love to help our family. I look at it this way: we have nothing to lose."

"Are they going to send you to rehab?" Brian asked.

"I don't know, maybe. I really just want help and advice about Max," I said, vaguely, as the disease was starting a war in my head. Many addicts, including me, fight rehab, even when the logical brain knows it needs it. The disease always fights to survive; the denial and resistance can be maddening.

As the days wore on, we made plans to go to Los Angeles to sit and be taped with Dr. Phil. No audience, just the three of us—Brian, me, and Dr. Phil. How hard could that be? Ha! I was about to find out. But first Shelly was sent to our home to chronicle my life as an active drug addict and to learn about the effects my drug addiction was having on my children and Brian.

It was very early spring, and Easter was around the corner. It was that time of the year when the trees are just starting to bloom again. My aunt Margaret aptly described the foliage to me once: "The trees look all lacy, with their light-green color." So with lacy green trees, a few early bulbs in flower, and the cold nip finally receding from the air, Shelly showed up at our door. It was late Saturday afternoon, and I had worked all day at the rehab center. Before coming home from work that day, I stopped to buy the ingredients to make our traditional "bunny cake" for Easter. Just as I set my grocery bag down inside, the doorbell rang.

I felt instantly comfortable with Shelly. Some might conclude this was not a stretch considering how many prescription drugs I was on, but I was still standing up and fulfilling work responsibilities. I was in that nebulous category of a functioning addict.

We stood apart, the kitchen island separating us, as we initially got to know one another. Shelly had an immediate and warm smile, short light-brown hair, and a lovely face. I tell her today, "You were one part field producer and two parts social worker." I melted into her kind demeanor. I have been surrounded by many people in my life as a mom, wife, and RN, but no one really knew me, no one knew I was dying, until Shelly came along, assigned by the *Dr. Phil* show to document my life. I sensed when she and I first met that she, too, did not always fit in. There was an aura about her that allowed me to trust her almost instantly. I didn't know her story yet, but I was willing to go on this journey with her.

The next day my alarm went off at 5:30 a.m. to wake me for my usual Sunday morning work at the state center. Again, the irony that I was taking care of patients with the same disease I was struggling with rarely fazed me. On this still-dark Sunday morning, however, I woke up to find Shelly at the foot of my bed, silent, with her camera pointed directly at me as I climbed out of my bed. I had given her a key to the house the night before so she could quietly enter in the morning.

She had instructed me not to yell out, "Hey, Shell," or anything else. I was to get up as I normally would for work. So I got up and went to the downstairs bathroom. Standing in my long blue nightgown, my glasses on, I went through my usual routine. I prepared my morning shot and described to Shelly and her camera how I started each day. Rolling my sleeve up and taking down the antique bowl that held my supplies, I explained that I shot up only half of an ampoule of liquid narcotic; the whole amount made me too sleepy. I left the rest in its vial and carefully stood it on end for use later in the day. Shelly trailed me from the bathroom as I went to the kitchen to make coffee, swallowing it with my first Adderall capsule. Although Shelly was tired from her long day of travel the day before, she remained vigilant at the rehab center in documenting my days. During the time that Shelly filmed me I gave her complete access to my life, and she gave me immeasurable acceptance and love. No one had seen this ugly side of me, this tormenting secret demon that was surely killing me.

To this day the rehab where I was working is not happy with me. I told them Shelly was taping a family issue, and they consented to her cameras. I take comfort and pride in the number of health care workers who have been helped through seeing my struggles as an impaired nurse on the job. I have heard from many of them.

That day at work, after shooting up buprenorphine and swallowing twenty-four hours' worth of Adderall before lunch and as Shelly taped me, I taught a class to the rehab patients. "You deserve to get well," I wrote in chalk. The class was on a rotating schedule, one week on nutrition, then hepatitis C, followed by sexually transmitted diseases and, lastly, the addicted brain. But each Sunday, without fail, I scribbled those same words on the blackboard: "You deserve to get well." Looking back, I believe I was speaking to myself in a repeating and desperate attempt to try to get through to the sane part of my own addicted brain.

Shelly laughed at all my jokes. She was the best straight man ever—no pun intended. The biggest gift Shelly gave me in those three days together was this: I saw myself in the reflection of her eyes. In spite of my addiction, she liked me. She treated me with kindness and respect. I was worthy of her friendship even if I was a drug addict. She was helping me believe that I did indeed deserve to get well. And she was a field producer for a Los Angeles TV show who landed on my doorstep, a stranger.

Shelly and I are friends today. I traveled a few years after our original time together to her home in Portland to document her wedding to Wendy. Under a romantic train trestle as they spoke their vows to one another, I turned the camera on Shelly and her beloved, as I joyfully attempted to pay back an immeasurable debt to her. God does speak to me through people. Like a soft song, many times best heard in hindsight, the cool breeze of spirituality has been bestowed upon me through others.

Shelly gave me the courage to walk the journey in front of me. Both she and Stephanie opened a door for me; their combined love, wisdom, and friendship were instrumental in my getting well.

The trip to L.A. from the East Coast to see Dr. Phil felt like a dream to me. I was always under the influence of mind-altering medication, and just as the trip got closer, I started consuming even more of my prescription drugs. The monster in me seemed intent on killing me before I could reach the portal of my recovery. Sitting with Dr. Phil, I was given the gift of truth, but my addiction fought hard. It felt like an exorcism of sorts: good and bad, sick and well waged a war between us, and finally the light won out.

I left the set of the *Dr. Phil* show and immediately went to La Hacienda treatment center in Hunt, Texas, about eighty miles northwest of San Antonio, with an unforgettable man named Rich Whitman, chief operating officer of La Hacienda and a valued liaison between the rehab center and the show. In the coming months, Rich hung onto me with a tenacity that at times drove me crazy. But his love and concern got me through a mind-bending detox, when I was too sick to care whether I lived or died.

I was not expecting to go to rehab that day. Like many drug addicts, I knew I needed intensive treatment, but I needed it *someday*, not today. And the prospect of leaving my two young children behind was almost too painful to bear. People have asked me how I could go to be taped with Dr. Phil for a prime-time special as a drug addict and *not* know I would be going to rehab. I think there were two reasons: First, I simply had never seen his show. And second, I was under the influence of three powerful prescription drugs. My mind was not working clearly. I was in a strange, suspended state of being and in survival mode, rarely thinking past a few hours at a time, as I continued to carry around my makeup bag with antidotal drugs to save my life in case of another overdose.

But I did go. I left my heart on the curb in Los Angeles as I climbed into a big town car and said good-bye to my kids. For three months my singular focus was returning home to them and Brian. First, though, I had some healing and work to do. It was brutal, and many times I was ready to bail.

We showed up at La Hacienda at around one in the morning. It is dark in deep Texas in the middle of the night. At times, as the drive went on and on from the San Antonio airport, I had the recurring thought that I was being abducted to Mexico. I was disoriented, exhausted, and starting to go into withdrawal. For the better part of a week, I had no idea where in Texas I was. It would take a long walk up a hill to the community room, known as the Bodega, before I would find a map on the wall in the coffee room that identified where in the world I had landed.

I did not want to walk up that hill. For the first long weekend, I stayed in bed in the detox ward, huddled in a ball with a cardiac monitor strung around my neck. Once a day, prodded out of the ward by the nurses, I would shuffle a short distance to the doctor's office for my mandatory daily assessment. That done, and saying almost nothing to anyone, I would crawl back to bed.

On the female side of the detox ward there were six beds in a row, separated by flimsy, hospital-type curtains. At the foot of each bed was a big plastic container where your belongings were deposited after they were inspected by the staff for any contraband drugs. The roommate to my right I affectionately called Scarlett O'Hara. She was a Texas oil baby and had the entitled attitude to go with her station in life. She and I got along fine. That first long weekend we joined forces and, with our combined shitty attitudes, managed to keep the nurses at bay as we refused to get out of bed. I hunkered down for what I thought would be at least a week, until Rich showed up again on Monday.

"Hey, there you are. How's it going?" Rich asked as he pulled the curtain back.

"Well, you figure it out. I'm in detox," I tartly replied. Rich was the enemy; he was the guy who flew me to this inferno, and I hated him. He ignored my nastiness, which I had hoped would motivate him to move on, but no such luck. He launched into a cheery little plan that included me getting out of bed and walking around campus.

"You have got to be kidding," I said. "I can't walk. Plus Scarlett over there keeps having seizures as she comes down from her daily dose of a hundred Xanax pills. Need to keep an eye on her."

"You aren't the nurse here, Joani. You are the patient," Rich informed me.

Well, that little comment infuriated me. Yes, I was used to working at a rehab, not being the patient in one, but I really did not have the strength to spar. Not yet, anyway. Rich and I would go at it a few more times in the months to come. He was the target of uncontrolled rage in me at times. As I slammed my fist through a bathroom door late one afternoon, I envisioned it being his face. It would take a wise therapist named Sunny and a lone spiritual moment on my own before I could pinpoint the source of my anger, own it, heal from it, and move on.

But at the time, I was bone tired. I was sleeping off a year of amphetamines and being weaned off the injectable narcotic buprenorphine with under-the-tongue Suboxone, and my hands and feet had begun to have a strange, tingling feeling, like they were always falling asleep. It was a neurological reaction as I was withdrawing from the tranquilizer Klonopin. For that I was given the barbiturate phenobarbital.

"Yeah, yeah, yeah, go away. I'm going back to sleep," I wearily told Rich.

"No, you're not. *Get up.* I want to show you the campus," he said, as he threw a fresh pair of scrubs my way. Surgical-type scrubs are frequently worn in detox in many rehab centers. They are like wearing a neon sign that says, "Steer clear: bitchy detox patient coming through."

Rich did not look like he was going away; his steely demeanor showed that there was no room for negotiation. *Crap*, I thought. Pulling myself out of bed and feeling clammy all over, I gruffly pulled the curtains back and changed into clean scrubs.

Dear Jesus, it was so bright outside. Was the sun brighter in Texas? And then there it was—this *huge* hill. I stopped dead in my tracks, as Rich was providing commentary, proudly pointing out the highlights of the beautiful grounds. "I can't walk up that fucking hill," I said, interrupting his narrative.

"Yes you can. The community room, the store, laundry room, and the best, Serenity Hill, is even farther up. It's all up there. Look at the flowers, all in bloom. April is such a great time of year here in the hill country. Did you know we're a bird sanctuary here in Hunt, Texas? Yep, we're smack in the middle of a migratory route of many different types of birds."

I stood and stared at him. I couldn't care less about birds and flowers. What an idiot. I just wanted to go back to bed . . . and die. Death seemed easier than trying to make it up that hill.

"No, I cannot fucking walk up that hill," I repeated.

"You can walk up this fucking hill," Rich said, as he continued to walk on ahead. "Joani, you don't smoke. I'm sure you can do it."

Again I just stood there. Rich turned back, took my elbow, and slowly and gently guided me up the hill. And I made it to the top. And so it was with my recovery. Many times I would slide back down, and cry, bitch, and moan that I was incapable of going any farther, and every time the amazing staff at La Hacienda picked me back up and led me on. It took me six weeks to completely detox from buprenorphine, and Rich was there every step of the way. God was all around me, working steadily through those around me.

CJ continues to have a rough road. Coming out of rehab, she went into a halfway-house setting. She did not cope or adjust well, culminating in heroin-possession and forged-check charges. At the time of this writing, she is serving out a year's sentence in the Texas penal system.

Paula has earned a college degree and gone into private practice as a therapist, and she remains cancer free. She and Jim are leaders for Celebrate Recovery and are helping other parents who are struggling with their children's drug addiction.

During her incarceration, CJ became active with a church missionary group. Paula says, "She may be physically behind bars, but her mind is free, whereas before, her mind was in prison." For the first time, Paula adds, CJ sees addiction as "the 'thief who came to kill, steal, and destroy' her. She is fighting back."

I hope she and I meet again, to catch up and talk about how good it is to live the sober life.

CHAPTER 15

The One Who Got Away, and a Breakthrough

Early in my career, I get a call from a young professional woman. Katherine is so young and newly out of college that the word "girl" might describe her better. On the phone, even though her communication is crisp and articulate, it's clear she is frantic over her mother's long history of alcoholism. Katherine also tells me that she has two younger sisters, one preparing for her wedding and another still in college. Katherine is the typical oldest child of an alcoholic—organized and overly responsible, the unspoken caretaker of the family, even though her father, Dan, is home in Delaware with her mother while Katherine lives in a fashionable neighborhood in Washington, D.C.

Her mother, Maureen, is an RN like me. She works on a maternity unit, familiar to me because I've worked a similar floor for over seventeen years during my career. She and I are also moms, wives, and close in age. The dissimilarity between us is in our poisons; where she prefers alcohol, mine was almost always prescription drugs.

In a voice often shrill with emotion, Katherine tells me, "My mom was missing the other night. First she called my dad saying she had a flat tire and was calling AAA. But she never made it home. My dad found her passed out in the car in the parking lot of the liquor store."

"How did your dad know to look at the liquor store?" I want to know.

"Apparently she had been to an after-work get-together, a baby shower for a co-worker. My dad knew if she had had something to drink there, she would need more, so he looked at her usual liquor store."

Without my having a chance to comment, Katherine breathlessly continues: "She's been drinking heavily for years. She always says she's going to get help, but then something gets in the way. Right now her excuse is that she's cross-training to another nursing unit and can't take time off from work. I guarantee when she's done with that, it will be something else—Christmas, spring flowers needing tending, and on it goes. My sister's wedding will be a disaster. We're almost dreading it, knowing she'll get hammered and ruin it, like so many other events."

"Have you considered telling her she's only welcome at the wedding if she is sober?" I suggest.

Katherine is silent, like it never occurred to her to set limits on her mother's drinking behavior. "No, we really never considered that. Do you think that's okay?"

"Absolutely."

Katherine is not done venting. "What I really want is for her to get well for good or get out of our lives. I am so tired of it all. My little sister, who's still at home, has to deal with all of it. My dad is clueless on what to do. He is toast from years of this wasteland of alcoholism."

From this complicated muddle of emotions, we plan an intervention. It is autumn, and Katherine is having Thanksgiving at her apartment. Her parents and sisters are planning to come down for the holiday. We organize the intervention for the Friday after Thanksgiving. I can't help but wonder how stressful this will be for the family, knowing that the day after the holiday we will be intervening. But logistics seem to indicate that this day is the best option.

Between college and wedding expenses, this family's finances are tight. Dan, a carpenter, tells me that in an effort to cut their monthly costs they have chosen a less expensive insurance plan, an HMO, which, like most

HMOs, is woefully inadequate when it comes to covering alcoholism treatment. Luckily, I know of one sweet, unassuming rehab center that most folks can afford.

As Maureen and her husband walk the neighborhood, I slip into Katherine's apartment. The faint smell of Thanksgiving leftovers is in the air. It's a gray day. All the leaves have fallen, and from a large window in Katherine's living room I can see the bustling street below, full of Black Friday shoppers. It's an unusually large room for a city apartment, and it's furnished in a modern monochromatic design.

But in contrast to the flat decor, the three beautiful girls before me shine—smart, refined, fair-haired, and freckle-faced—bringing their Irish last name alive. The nervous energy in the room is palpable, and I do my best to settle them down in my usual low-key manner, making small talk about Thanksgiving and the upcoming wedding and giving out casual hugs for courage and, I hope, comfort.

Maureen and Dan ring the bell to announce their return. I answer the door with the three girls standing behind me. At first Maureen's face is animated as she deduces that I'm an unexpected friend from the building. She has the same pale Irish skin as her girls and a lightly freckled face with pale blue eyes, matching my Scottish coloring almost completely. Her cheeks, though, possess that unnatural ruddiness that alcoholics take on as their drinking continues.

Shaking her hand now, I jump right in. "Hi, Maureen, my name is Joani. I am an RN. Your girls and husband have asked me here today because they are concerned about your drinking."

Spitfire is the word that comes to mind to describe Maureen's reaction. Nurses, after all, are called on to react quickly in our jobs in the life-or-death atmosphere of a hospital.

"Well, I'll be damned," she blurts out, with a residual Boston accent from her years in New England. "I don't believe this is appropriate, do you, girls?" she says, immediately deflecting blame. *Crap,* I think, as I contemplate the difficult job in front of me.

Her ruddy cheeks become even redder as her emotions quickly escalate. Touching her arm gently, I say, "Please, come sit. Your girls have some letters full of love that they want to share with you."

"Get your hands off me," she replies. "I don't know you." My job is to try to calm her down.

"Okay, but all you need to do, Maureen, is to listen to some beautiful letters your family has prepared and then the decision on what you do today is yours," I say, putting the control in her court.

Flopping down on the couch, she stares at us defiantly. She is clutching her handbag close to her body, as if she needs to be prepared for a quick departure.

"Okay, Ellen, you read yours first," she demands of her youngest daughter, who lives at home. "I can't wait to hear what lies you have been spreading about me."

"No, Ellen is not prepared to read first," I counter, trying to maintain some authority and control. "Please, Jessica, read your letter."

All three girls are tearing up and practically cowering, and their dad looks helpless. Jessica can barely get her words out as she gazes down at her letter. "Mom, I will always love you. I remember when I was little, you were the best mom, always doing projects with me. Remember all the cookies we used to decorate?"

"What the hell has this to do with my drinking?" she says, with a pompous air.

I am appalled at Maureen's behavior. How in God's name can she be so cruel to these obviously emotionally distraught girls? I hate this woman for the anguish she's causing these kids. No, I just pure hate her. In my anger, I forget my number one truth—the alcoholism/addiction will always fight to survive—as my objectivity slips away. I am taking the bait, and suddenly everything has become personal, a big mistake for a clinician in the field. I see myself in Maureen, a mom and a nurse with an attitude problem to match her addictions. Her entitled posture is a mask, which to this day I have to be careful about donning. It's my favorite defense mechanism for keeping the world at bay. Maureen is representing the worst part of me, and I can't pull back from my own emotion and self-hatred.

"You need to shut up and listen," I retort.

"How dare you address me that way. And you call yourself a professional?" she says in one smooth, disdainful comeback. I am not going to win this one.

This intervention is early in my career. In the future, I will face other nasty, condescending patients. With time and experience, I will learn how to better manage the situation and not let my personal feelings and projections sabotage the process. But I'm not there yet.

We manage to get through the letters with a lot of stopping, starting, and sniping as Maureen interjects ugly and irrational comments. Today, when I find myself in a similar situation, I calmly set boundaries, no matter how unglued or angry I might feel inside. The patient is not allowed to respond until his or her loved ones have read their letters, expressing their love and sharing some memories. Then I invite the patient to voice his or her thoughts and concerns. Some people—having heard all the love and examples of how badly things are going in their lives because of drugs—need to bitch and carry on before deciding if they will go to treatment. Maureen is one of those people.

The process is very difficult for the three girls. Love, tears, and a solid, affordable plan for treatment are unable to convince Maureen to rein in her caustic remarks. Her behavior is reprehensible to me, and instead of allowing her to continue to blow off steam at the kids' expense, and probably mine as well, I let her have it, threatening her if she does not accept the help of treatment being offered.

"If you don't go to treatment, your family is prepared to call the Board of Nursing and report you as an impaired practitioner."

Maureen laughs. "Well, goodie for you all."

"And Mom," Katherine adds, "you are no longer welcome in my home until you sober up for good. And that means tonight."

"Where do you expect me stay? My plane doesn't leave until tomorrow."

"I don't know, but not here. Go to treatment or leave. I can't go through this anymore," Katherine says, through an explosion of tears.

The interactions escalate to a level I am not proud of. I *never* get to this point in my interventions any longer. I shut the process down, with options, doors left open, contracts, and realistic consequences, framed when all the heads in the room are cooler. But on this day, I fail to do my best job, and I feel personal and professional regret over the outcome.

My days at La Hacienda treatment center seemed to drag on. I eventually made it out of detox, only to end up back in. There is not much literature or experience out there with people maintained on buprenorphine for two and a half years. Within a few days of the doctors' concluding I was completely detoxed off the buprenorphine, I was put on the drug naltrexone, or ReVia, for potential relief from continuing and protracted withdrawal symptoms from the buprenorphine. Within hours of my first dose of naltrexone, I was catapulted to hell. As the drug did what it was supposed to do—block my opiate receptors—it must have bumped out what little bit of buprenorphine I had left in my system, and I experienced the worst withdrawal symptoms of my life. I can barely describe what I went through and my state of consciousness. It was like being brutally awake, aware of every nerve ending. Even the touch of the pillowcase on my face hurt. If I had had a gun, I would have gladly shot myself in the head.

A fellow patient, a pop artist songwriter, came and sat on the end of my bed in the detox unit, offering me support and sips of liquids as I attempted to return to the living. Addiction is the great equalizer: the rich, the poor, the famous, and the ordinary all go through the same physical and mental torment when getting off of drugs and alcohol.

I was ultimately started back on eight milligrams of Suboxone because my unanticipated intense detox reaction following the naltrex-one was just too physically hard on me, but I had to be weaned down all over again. It seemed to go on forever, but with much tenacity, expert-ise, patience, and love from the capable staff at La Hacienda I did it. I succeeded.

But sobriety was not sweet. Not yet. Sober, I was raw with anger, and I continued to direct irrational animosity at Rich Whitman. I also went to the mat with my first therapist, Doug. I became convinced that he held his hand too close to his crotch, and I monopolized an entire group session one day ranting and raving over the issue of where he placed his hand in his lap. I was soon transferred out of his group to a wonderful, soft, sweet female therapist who only had women under her care—women who had all been abused. We sat on the floor every Friday and ate popcorn and watched movies. I liked this group, but I would be transferred out again, for reasons I suspect but was never told.

One afternoon my rage over Rich reached a fever pitch, and I slammed my fist through my wooden bathroom door. Marching to the doctor's office, I warned the physicians to keep Rich away from me. Blinded by tears of fury, I stormed up to the top of Serenity Hill, the highest spot on La Hacienda campus. At the top was a circular fire pit with a flame that was always lit. The smell of the burning fire is marked indelibly in my mind. Its warmth on cool mornings when reciting the Third Step prayer with others from the community quelled my nerves. Outside of the circular fire pit was a quiet area for worshiping, meditat-ing, or just stopping to gaze or gossip with a walking partner. An open-ended, A-frame roof covered pews, a cross, and a large bell that resonated across an expansive ravine below that opened to the Guadalupe River in the distance. A pure-white feral cat we called Ghost Kitty would occasionally appear during a quiet moment of solitude, creeping out of the brush. I imagined she embraced the spirits of those who lost their lives to the disease of addiction. At my feet, and elsewhere around the campus, were rocks painted with dates and inspirational sayings, as well as two with my children's names, Mary and Max. The kids and I had painted them one afternoon during leisure time, and we left them behind when we departed La Hacienda, so that a tiny bit of ourselves remained at the place that has meant so much to so many of us.

But on this afternoon I was unable to read or absorb any inspiration from the rocks, or even care if Ghost Kitty would grace me with her presence on Serenity Hill. I was blind with fury as I stormed up the hill. I was so tired of being mad, but I could not soothe the anger that permeated my days and nights. I had thrown so many phones at the wall in my room, breaking them apart, that I was told if I destroyed one more phone, it would not be replaced. I never threw another phone.

At the top of the hill, I slumped down on a concrete bench overlooking the ravine. In front of me was a garden statue of an angel. Taking my sandaled foot, I knocked her over and, with great satisfaction, watched her roll down the steep hill and disappear over the ridge. Then in the distance I heard the familiar hum of the golf cart. The grounds of La Hacienda spanned acres and acres of land, so staff members frequently rode golf carts to get around and keep an eye on things. Staff was typically dispatched on a search-and-find mission when one of the flock had taken off in a huff of despair. So if you were unglued and heard the hum of the golf-cart engine, you knew they were onto you and your emotional distress, and it was usually an "Oh crap, here *they* fucking come" moment.

I heard the engine cut off and then heavy footsteps on the gravel behind me. By the sound of the footsteps, I assumed it was a man, and I was right. It was Raymond.

"Hey, can I sit with you?" he asked, respectfully.

"Do I have a choice?" I snarled back, sounding a lot like Maureen, my future patient with an attitude.

"No, you don't," Raymond said, playfully, smiling as he took a seat. "Having a rough day, huh?"

I didn't need any coaxing. I immediately started a crazy tirade about the social injustices in the state of Texas. "How can you fucking stand to live down here in Texas? It is such an old boy's school, a disgusting network of *white* men. The Caucasian man rules the land; it sickens me." Raymond, who was black, just sat quietly for a minute, no doubt trying to figure out where the heck I was coming from.

"No, honey, I think you might be wrong about that," he said, gently, while mimicking my posture: chin resting in my hands, elbows on my knees. "I have lived here my whole life, and there are lots of good and bad people of every race in Texas. White guys don't run everything down here."

"Oh," I said, seemingly unable to debate the issue.

"And I know this, Joani. You are about the angriest patient we've seen in long time. When you are walking across the lawn to dinner you look mad. You've got to figure out what is eating at you and let that bird fly," he said, with a slow Texas drawl.

"Or crawl," I said, trying to avoid his point. "Everything seems to crawl out here. Snakes, tarantulas, lizards. Hell, it's like going to rehab in the *Wild Kingdom*. A spider bit me in the ass the other day in the nurses' station!" Then it dawned on me. "Oh, I look mad when walking to dinner because I have to walk by Rich's office," I said, with a slight laugh. Even I knew I was off base with my anger.

Satisfied that I was not suicidal or ready to run for the hills, Raymond left me on the hill. As I contemplated his words, I could hear the faint hum of the golf-cart engine as he retreated back to the main campus. What was I angry about? Everything Rich did pissed me off, but the actual cause of my wrath was out of my reach. In my pure exhaustion and desperation, and ultimately in search of an answer, I walked a few feet to the wooden pews underneath the A-frame roof. Sinking to my knees, I folded my hands onto the bench in front of me, laid my weary head down, and cried. At first I did not give voice to my prayer, as pure sorrow poured out of my body onto the altar of whatever was out there. All the hurt and fear that was hiding behind my anger was on the surface. I was sober and desperate with emotion that had no name, and this was my prayer: "Dear God, show me the way. Help me to figure this out. I am lost, lost, lost, lost."

The word "lost" echoed in my head as I wept, my mind adrift in grief that refused to identify itself—until I slept that night.

The phone was ringing. Over and over, I could hear it, not blaring out, but a soft and distant ring. I recognized the unique sound, and the color, olive green, reminded me of something or somewhere long ago, a place maybe. But I couldn't locate the phone, even as the ringing continued. And then, like a sharp stab, there was a smell, a familiar odor, the smell of love, sex, hate, and shame, all mingling together and producing in me a mix of emotions and ambivalence, of lust and hate. The odor was as strong as the ringing of the phone was weak; it was Brut cologne, and it permeated the air all around me. I desperately needed to find the phone. I was asleep but seemed to be aware that I was dreaming. Everything blurred together as I tried desperately to climb back to consciousness and safety. But the phone kept up its insistent ringing as the smell of Brut threatened to make me either vomit or reach orgasm. Finally, my hand grabbed the phone, only to knock the receiver to the ground. I was falling out of bed as I reached for the phone and heard a barely audible voice that I thought I recognized, but I couldn't hear her words. "Mom? Is that you? Mom?" I called out to my mother, over and over and over again. I knew she was there, but I could not get through to her. We did not speak—the connection was never made—and I woke up.

This was the first and last dream I ever had about the man who abused me as a girl of eleven and the helplessness I felt when facing the situation. Upon waking, it was like a clear day after a strong thunderstorm. I was graced with just a grain of clarity, but from that grain came some of the most important self-growth I think I have ever experienced. My prayer that day on Serenity Hill was like cracking a door open. Prayers, I believe, give voice to what we feel is impossible, and as we open our minds, the possible flows in.

I was excited when I woke up. I reported my dream to the doctors and my therapist, Nell, right away. I knew it was a significant moment for me. There had been recent talk of transferring me to another rehab center. The prevailing opinion at La Hacienda was that I was a nut that just could not be cracked—until my dream. That afternoon as I walked back to my room, an attractive, dark-haired woman squealed up to me in her rough-riding four-wheel-drive vehicle, a deer guard affixed firmly to the front fender. Sunny had a Marlboro at her mouth, ready to be lit, as she said to me in her native Texas accent, "Honey, do you want to go to another rehab?"

"Nope. I want to go home to my kids."

"Well, listen. I hear you got yourself some unfinished business in that head of yours. I think it's time for you and me to put those puppies on the table and put them to bed. What do you say, you in?" It was not that I didn't remember most of the details of the traumatic sexual abuse that occurred in my life. I just hadn't talked about them much in a therapeutic environment.

I was intrigued. I had seen Sunny around the campus, and honestly, she scared me a little bit. Instinctively, I seemed to recognize that the Texas lady therapist named Sunny Pawlik had something to offer me. Sunny was a straight-shooting therapist; behind her back we patients called her office "the no-bullshit zone." So she and I went on a journey. Through a mixture of guided imagery combined with cognitive recall on paper, deep relaxation with music, aromatherapy, and visualization, the painful episodes in my life were processed.

I went through the process three times. I believe each of the sessions took about two to two and a half hours, but I'm not sure because they were so intense and the time became blurred. I went back in my memories, memories that I put to paper, about Bruce and that dark period of time in my childhood. Then, with Sunny sitting behind me, as soft music played in the dimly lit office, she took me down a road of visualization. First, I visualized some of the specifics of the sexual abuse. Then, as I recall, we fried the son of a bitch to ashes before we saw him as someone ill and in need of forgiveness.

I repeated this process in the coming weeks, focusing first on my mom and the grief I felt over her death. Then I dealt with my painful and rage-filled memories of my father, his lack of involvement in my life, and his bizarre lack of communication and self-centeredness.

I read a Buddhist quote once that reminded me of my time with Sunny: "Three things cannot be long hidden: the sun, the moon, and the truth." With Sunny's incredible abilities as a mental-health therapist and my courage and willingness to go through the process, I came out on the other end a much less angry and burdened person. I was far from being completely well—and it will not be the last time that residual effects of sexual abuse and memories of my childhood will affect my life—but I was much, much better, well enough to start working the Twelve Steps of recovery.

Close to my discharge, after three months at La Hacienda, a new community of patients was on campus. I was strolling past Rich's office on my way to lunch, when a patient who had known me only a few weeks said to me, "Joani, you are always so calm. You never seem mad about anything." Ah—the payoff of walking through the pain. And the best was yet to come.

Maureen storms out of her daughter's apartment and stays alone in a hotel room the night of the intervention and then flies back home the next morning. I strongly suggest to the girls that they get into their own recovery program, Al-Anon or Adult Children of Alcoholics. They come to their own decision that they don't want to be around their mom until she gets well, and I support that decision. Ellen, the daughter still living at home, moves in with an aunt. Dan stays by Maureen's side.

Maureen and I talk on the phone a few times following the intervention. I try to get her to compromise on going to treatment when she finishes her training program. Our conversations could be frustrating as we talked about options for getting her help.

How could I have blown this one so badly? Maureen and I were so similar to each other in many ways: our age, gender, and nursing careers mirrored each other, and we even graduated from college the same year! Even our freckled Irish/Scottish skin and last names are similar. Unfortunately, I suspect that I brought my feelings about myself to this intervention. A projection was in our midst, as I saw too much of myself in Maureen, the side I hate, and I did not do my best job.

But all was not lost. Months later I got a phone call from her eldest daughter, confirming what the statistics tell us: around 85 percent of people enter treatment on the day of their intervention; about 5 percent go into rehab in the days and weeks following the intervention; and sadly, 5 percent never receive treatment for their disease. Maureen was in that 5 percent who enter rehab *after* the intervention. I tell families frequently, "If your loved one does not go to treatment with me tomorrow, the intervention is not over. Hold firm to your boundaries, get help and support for yourselves, and your family member will likely go to treatment. You have started a powerful conversation and have offered a solution in a loving and respectful manner. Keep the faith, stay calm, and let's see what happens."

CHAPTER 16

Relapse, Fear, and a Long, Strange Night

OUR GREATEST GLORY IS NOT IN NEVER FALLING
BUT IN RISING EVERY TIME WE FALL.
—*Confucius*

My first day home after three months at La Hacienda was frightening for me. The thought that Max might have autism left me feeling fragile and very afraid for my family. That evening at dusk, I was at an automated bank machine withdrawing money. I had read somewhere that the most common time people are shot dead by criminals at bank machines is in the early evening hours. I clearly remember that as I faced the bank machine, I hoped someone would shoot me in the back and kill me. I was that afraid and unsure of how I could live my life sober with the responsibilities that lay ahead of me.

Returning home from the ATM still alive, I came up with plan B: I went out to find a support meeting. My first therapist at La Hacienda, Doug, had a phrase on his blackboard that I never forgot: "If you attend a meeting on the first day you are home from rehab, you have a 50 percent better chance of staying sober." I figured I needed all the help I could get, so, taking out my *Where and When,* an AA pamphlet that lists all the recovery meetings in the area, I mapped out my destination. I had made a promise to myself. Feeling very much like a foreigner from up north one evening at a meeting in Kerrville, Texas, while still a patient at La Hacienda, I proclaimed to the group, "I have no idea if all of this recovery stuff will work for me or not, but I tell you this, and this is a promise to myself: I will do everything I am told to do in regard to my recovery for one year, and I will get back to you and let you know if it worked out or not."

Well, I'm getting back to you. It worked. In spite of the enormous challenges our family faced in regard to Max and his diagnosis of autism and all that that entailed with treatment, doctors, downright worry, and at time sadness that could take my breath away, life got easier and more peaceful. And I found a sense of purpose. I attended a meeting every day, sometimes two. That first night, after my ATM death wish, I ran to the first meeting I could find that was close to me. It was a Narcotics Anonymous meeting.

Many meetings have a flavor to them, meaning certain subgroups of people will find each other and, having some aspects in their lives in common, will tend to gather at the same meetings. Well, this was an unofficial biker meeting. Lots of tough, tattooed, pierced, and sober folks gathered together on this night. I seemed a bit out of my element, but I didn't care. I was feeling desperate and scared, and as far as I knew, that blackboard saying in Doug's office did not say, "Find a meeting with people just like you." So I went in and took a seat. When it was my turn to speak up, I said, "My name is Joani; I am an alcoholic and a drug addict."

"Hi, Joani," everyone answered in the usual way before I continued, "And this is my first day home from rehab, after being there for three months, and I am so scared and tired." With that I put my head down on the table and bawled like a baby. And what a baby I must have appeared to be. Three long, privileged months in one of the best rehabs in the country, with nothing to do but get well, and I was whining away.

But no one in this group treated me like I was being frivolous. I will never forget the warmth and support this unlikely group gave me that night. I have not been back to that meeting; as birds of a feather will flock together, I sought out other groups with people who looked more like me. But those chained and tough recovering bikers gave me hope that first night, and I will forever be grateful to them.

So it was with every meeting I went to: I found support, friendship, and knowledge about how to stay sober with the Twelve Steps. And I was having fun. Recovery is not all about meetings and Steps. We socialize, go to movies, visit each others' houses for potlucks and barbecues, and talk and gossip like any other social group. I love the saying "AA is not my whole life, but it makes my life whole." Amen.

In the beginning, there were times when recovery did feel like it was my whole life, but that was okay: the alternative—unrelenting drug addiction—was far worse. I found volunteer work to be a welcome reprieve from the worries of my own life, and the sense that I was needed and contributing, or giving back, was invaluable to my recovery. I formally went through the Steps for a second time, having worked them the first time in treatment, and then found my greatest reward in the Twelfth Step, helping my fellow alcoholic/drug addict who was suffering.

My work bringing alcoholics and addicts to the *Dr. Phil* show began with that angel producer Stephanie Granader. I was on a Twelve Step call close to my home. A girl named Lana had called our central office earlier that day and was intoxicated and talking about suicide. I volunteered once a week answering the phones in the office, and Lana called during my shift. "Hold on, sweetheart. Give me your address. I'll be right over."

During my drive to Lana's house, Stephanie called me to catch up and say hello. "Hey, it's me, Steph. What are you doing?" she asked, her standard opening. The wonderful thing about Stephanie is that she always seemed sincerely interested in what I was doing.

Today I was prepared to keep it short. I felt some urgency to get to Lana's house.

"Hey, hi. I'm on my way to a girl's house, an alcoholic who called our intergroup office for help this morning. So I can't talk long. Can I call you back later?"

"Wait. Tell me about her."

I gave her the few basics that I knew.

"Well, maybe you can bring her to us," Stephanie suggested.

And that's how it all got started. Since then I have brought eight young women and one young man to the *Dr. Phil* show for help. The show has been exceedingly generous in support of the people I have brought there, and it has been the most gratifying and unexpected journey of my life to watch lives turned around with the help of Dr. Phil and the resources he and his staff provide.

Life was stable. Not perfect, but we were moving forward, navigating the usual family issues. Max had received the official diagnosis of autism from Kennedy Krieger Institute in Baltimore after a three-day evaluation, and we were learning what we needed to do for him to assure he had the best chance in this world. Mary also had some adjustment issues as she entered third grade. With a mom who was absent because of numerous rehabs and a little brother with autism, her world had been far from steady. Anxiety seemed to be plaguing her as it had me as a child, and we sought help through professionals for her as well. All in all, though, we were a thriving family. Brian was active with our local Episcopal church, which is where the kids went to Sunday school and where they had been baptized, and where Brian and I had been married. With the help of therapy and Al-Anon, Brian's and my relationship was strong and committed. We were lucky to have come through a few powerful storms in our family's life. I continued to be active in my recovery and formed some tremendous friendships with the people I had taken to the *Dr. Phil* show. And then, after almost two years of sobriety, it fell apart. And quickly.

Sometime during the fall of 2006, I started to have nagging lower back pain. This was really the first time since my spinal fusion that I had pain. I ignored it at first, thinking it would abate soon. But it did not; instead, it intensified and migrated to my lower abdomen as well. After about a month, I told Brian I couldn't tolerate my discomfort any longer, and I made an appointment with a doctor. I knew I was in a danger zone, but I simply did not care. I remember Brian watching me leave for the doctor that morning. His face said it all—worried for me and no doubt the whole family.

"We'll get an MRI to make sure there is no further pathology," said the doctor, in response to my symptoms. "I think a short course of steroids and the drug Ultram for pain will be helpful and get your back to calm down."

In the recent past, Ultram had flooded the market. Initially it was reported—by the pharmaceutical company that manufactured it and had a financial interest in its sales—that it was not addictive and was generally safe for narcotic addicts to take. That opinion has since been refuted, because many people have become addicted to the drug. In all honesty, when it was prescribed to me, I knew there were rumblings that the drug was causing dependence in some people. But I was hoping it would be okay. I got my prescription filled but did not take it the first day. I was reluctant. On the second day, on my way out the door to a day-long program about the public school system that my children were enrolled in, I threw the bottle into my bag. My thought was that sitting all day could be a challenge, and I might need some relief. I was looking for an excuse to take the pills. They were softly calling me home to them, and I had some recognition of this, but I was unable to change course.

Close to lunch, I felt I was in enough pain to justify taking an Ultram. I took one pill. Within fifteen minutes I felt a nebulous, hard-to-define state of consciousness envelop my brain with a divine—and false—sense of well-being. I knew it was false, but I didn't care. I just wanted more.

Excusing myself from the table, I went to the bathroom. All roads seem to lead back to the bathroom for relapsing addicts. It is not glamorous. Entering a stall, I eagerly, almost frantically, fished around in my bag for the bottle of Ultram—white and square, with clear blue lettering that said "ULTRAM." *Just one more won't hurt,* I said to myself, and Father Martin whispered back to me, saying clearly from his podium in my past, "One is too many and a thousand is never enough." But it was too late. I'm not a lightweight drug addict; I don't pull back easily. Like the alcoholic who sidles up to the bar intending to have just one drink but then goes off on a bender, I was already gone. With just one pill, my brain was hijacked, and I knew it. Although I knew I didn't want to go down this miserable road again, I could *not* stop it, which *is* the definition of addiction.

Within days I needed another bottle. I easily resurrected my old skills and simply went to another doctor and requested Ultram for back pain. Remember, most doctors at this time thought Ultram did not present a problem to addicts. My request for the drug was granted—with three refills posted on the prescription—by a doctor who knew my history.

It was the holidays, a magical time in historic Annapolis. It is one of my favorite times of the year in Maryland, and also one of the most difficult for me to navigate emotionally. Holidays are a mixed bag for many people. I am a chronic relapser, and, almost exclusively, my flare-ups have occurred in the fall as the leaves burn bright and the holidays are on the horizon. Was the back pain that autumn just a cruel game my mind was playing on me to make my return to prescription drugs seem more acceptable? I don't know, but I can't help recognizing the timing of my last relapse and the recurrence of back pain.

I did not use my insurance to get the Ultram prescription filled, and I went back to my old haunt, an independent pharmacy, where fewer questions are asked and refills are more easily accommodated. As Christmas approached, I was running low on the Ultram, and I was running out of my usual tricks. A few days before Christmas the pills were gone, and I thought I might be okay. But I was not okay, and on Christmas Day I found myself needing a drug badly.

I had been in the process of taping, on and off, a man named George. George would later become sick with pneumonia, a complication of being HIV positive from his needle addiction to heroin, and he died in a city hospital before our project was complete. He was a tall, strong, and streetwise man I met in the housing-project part of town while working with other addicts. The hood can be a scary place, and George always helped me when I needed to find an addict I was working with. He had a genuine spirit that shone through, and we became friends that summer. When he would approach my van, I knew a friend was coming to say hello.

On Christmas afternoon, after all of the excitement with the kids had died down and our traditional Christmas Eve dinner was long over, I telephoned George. I went back to my office in the house so Brian and the kids couldn't hear me. Through my work with other addicts, I had found out how easy it was to get heroin on the streets of Annapolis—easier in many ways than doctor shopping for narcotics.

"Hey, George. Merry Christmas."

"Hey, girl, how are you?"

"Okay. But I need a favor."

"Anything babe. What's up?"

"I've been on the drug Ultram for about a month. Ran out and I'm sick. Can you help me score some heroin?" I said, straight to the point.

"Oh, girl, no. Please tell me it ain't so."

"It's true, and I feel like shit."

"Are you sure you want to do this?"

"Yes."

George was silent.

"I will split what I get with you," I offered, attempting to sweeten the deal with a tactic known as "boosting."

"Okay, baby, come pick me up. I'm at my cousin's; you know, the white condo on the corner."

Trying to sound casual, I told Brian I was going out to tape George doing whatever it is he does on Christmas. "Should make some compelling footage," I added, hoping I sounded truthful.

George was waiting outside when I pulled up. Climbing into the van, he gave me a long, warm hug. "I'm sorry" was all he said.

"Me too, but it is what it is," I replied. I was in withdrawal and short on words. I just wanted to get relief, and I suspect that for whatever reason—crappy childhood, probably—I needed psychological relief this Christmas, like almost every year. *Will I ever be well? Maybe two years is all I get,* I thought with sadness.

George and I went to one of three usual spots in Annapolis where heroin is available. As my van pulled up, it was immediately met by a few young men eager to fill my order. My van and, frankly, the color of my skin, seemed out of place for the neighborhood, but they saw George, whom they knew, and all was cool.

I bought two dime bags of powder heroin for twenty dollars. Giving one bag to George, I took him back to his cousin's place. I wanted to be alone.

"You going to be okay?" George asked.

"I don't know. Thanks, buddy. I'll be in touch."

That was the last time I ever saw or talked to George. He died shortly after our Christmas night together. I still have the footage I took of him. On tape, bright, wet tears slide down his dark brown face as he tells me of his addiction, his love of his children, and how he feels he will never be well. Pneumonia is most likely what is listed as the cause of death on the certificate, but like my dad, who died behind the wheel of his car, addiction and alcoholism are the more accurate truth. Again, that short friendship with George broke down another wall in me, built on a preconceived opinion that all black men who live in housing projects are no good and should be feared. George was a wonderful guy, full of love, especially for his children, but he was profoundly affected by addiction and had too few resources or advantages in his life.

I drove back home that Christmas night. Parking my van on the curb just outside our house, I sat quietly for a few seconds. I could see the kids and Brian through the gauzy front-room curtains, playing and assembling all the Christmas toys and goodies. Taking the dime bag out of the ashtray where I had gently laid it, I opened it with the tenderness of a mother's touch. I moistened my finger ever so slightly and then dipped it into the powder. Shoving my finger up my nose, I inhaled sharply. And then blessed relief was upon me as the heroin quickly reached my brain. Was it my imagination or was it real? Dear God, no, the feeling the heroin produced in me was even better than OxyContin. *Oh my God,* I thought, *I am fucked. What box have I opened?* Looking up, I could still see my children playing through the curtains. With tears running down my face, I sat in the van and continued snorting the heroin while watching Mary and Max play on Christmas Day.

The next morning, feeling a combination of fear and shame, I called Stephanie Granader with the *Dr. Phil* show once again.

"We're bringing you in. I'll call you with a date this afternoon," Stephanie confidently told me on the phone. "Hang in there, sweetie."

"I'm sorry, Stephanie."

"Don't, Joani. Don't beat yourself up. Got it? We love you. You just got sick, that's all. Now stop it."

"Okay, I love you, too."

Within the week I was back in Los Angeles, sitting with Dr. Phil and taping a show. Later that day I returned, safely and gratefully, to La Hacienda. It was a short relapse and a short stay in rehab, twenty-eight days—a refresher course, I called it. This was a new pattern for me. In the past, relapses lasted years, not a few weeks. As odd as it sounds, even my relapse represented growth. I had had two good years of recovery, and I wanted more.

But it would not be that simple. First I had to make it home from rehab. My stay at La Hacienda was unremarkable in many ways. I was never in detox; my physical dependency was that mild. But as my discharge home loomed, I had increasing anxiety, manifested in numerous somatic complaints. I felt comfortable at La Hacienda; it represented safety to me. I had spent a significant amount of time in institutions over the past ten years, and I knew the drill and felt at home there. But rehab is not home.

It started in the car as we pulled out of the La Hacienda driveway, leaving for the San Antonio airport. I felt short of breath as I looked out the window and watched the buildings of the rehab center fade. There was another patient in the car with me, and as I started a conversation, the feeling passed. We made the long drive without incident.

Then again, waiting to board at the airport, I felt a vague sense of danger, which was completely out of character for me because I am a calm flyer. I took a few deep breaths and got on the plane, which would take me to Florida, where I would connect with a flight to Baltimore. I texted Brian, telling him I was on my way and confirming the flight information.

Taking my seat, I noticed a pleasant-looking African American woman to my left, and I started a conversation. We exchanged the usual "What do you do?" banter. She had recently graduated from college at age forty-something and was very proud of herself. Her trip to Texas had been for a job interview. She was an inspiration. She had strong feelings about education and being a black woman in America. I listened closely. I felt privileged to hear her story and her cultural views.

She had also been addicted to crack cocaine as a young woman. She recalled how in her addiction she would sit completely naked and paranoid in her hall closet for hours. Periodically she would sprint out of the closet to the closed blinds in her living room and peek out, looking for imaginary predators.

During this part of her story, my symptoms started up again. Suddenly, the oxygen in the plane cabin felt as if it were diminishing. I couldn't breathe. I felt like I was in that closet. It's a funny thing about having a panic attack—you know you're having one, but you're equally convinced you're going to die. My companion seemed unaware of my plight as she continued to tell me harrowing tales of drug addiction past.

I excused myself to go to the bathroom. I thought a bit of distance between us might help. It didn't. While in the bathroom, I started to gag and dry heave as I sat on the toilet lid. I had had panic attacks in the past, but never this severe. I tried to take deep breaths to calm myself, but it didn't work. I started to seriously fantasize about Valium.

Back in my seat, I was increasingly convinced there was something seriously wrong with me. I was slowly but surely losing my mind, and I knew it, but I couldn't stop irrational thoughts of my impending death.

I told my new friend I was not well. "Do you have a car at the airport?" I asked her.

"Yes," she said, slowly, and looking at me intensely.

"I need to get to the hospital; there's something wrong with me. Could you drop me off on your way home?"

I have never been severely mentally ill, other than around issues of addiction and, yes, some anxiety, but never anything like this. This behavior was completely out of character for me.

She said that yes, she could take me to the nearest hospital.

Good, I thought, but then realized this might not be appropriate, so I decided to get the flight attendant involved in my imaginary hell. I had hyperventilated to the point that my stomach had blown up with air. I looked like I could be pregnant, or possibly suffering from some life-threatening ailment.

Showing the flight attendant my stomach, I declared myself to be critically ill. She seemed to believe me. Addicts are grand liars and manipulators, even when having the mother of all anxiety attacks. "Okay," she said, "we'll have the paramedics pick you up in the terminal and take you to the hospital."

When the plane landed, she announced that everyone was to remain seated. "We have a critically ill person on board who needs to deplane first." With that, the paramedics stormed the plane with a skinny little wheelchair and took me off.

Even as I write this, I can barely believe it myself.

While I was at the terminal, they transferred me to a stretcher. I

showed them my stomach, declaring this to be a new physical occurrence accompanied by nausea and vomiting during the flight. They
immediately started an IV and agreed with me that it might be a bowel
obstruction.

So now I was in an ambulance. Finally I was given oxygen via nasal
prongs, and I was hooked up to a cardiac monitor and an IV with 5 percent dextrose. With sirens blaring and at high speeds, I was taken to a
hospital somewhere in Florida, late at night on my way home from
rehab.

And I was finally calm. Institutionalized once more, I could breathe.

The emergency room was packed. I was quickly processed and told to
wait in my wheelchair in the waiting room. I called Brian and told him
not to expect me home that night. I think at this point in our marriage,
Brian expected the unexpected, but he still wanted to know what had
happened.

"Not sure what happened," I said, which was the truth, "but I had a
strong urge to not board the plane for Baltimore. I think I might be very
sick; I'll let you know what they find out."

"Do you think you'll come home tonight?" Brian wanted to know.

"Not sure; I'll let you know."

God only knows what he was thinking about me at that point. I have
never asked him. Some things are better left unknown.

Wheeling myself over to a vending machine, I got some snacks and a
bottle of water. I had a vague thought that I should not eat if I had a life-
threatening bowel obstruction, but I was hungry, and from the look of
the waiting room I thought it might be a long night. I snacked and made
casual conversation with others waiting to be seen. A sick child with a
high fever and an elderly woman with flulike symptoms were closest to
where I was parked. Considering that they might have been contagious,
I moved on.

It was cold. Wheeling myself back to the nurses' desk, I asked for a
blanket. I was quickly obliged. Finding the quietest spot with low lighting,

I propped up my feet on a chair. Covering myself with the blanket, I closed my eyes and slept deeply. As I drifted off, I could hear the reassuring noises of the ER that were so familiar to me as a hospital nurse for more than twenty years.

I wasn't sure how long I slept. As an orderly woke me to take me to a room to be examined, I had to remind myself where I was, being somewhat disoriented from sleeping so soundly. In the exam room, I put on a gown and waited for the doctor. A physician assistant came in to do my exam and interview. I told him my theory that I had a bowel obstruction. He lifted my gown to have a look, poking and probing my abdomen.

Looking at me disgusted and with disdain, he said, "You're not distended. You're a nurse; this is not distended." I looked down. During my long nap in the waiting room, I had deflated. The PA was looking at me like I was just another nut job in the ER on a Friday night.

I insisted on X-rays to make sure. He obliged me, no doubt thinking this would be the quicker way to get rid of me. For good measure, I asked for a chest X-ray, too. *Just radiate my whole fucking body, there is surely something wrong with me!* I thought.

So they X-rayed the hell out of me and did blood work. After the tests, a doctor, a gentler man, came in. No doubt the PA could not deal with me. Some practitioners just do better with the psych patients. I appreciated this man's softer style. I had fallen asleep again, and he was empathetic as he woke me up.

"You were sleeping so peacefully," he said, "that I didn't want to wake you." He added, gently, "There's nothing wrong with you. I understand you were on a flight on your way home from rehab."

"Yes," I said, and then I started to cry. "Could I have a Valium, please?"

"I don't think that's a good idea for a drug addict on her way home from rehab, do you?"

"Probably not," I replied.

Whoever this doctor was, you have to give him *huge* credit. How easy it would have been for him to tranq me up and get me out of his ER. He took the harder, longer road, and continued to talk to me.

"What do you want to do?" he asked. "Stay in Florida, go back to rehab, or go home?"

Relocation to the Sunshine State was not in the cards, and I could not just show up back at La Hacienda, so it was door number 3. "Home," I said, weakly.

He patted my shoulder and said, "Good luck."

I shuffled out to the nurses' station. With my elbows on the desk and my face cradled in my palms, I looked at the nurse. Defeated, I said, "There's nothing wrong with me."

"We know," she responded, not unkindly.

"Can you call me a cab to take me to the airport?" I still had no idea what airport it was!

"Sure, sweetie."

With the IV out and under my own power, I walked out of the ER into the darkest night I can recall. It was maybe four in the morning, that moment when it's pitch dark before dawn starts to creep in.

Two cabs were at the curb. One of the drivers instructed me to get into his cab, when the second cabbie blared his horn. They were fighting over the fare. The first driver immediately backed down, and I ended up in the second, horn-blaring cab. The driver informed me he was the one who got the call, and the other guy was trying to steal his job.

"How long is our drive to the airport?"

"Forty-five or so minutes," he said, with a heavy Middle Eastern accent.

Quiet at first, I gazed out the window. Every night at La Hacienda I used to look up at big skies and star-filled nights, among the many blessings that rehab center offered me. The North Star always caught my attention. Being from Maryland, north of Texas, it represented home to me. And home meant my children, my babies I had left behind at the tender ages of six and four.

On that early morning in Florida, the skies had shifted dramatically as the world rotated. About the only prominent star left in the sky was the North Star. It was a light-bulb moment for me as I realized that the North Star, which had become a symbol of comfort and hope for me at La Hacienda, would always be with me. I immediately started to feel calmer.

As is my nature, I started a conversation with the cab driver. I have a bit of Margaret Mead, the anthropologist, in me. I have a natural curiosity about others' lives and experiences. He told me he was originally from Iran and was a Muslim. "Are you Christian?" he asked in turn. "Yes," I mildly declared. "Organized religion leaves me cold," I added.

I asked him if it had been difficult for him since 9/11, a Middle Eastern man living in the United States. "No," he said. "I think people sense the goodness in others, and I am accepted here."

"Why are you coming from the hospital to the airport in the middle of the night?" he asked.

Finally, for the first time on this long night, I verbalized what was at the bottom of my heavy heart. With sudden tears that rolled down my cheeks, I told this stranger from Iran that I was afraid to return home.

"I got off the plane on my way home from rehab. You see, I'm a drug addict, I've been in over a dozen rehabs and have come home over a dozen times, and I have relapsed and gotten sick over and over and over again. I was convinced there was something wrong with me, so I had them take me to the hospital. It was a fucking anxiety attack. I'm a drug addict who can't get well, that's what's wrong with me," I said loudly. Then, quietly, "And I am so tired of trying."

He was quiet as he handed me a tissue over the seat. A smart man knows when his silence is all that's needed. After a time, and as my crying ended, with equal quietness he said, "I am sorry you are in pain."

Rapidly, the airport appeared. I fished out the money to pay him. Getting out of the cab, I stood on the curb as the driver got my bag. Then the briefest of moments changed everything for me on this strangest of nights. He was extremely tall, and he loomed over me on the curb. He was Iranian dark, with a huge amount of thick, brown hair. Taking both of my hands in his, he gently said, almost in a whisper, "I sense goodness in you."

Looking down, I avoided his gaze. I felt like shit about myself for having to go away to rehab again. He lifted my chin, looked me right in the eyes, and repeated, "I sense goodness in you."

I bit my lower lip, trying to control my crying. Then, holding both sides of my face, he gently and firmly added, "Go home and live your life as God intended you to. Live your life in God's grace."

Then he walked back to his cab. He turned toward me, and we both waved good-bye. I stood on the curb and watched until his cab was out of sight. I felt a lightness of being after my encounter with the man from Iran. I never knew his name. I walked into the airport, got a Starbucks, and sat down by a fountain. As I sipped my coffee, I could hear the rhythmic tinkling of the water. I remember feeling grateful for the girl who worked the night shift at the Starbucks at the airport. My heart was joyful; I was relieved of my intense fear of returning home, and I was happy. I watched a family walk in with the usual Disney World sweatshirts and hats on, and I couldn't wait to see my own kids.

And I was at peace. No longer afraid, I had the courage to return home and give recovery another chance.

Was it a chance encounter with that Iranian man? Probably. But there is a part of me that feels that the whole night, the entire sequence of events, was leading up to meeting this man and hearing his words. It was a spiritual experience for me.

When I landed in Baltimore, I had to find my bags, which had arrived much earlier than me. With my back turned while I was looking for my luggage, I heard the familiar squeal of two little kids: *"Mom!"* I turned and saw my two children running to greet me. I knelt down as they ran into my arms.

I have been sober now going on four years.

Epilogue

Addiction is not a simple disease, and when it manifests itself in people's lives in all its glory and destruction, it is always a multifaceted malfunctioning of health. It is not just the biological or genetic components that push a person to the edge of active addiction; it is generally agreed that when addiction plays out in a person's life, it is threefold in its pathology: biological, psychological, and social. The biological involves the physical body, brain chemistry, and the genetics influencing it. The psychological has to do with elements such as family dynamics, emotional turmoil, and negative thinking. And the social aspect relates to how factors such as socioeconomic status, culture, poverty, technology, and religion can influence health.

When those three big components collide, addiction comes to life in all its ugly destruction, with the mind affecting the body and the body affecting the mind and the social factors interplaying with both. Psychiatrist George L. Engel theorized the model in 1977. There are striking similarities between Dr. Engel's theory and that of Bill Wilson, who cofounded Alcoholics Anonymous in 1935. When describing the alcoholic condition, Wilson wrote in the Big Book that alcoholism has a threefold aspect: body, mind, and spirit. Part of AA's success is that its roots are firmly planted in what have turned out to be facts about the disease of alcoholism substantiated by modern medicine. In many ways we have come a long way since the writing of *Alcoholic Anonymous* in 1939, treating alcoholism and addiction as a disease and not a moral failing. But just as we have come a long way, we need to look back to our roots in AA and keep recovery and its meetings firmly planted in a solution that has worked for millions of people—the Twelve Steps.

I am clean and sober, but my family is still in chaos—the good chaos of Boy Scouts, Girl Scouts, karate, drawing classes, making fudge, speech class, homework, PTA, jobs, writing, speaking engagements, a dog, a cat, and two hamsters! I consider my sobriety a large accomplishment, but it is not my final frontier. Clarity is the huge gift and benefit that comes with documenting one's story. It's clear to me that I still have work to do. My greatest hope is that through this work I will grow in my capacity to let people *in,* to trust more, and to love more authentically. That, I believe, is the most enduring gift I will give myself and my family.

An integral part of AA and the Twelve Steps is giving—giving back what's been given to us. I literally come alive when helping another. No matter how many interventions I do, I still crackle with purpose when someone shows me their daily hell with their addiction. And a phone call from an anguished family member reliving a loved one's nightmare can still stop me in my tracks . . . and ultimately keep me sober. As Father Martin used to tell me, "Sobriety is a circle—the circle of life. As you help someone else, you help yourself."

Acknowledgments

The lessons I have learned in my time on Earth have come from Mormons and Muslims and a whole lot of folks in between.

Undoubtedly, I gained a sense of humor from my mom. She had the ability to belly laugh about life and herself. She was my best friend for a large portion of my life, and I still miss her intensely. She also taught me how to make fudge and peanut brittle, which my kids greatly appreciate! My daughter and I read from my mom's original peanut brittle recipe, which was lost to us for thirteen long years before falling out of a long-forgotten paperback book, much to our delight.

I could not have written this book without the help of my editor, Ron Silverman. He had the uncanny and professional ability to put my words in the proper order without altering my voice, while still paying so much attention to detail. Amazing. I am ever so grateful to him.

To Sid Farrar, the editorial and trade director at Hazelden, thanks for believing in the project. To Karen Chernyaev, my editor at Hazelden, thanks for putting my story together in a way that flowed. A fresh pair of eyes is a gift! A big thanks to the final and hardworking prepress editor, Sara Perfetti, who has amazing attention to detail.

Therese Borchard, my friend and an author herself, helped me shape the book proposal in a way that made sense. While she is a professional author and all that that encompasses, I am a storyteller, and her input into the beginnings of the book was a great help. Her book *Beyond Blue* chronicles her own journey with bipolar mental illness. Her ability to write down her pain and discoveries gave me the inspiration to complete this book.

My friend Barbara Mehr was my unofficial life coach. (I offered to pay her, but she turned me down.) She would meet me at the coffee shop and bookstore to give me a kick in the ass to get started writing. She reminded me of a Nike commercial: Just do it! Thank you, Barbara!

Thanks also to my agent and friend Laura Strachan, who believed in this project and with her no-nonsense style helped me complete it. And she always answers her phone, which I love!

Dr. James Kehler, thank you for spanning the decades of therapy with me. You have always been there for me.

And Chris Raymer, thanks for beautifully building on to what Father Martin taught me years earlier, in a way that made complete sense to me, finally! Rock on, you beautiful Big Book thumper. Body, Mind, and Spirit, you explain the book *Alcoholics Anonymous* in a way that would make the founders and Mark Houston proud. People get it when you explain it. What a gift!

Thank you, Rich Whitman, for putting up with me! And Michelle Savage, the therapist who flew with me and Rich to La Hacienda from the set of the *Dr. Phil* show, thanks for listening to me bitch the entire way! To doctors and brothers Daniel and James Boone at La Hacienda, wow, what wonderful doctors and proud Christians. Thank you for your care. And all the nurses, thanks for letting me pretend I was at work and not a patient! To all the staff at La Hacienda, thank you for changing my life.

What can I say about Colleen Schneidwind? Colleen has been my friend and trusted childcare provider for both my kids. She loved and cared for my children, especially Max, when I was too sick to do it myself and when I was away at rehab. Thanks, Colleen; we never worried about our kids when they were in your care.

I salute all the baristas at Café Pronto in Annapolis, Maryland. All those kids, while providing the best coffee ever, also cheered me on as my dog, Lucy, and I sat at a table and wrote this book. And to the regular patrons, especially my good friend Lori, thanks for your company and support; you kept it interesting.

To Dr. John McClanahan, who gave me my start in private practice as an interventionist, thanks; your guidance and belief in me has brought me confidence and a career.

To all the families who allowed me to be part of their struggles and triumphs while working with their loved ones through the process of intervention: you have been an inspiration to me, and yours is definitely the road less traveled as you have taken a proactive position in fighting the disease of addiction.

To Aunt Margaret, my mom's identical twin, thank you for always wanting to know when I'm on the *Dr. Phil* show and for being proud of me. Also, thank you for being with me when I needed you the most, at my mother's death. I will always love you.

To Dr. Phil, his wife Robin (who gives great hugs), and all the production people behind the scenes at the show: I always look forward to seeing you all and hearing about your summers and families. You make TV real—Shelly, Stephanie, Angie, Julie, Brooke, Annette, Allen, Anthony, Leah, Marsha, Christopher, Elizabeth, Emily, and women who mike me up before I go onstage. Your cheering me on has meant the world to me. And special thanks to Dr. Phil. I am forever in your debt. You told me the truth (even if it did piss me off!) and provided me with a tremendous opportunity in La Hacienda treatment facility. You saved a family, my family. There is no greater good. Thank you, Dr. Phil.

Just recently, as I was finishing this book, I received a wonderful surprise and gift from Cindy and Craig Rosen and their son Corey. The Rosens made a generous donation to the Kennedy Krieger Institute in Baltimore, in my family's name, toward autism patient and family-support services. Because my son, Max, was diagnosed with autism through Kennedy Krieger, their gift means so much to me and my family. Thank you, Cindy, Craig, and Corey.

Brian, my husband, took a lot of hits during my addiction. He was labeled The Enabler. Yes, he enabled my disease, but he has enabled my success every step of the way. He is more than I deserve. He is my best friend and a wonderful dad to our kids. He has truly been the glue that has kept it all together. Thank you, Brian. I love you more than I can say.

And to my children, Mary and Max, your love has transformed my life. In simple terms, you saved my life. In the end, mine is a mother's story, a story as old as time.

Alcohol and Drug Treatment Facilities: A Selected List

These are the alcohol and drug treatment facilities I respect and work with, in alphabetical order. Certainly there are other good rehab centers, but these are the ones I have experience with and trust to do a consistently superior job.

Caron Renaissance, 866-915-0290, www.caronrenaissance.org

Caron Treatment Centers, 800-854-6023, www.caron.org

Clarity Way, 877-251-6604, www.clarityway.com

Farley Center, 877-389-4968, www.farleycenter.com

Father Martin's Ashley, 800-799-4673, www.fathermartinsashley.com

Hazelden, 800-257-7810, www.hazelden.org

Kolmac Clinic, 301-589-0255, www.kolmac.com

La Hacienda, 800-749-6160, www.lahacienda.com

The Meadows, 800-632-3697, www.themeadows.org

Origins Recovery Center, 888-843-8935, www.originsrecovery.com

Phoenix Recovery Center, 800-671-9516, www.phoenixrecoverycenter.com

Pine Grove, 888-574-4673, www.pinegrovetreatment.com

Seabrook House, 800-761-7575, www.seabrookhouse.org

Resources

The following books can give you more information about interventions, addiction, and recovery.

Intervention

Get Your Loved One Sober: Alternatives to Nagging, Pleading, and Threatening by Robert J. Meyers and Brenda Wolfe. Center City, MN: Hazelden, 2004.

Intervention: How to Help Someone Who Doesn't Want Help by Vernon E. Johnson. Center City, MN: Hazelden, 1986.

Love First: A Family's Guide to Intervention, second edition, by Jeff Jay and Debra Jay. Center City, MN: Hazelden, 2008.

Stop the Chaos: How to Get Control of Your Life by Beating Alcohol and Drugs by Allen A. Tighe. Center City, MN: Hazelden, 1998.

For Family Members and Loved Ones

Addict in the Family: Stories of Loss, Hope, and Recovery by Beverly Conyers. Center City, MN: Hazelden, 2003.

Codependent No More: How to Stop Controlling Others and Start Caring for Yourself by Melody Beattie. Center City, MN: Hazelden, 1986.

Courage to Change: One Day at a Time in Al-Anon. Virginia Beach, VA: Al-Anon Family Group Headquarters, Inc., 1992.

Everything Changes: Help for Families of Newly Recovering Addicts by Beverly Conyers. Center City, MN: Hazelden, 2009.

It's Not Okay to Be a Cannibal: How to Keep Addiction from Eating Your Family Alive by Andrew T. Wainwright and Robert Poznanovich. Center City, MN: Hazelden, 2007.

The Language of Letting Go by Melody Beattie. Center City, MN: Hazelden, 1990.

Early Recovery

Alcoholics Anonymous, fourth edition. New York: Alcoholics
    Anonymous World Services, Inc., 2001.

Narcotics Anonymous, sixth edition. Van Nuys, CA: Narcotics
    Anonymous World Services, Inc., 2008.

*Now That You're Sober: Week-by-Week Guidance from Your Recovery
    Coach* by Earnie Larsen with Carol Larsen Hegarty. Center City,
    MN: Hazelden, 2010.

A Program for You: A Guide to the Big Book's Design for Living. Center
    City, MN: Hazelden, 1991.

Twenty-Four Hours a Day. Center City, MN: Hazelden, 1975.

Undrunk: A Skeptic's Guide to AA by A. J. Adams. Center City, MN:
    Hazelden, 2009.

A Woman's Guide to Recovery by Brenda Iliff. Center City, MN:
    Hazelden, 2008.

About the Author

Joani Gammill, RN, BRI I, CNDAI, CNDCS, lives in Annapolis, Maryland, with her husband and two children. She is in private practice working as an RN doing interventions. She is a frequent guest on *Dr. Phil* and enjoys speaking around the country on issues concerning addiction and recovery.